John Charles Earle

Manual of the Lives of the Popes

From St. Peter to Pius IX.

John Charles Earle

Manual of the Lives of the Popes
From St. Peter to Pius IX.

ISBN/EAN: 9783337064228

Printed in Europe, USA, Canada, Australia, Japan

Cover: Foto ©ninafisch / pixelio.de

More available books at **www.hansebooks.com**

COLLEGE OF ST. FRANCIS XAVIER,

Second Grammar Class,
1st. Section.

...... *Greek* ....

1st Prize

AWARDED TO

Charles E. McDonnell

New York City, June 29th, 1868.

Jos. Loyzance, S. J. *Prest.*

NEW EDITIONS, &c.

Recently Published by MURPHY & CO., Baltimore.

Just Published, a New Edition on Fine Paper.

BUTLER'S LIVES OF THE SAINTS,

(Metropolitan Edition.)

THE LIVES OF THE FATHERS, MARTYRS, AND OTHER PRINCIPAL SAINTS, compiled from the original Monuments and other authentic Records, illustrated with the remarks of Judicious Modern Critics and Historians. By the Rev. ALBAN BUTLER. *Embellished with Fine Tinted Engravings.*

No. 1——2 vols., 8o., cloth	4 plates		$7 00
" 2——4 vols., cloth, fine paper	8	"	8 00
" 4——4 vols., roan	8	"	9 00
" 5——4 vols., library style	16	"	12 00
" 6——4 vols., cloth, gilt sides and edges	16	"	14 00
" 7——4 vols., imit., gilt sides and edges	24	"	16 00
" 8——4 vols., super extra	24	"	20 00

APPROBATION OF THE MT. REV. ABP. KENRICK.

The "Lives of the Saints," by the Rev. ALBAN BUTLER, being a work of acknowledged merit, full of sound instruction, and abounding in edification, originally published by the Metropolitan Press, and now re-published by John Murphy & Co., I hereby approve of, and recommend it to the faithful.

Given under my hand, at Baltimore, this 13th day of March, 1854.

✠ FRANCIS PATRICK,
Archbishop of Baltimore.

To a work so well and so favorably known as the LIVES OF THE SAINTS, it is deemed unnecessary to say anything by way of commendation. Suffice it to state, that this *Metropolitan Edition*, has been gotten up with the greatest care, under the supervision of the eminent Professors of Saint Mary's College, Baltimore. It is printed on fine paper, from a good, clear and bold type, illustrated with Fine Tinted Engravings, and may be justly considered the MOST COMPLETE, as it is unquestionably *the cheapest and best edition published.*

Now ready, in 1 vol., 8o., cloth, price $2.50. Library style, $3.

A New and Improved Edition of

Hughes and Breckenridge's Oral Discussion of the Question, is the Roman Catholic Religion, in any or in all its Principles or Doctrines, inimical to Civil or Religious Liberty? And of the Question, is the Presbyterian Religion, in any or in all its Principles or Doctrines, inimical to Civil or Religious Liberty?

By the Rev. JOHN HUGHES, of the Roman Catholic Church.
And the Rev. JOHN BRECKENRIDGE, of the Presbyterian Church.

MURPHY & Co. *Publishers and Catholic Booksellers, Baltimore.*

April, 1867.

NEW BOOKS AND NEW EDITIONS,
Recently Published by MURPHY & CO., Baltimore.

New and Uniform Editions of

ARCHBISHOP SPALDING'S WORKS,
In 5 vols. 8o. various Bindings.

☞ These works ought to occupy a conspicuous place in every Public and Private Library in the country, as COMPLETE and RELIABLE WORKS of REFERENCE.

Just Published, in 1 vol. 8o., *cloth*, price $3.50. *Another Edition, on fine paper*, 2 vols., 8o., *cloth, bevelled*, $5. *Library style*, $6. *Half calf*, $7.00.

A New, Improved and Greatly Enlarged Edition of

MISCELLANEA—Comprising *Reviews, Lectures* and *Essays*, on *Historical, Theological*, and *Miscellaneous Subjects*. By Most Rev. M. J. SPALDING, D.D. Abp. of Balt.

This New and greatly Enlarged Edition of this learned and popular Work has been carefully revised, and enlarged, by the addition of upwards of 150 pages of interesting and highly important matter, embracing among many other things, an ESSAY ON COMMON SCHOOLS, THROUGHOUT THE WORLD—A LECTURE ON THE ORIGIN AND HISTORY OF LIBRARIES—AN ESSAY ON DEMONOLOGY and the REFORMATION, &c. &c.

Th. Extensive Work, of upwards of 800 pages, large 8o. comprises ESSAYS, REVIEWS and LECTURES, on upwards of FORTY DIFFERENT SUBJECTS, most of them Historical, and all of more than ordinary interest, being peculiarly adapted to the wants and circumstances of the American people. That such a work should have reached a Fourth Edition, in a few years, is a sterling proof and gratifying evidence of its merits, which have made it quite as great a favorite with the Protestant as with the Catholic community.

Just Published, an entirely new Edition, in 1 *vol., 8o., cloth,* $2. *Another Edition, on fine paper, cloth, bev.* $2.50. *Lib. style*, $3 *Half calf*, $3.50.

Lectures on the Evidences of Catholicity. Fourth Revised Edition. By the Most Rev. M. J. SPALDING, D.D. *Archbishop of Balt*

These Lectures are intended to exhibit, in a plain and strait-forward manner, the principal Evidences of the Catholic Church. They are now offered to the Public in a Fourth Edition, with the hope that some sincere and candid souls, now wandering amidst the mazes of hereditary error, may be led back by the perusal of them to the bosom of the true Church, from which their fathers in an evil hour separated, to follow after the devices of their own hearts.

To every lover of the Christian Religion it must be apparent, on sufficient examination, that the Evidences which sustain Catholicity are substantially identical with those which establish Christianity itself. The scope of these Lectures is to establish this identity.

Recently Published, in 1 *vol. of* 1000 *pages,* 8o., *cloth, price* $3.50. *Another Edition, on fine paper*, 2 *vol.,* 8o , *cloth, bevelled.* $5. *Library style,* $6. *Half calf*, $7.00.

History of the Protestant Reformation, In Germany, Switzerland, England, Ireland, Scotland, The Netherlands, France, and Northern Europe. In a Series of Essays, Reviewing D'Aubigne, Menzel, Hallam, Short, Prescott, Ranke, Fryxell, and others. Fourth Edition, carefully Revised. With a New Preface, and a New and Complete Index. By the Most Rev. M. J. SPALDING, D.D. *Abp. of Balt*.

In announcing a New Edition of this celebrated work, the Publishers feel that they are offering the most Comprehensive, Elaborate, and Complete HISTORY of the REFORMATION ever published. It is replete with facts, well arranged, and thoroughly digested. It abounds with References to the Original Authorities, most of them Protestant. All the hidden springs of action are developed and the actors themselves, in the stirring drama of the Sixteenth Century, are brought upon the stage and portrayed, as represented by themselves, or depicted by their contemporaries and friends. The various influences of the Reformation, in the different countries of Europe, are also thoroughly examined, and its claims to have given a new impulse to Liberty, Literature, and Civilization, are carefully scrutinized. Facts and authorities are succinctly and methodically arranged.

MURPHY & Co. *Publishers and Catholic Booksellers, Baltimore.*

THE APOSTLESHIP OF PRAYER ASSOCIATION.

☞ Especial attention is respectfully solicited to the following Works, on the *Apostleship of Prayer.*

Published with the Approbation of the Most Rev. ABP. SPALDING.

Just Published, in a neat volume, 12o., *cloth, price* $1.50.

The Apostleship of Prayer. A Holy League of Christian Hearts united with the Heart of Jesus, to obtain the Triumph of the Church and the Salvation of Souls. Preceded by a Brief of the Sovereign Pontiff Pius IX, the Approbation of several Archbishops and Bishops, and Superiors of Religious Congregations. By the Rev. H. RAMIERE, of the Society of Jesus. Translated from the latest French Edition, and Revised by a Father of the Society.

Just Published, in a neat volume, 32o., *cloth, price* 40 *cts.*

The Manual of the Apostleship of Prayer. Enriched with ample Indulgences by His Holiness Pius IX, and Approved of by a large number of Archbishops and Bishops, and Affiliated to the Association of the Sacred Heart, established in Rome, in the Church *della Pace*. By the Rev. H. RAMIERE, S. J., Director of the Association. Translated from the French.

The Apostleship of Prayer Association. Explanation and Practical Instruction by FATHER RAMIERE, S. J. Translated from the French by a Father of the Society. Price, 5 cts., per 100, $3.

The Rosary of the Apostleship, In small pamphlet form.

☞ The large and constantly increasing demand for these Works, is an evidence of their merits, and the great popularity of this Association.

Just Published, per dozen, 60 *cents, per* 100, $3.50, *net.*

Circles of the Living Rosary, Illustrated.

Published with the Approbation of the Most Rev. Archbishop SPALDING.

This is an entirely New Translation, conformable to the Brief of HIS HOLINESS, POPE GREGORY XVI, January 27, 1832, each Mystery is accompanied by the Instructions, Prayers, Meditations, and a List of all the Indulgences, granted by the Sovereign Pontiffs, to this widespread Devotion. ☞ The Circles are beautifully Illustrated, and Printed on Fine Paper.

Recently Published, 32o., *cloth,* 50 *cents; in finer bindings, up to* $2.

The Month of Mary, for the Use of Ecclesiastics.

Translated from the French.

APPROBATION OF THE MOST REV. ABP. SPALDING.

WE have examined, and WE cordially approve the publication, in an English translation, of the Month of Mary, for the use of Ecclesiastics, and WE recommend it to the Clergy and Seminarians of OUR Archdiocese. M. J. SPALDING, *Abp. of Balt.*

This little Work, in honor of the "Immaculate Queen of the Clergy," has been already heralded by, at east, six editions in French. This first English Edition, is confidently recommended to the Ecclesiastics of this country.

Church Registers.—*Registers of Baptisms, Marriages, Confirmations, Interments. Registers of Pews.—Parish Records.*

☞ These Books are carefully prepared with Printed Headings, and conveniently arranged, for keeping Church Records, in such a manner as to save time and labor to the Pastor, and affording great facility for reference at all times.

The PEW BOOKS are admirably arranged for keeping the Accounts in the most simple manner, showing at a glance the state of the Pew-holder's account. They are put up in Books of 2, 3 and 400 pages, and can be ordered to correspond to the number of Pews in a Church—a page being appropriated to each Pew.

This series of six Books are printed on Fine Cap Paper. They are uniformly bound in Books of various sizes, and may be had separately or in sets, done up in neat Walnut Cases.

MURPHY & CO. *Publishers and Catholic Booksellers, Baltimore.*

New and Uniform Edition of FATHER FABER'S Works,

In 8 vol., 12o., cloth, $1.50; gilt edges, $2 per vol. The complete set, in boxes, 8 vols., cloth, $12; cloth, gilt, $16. In half calf, $24.

All for Jesus; or, the Easy Ways of Divine Love.
The Blessed Sacrament; or, Works and Ways of God.
Growth in Holiness; or, Progress of the Spiritual Life.
The Creator and the Creature; or, the Wonders of Divine Love.
The Foot of the Cross; or, the Sorrows of Mary.
Bethlehem.   *Spiritual Conferences.*
The Precious Blood; or, the Price of our Salvation.

☞ Upwards of 50,000 copies of Father Faber's Popular Devotional Works have been sold in this country, and the demand is constantly increasing.

One of the most eloquent and distinguished clergymen in the United States, in writing an Introduction to one of Father Faber's works, says:

"We turn to this last work of the Rev. Dr. Faber, with sentiments of gratitude to heaven, and hope for its abundant blessing on the teachings of such a guide, which our most earnest language would but faintly express. If the power to conceive and convey to others the sublime, and at the same time the most practical truths that can interest the human mind, be a title to the homage of men, then has Father Faber established for himself a claim which no length of years nor change of circumstances can efface. Few writers, since the days of St. Francis de Sales, have made more Christian hearts bow in loving adoration before our tabernacles than the author of 'All for Jesus,' 'The Blessed Sacrament,' &c. &c. &c.

Recently published, in 1 vol., 18o., cloth, 75 cents; cloth, gilt, $1.25.

The Love of Religious Perfection; or, How to Awaken, Increase, and Preserve it in the Religious Soul. From the Latin of Father Jos. BAYMA, S. J.

Published with the Approbation of the Most Rev. ARCHBISHOP SPALDING.

No one can read, in the proper Spirit, this valuable Treatise, without perceiving it well deserves the reputation it has won. Learning, wisdom and piety, unite to recommend it to all who wish to advance in that best and purest of all Sciences, the Science of Salvation. Like two other similar works, the Imitation of Christ, and the Spiritual Combat which have helped to enlighten and encourage thousands on their way to our only true home, you may open this little book at almost any chapter, and find something to turn your thoughts heavenward; to raise your heart to God, to purify its affections, to warn you against the deceitfulness of Sin, and the allurements of the world in the midst of which we live.

Catholic Sermons.—The Catholic Pulpit, Containing a Sermon for every Sunday and Holiday in the year, and for Good Friday, with several Occasional Discourses. One large volume of 763 pages, 8o., cloth, $3.50. Library style, $4.

Universally esteemed the best collection of Sermons in the English Language.

"We know of no language sufficiently forcible in which to urge upon our readers the excellence of The Catholic Pulpit. The Sermons contained in it may well compete with the most elaborate productions of Fenelon or Bossuet. Though no Anglo-Saxon, we feel a kind of pride in contemplating the gorgeous form in which the English language can clothe ideas, of which the work before us is a standing testimony."—*Toronto Mirror.*

Archbishop Dixon's General Introduction to Sacred Scriptures. 8o., cloth, $3.50. Library style, $4.

☞ As this work has not been stereotyped, and the Edition is nearly exhausted, such as may desire to secure one of the most learned works of the age, will do well to send early orders. Every one that has an English Bible should have Dixon's Introduction to explain the Text.

An Essay on the Harmonious Relations between Divine Faith and Natural Reason. To which are added Two Chapters on the Divine Office of the Church. By Hon. A. C. BAINE. 12o. cloth, $1.25.

The New Glories of the Catholic Church. Translated from the Italian, by the Fathers of the London Oratory, at the request of the Cardinal Archbishop of Westminster. With a Preface by His Eminence Cardinal Wiseman. 12o., cloth, $1.25. Gilt edges, $1.75.

MURPHY & Co. *Publishers and Catholic Booksellers, Baltimore.*

New and Improved Editions of Highly Important Works.

LADY FULLERTON'S TALES.

A New and Uniform Edition, in 3 vols., 12o., cloth, $1.50. Cloth, gilt edges, &c., $2 per vol.

Lady Bird.   **Ellen Middleton.**   **Grantley Manor.**

No less accomplished as an authoress than pious and unostentatious in private life, Lady Fullerton gives her works a character of instructiveness and practical wisdom which we look for in vain in many of our professedly religious tales. The young of her sex will find in her pages entertainment of the highest order, interest, beauty of style, elegance of description, without a line to pamper the silly or romantic ideas that too often unfit them for real life. The signal success of her works, not only in England, but in America, and their translation on the Continent, are the best evidences of their decided merit.

Pauline Seward. A Tale of Real Life. By J. D. BRYANT, M. D. Sixth Revised Edition. Two volumes in one. New Edition, 12o., cloth, $1.50. Cloth, gilt edges, $2.

"No prose writer of America has yet, to our knowledge, penned a more graceful or more unaffected tale than this."—*London Sun.*

The Genius of Christianity; or, the Spirit and Beauty of the Christian Religion. By VISCOUNT DE CHATEAUBRIAND. With a Preface, Biographical Notice of the Author, and Critical and Explanatory Notes, by the Rev. C. I. White, D. D. Embellished with a fine Steel Portrait. 800 pages, large 12mo. Cloth, $2.25. Cloth, extra full gilt, $3.

The *Genius of Christianity* is now presented to the Public for the *first time* in a Complete English translation, accompanied with a Biographical Notice of the distinguished Author.

This work was originally published in France, more than fifty years ago, and it has been pronounced by the best critics one of the most eloquent, instructive, and interesting productions of which the literature of the 19th Century can boast.

Balmes on European Civilization. Protestantism and Catholicity compared in their Effects on the Civilization of Europe. By Rev. J. BALMES. 8o. cloth $3. Library style, $3.50.

"This Book, to be known, must be read, and we would recommend all who would possess one of the great Books which has appeared in our day, to lose no time in procuring it."—*Brownson.*

Life of St. Francis Xavier. Apostle of the Indies and Japan, from the Italian of BARTOLI and MAFFEI, with a Preface, by the Rev. Father FABER   12o. cloth, $1.75   Cloth, gilt edges, $2.25.

Life of St. Vincent de Paul. Founder of the Congregation of the Mission, and of the Sisters of Charity. By M. COLLET. New Edition, fine paper, 12o. cloth, $1.00. Cloth, gilt edges, $1.50.

The Studies and Teachings of the Society of Jesus, at the Time of its Suppression, 1750–1775. Translated from the French of the ABBE MAYNARD, Honorary Canon of the Pointers, &c. 12o. cl. $1.

Milner's End of Religious Controversy. In a Friendly Correspondence, between a Religious Society of Protestants, and a Catholic Divine. By the Rt. Rev. JOHN MILNER, D. D. A New Edition, just published, in small 8o. Cloth, $1.

Catholic Tracts, for General Circulation. Price $5 per 100 net.

The "Catholic" Church, and the Roman Catholic Church In a Friendly Correspondence, between a Catholic Priest, and an Episcopal Minister.

Faith, Hope, and Charity. The Substance of a Sermon. By Bishop BAINE.

MURPHY & Co. *Publishers and Catholic Booksellers, Baltimore.*

MANUAL

OF

The Lives of the Popes.

MANUAL

OF THE

LIVES OF THE POPES,

From St. Peter to Pius IX.

By John Charles Earle, B.A.

> "Siate, Christiani, a muovervi piu gravi;
> Non siate come penna ad ogni vento,
> E non crediate ch' ogni acqua vi lavi.
> Avete 'l vecchio e 'l nuovo Testamento
> E 'l Pastor della chiesa che vi guida;
> Questo vi basti a vostro salvamento."
> Dante, *Il Paradiso*, Canto V.

First American, from the Last London Edition.

BALTIMORE:
PUBLISHED BY JOHN MURPHY & CO.
182 Baltimore Street.
1867.

RE-IMPRIMATUR.

MARTINUS JOANNES,
Archiep. Balt.

PRINTED BY
JOHN MURPHY & CO.
BALTIMORE.

PREFACE TO THE AMERICAN EDITION.

AN English periodical, second to none in our language, and distinguished for its ability and impartiality, thus speaks of the work which we now present to the American public.

"We notice with pleasure the appearance of this invaluable Manual. No division of Ecclesiastical History is so convenient as that by successive Pontificates; and such a volume, therefore, as the present is not more useful towards *acquiring* the knowledge of Ecclesiastical History, than towards recalling what has been already learnt."

* * * * * *

"The Manual admirably meets a want long felt in English Catholic literature; and will be exceedingly useful in our Colleges and Schools. The biographies, though necessarily brief, contain all the material facts, civil and ecclesiastical, of each Pontificate, carefully summarised; and the narrative throughout is written in a very clear, concise, and graceful style."

The sincere inquirer after truth, and we cherish the hope, that there are many such in our country, will hardly require any additional commendation of this little volume after the above favorable judgment from such competent judges.

It is not many years since one of our public men said: "There is nothing of which the present age stands so much in need, as of peace-makers." Peace through Truth is the only peace that can be lasting: and in promoting this always desirable state of society, few agents are more potent than historical truth. How much it has already accomplished within the present century, is one of the brighter signs of our times, dark and foreboding as they must appear to many. Whatever clouds passion and prejudices may spread over the minds of men sooner or later truth resumes her sway, and triumphs over all error. Falsehood can exist only for a time: it may be embellished by learning, sustained by self interest, genius and the power of party spirit, but it cannot bear the test of patient inquiry, scientific research and candor. Before these united, how many great historical errors have already disappeared: how many noble, but long-misrepresented characters of former days, have come forth from the gloom, in which their deeds, their virtues and sufferings remained so long hidden to wear the honors so unjustly, and for so many generations withheld from them. For the intelligent reader it will be enough to name a Gregory VII., an Innocent III., a Thomas à Becket, to remind him of what the present age has done in this regard.

What is true in matters of faith, holds good to a great extent in matters of history. It is the Truth will make you free.

May our present addition to the solid literature of our country contribute to the enlightenment of many and to the promotion of that taste for valuable knowledge, still so desirable, is the cordial hope and desire of the publisher.

BALTIMORE, *March* 25, 1867.

Author's Preface.

Though the larger part of this volume has already appeared in a Catholic periodical, it is not without much diffidence that I now offer it to the public complete. The history of the Papal line is encumbered with peculiar difficulty, in consequence of the conflicting accounts which exist respecting many Pontiffs, the insufficiency of information regarding others, and the variety of sources from which their annals are derived. These circumstances would make it difficult to satisfy all parties even in an extended history; but in a Manual, where everything must be compressed into a small compass, it is almost impossible to obviate all objections. If my humble attempt should fall into the hands of any who are learned in ecclesiastical history, I entreat them to remember that I have not presumed to write chronicles for them. This compilation is intended—as its title indicates—for students, and has grown out of notes made, in the first instance, for my own instruction and amusement. If it should prove to be as accurate as I have endeavoured to make it, it may perhaps find a place by the side of larger works, ancient and modern, on the same subject; and, by reason of its elementary character, be sometimes, and for special purposes, preferred to more elaborate treatises. The scholar and the teacher, as well as the learner, may—such is my hope—find it convenient to turn to a volume which will help them in the confusion that arises, even in the best memories, when trying to recall in an instant the chief events in the pontificate of one Pope, whose name is common to ten or twenty others, and they may be glad of a compendium of Papal history that supplies them readily with the dates they require.

I have avoided all vexed questions and all controversy; and though I write as a Catholic, in the love of Catholicism, and in devoted submission to Papal authority, I do not think

Protestant readers and Protestant students will find anything in the series to repulse them, or cause them to exclude it from their bookshelves. I recognise all good wherever I find it, as affiliated to the Catholic Church, and earnestly deprecate hostility where I intend and feel nothing but kindness and love. If in any of my statements I have unconsciously been led into error, I shall be grateful to any one who will point out the mistake, and it shall be rectified at the earliest opportunity. The confidence I have in the Papacy as a divine institution relieves me of all anxiety as to the effect of recording in each instance the plain, though sometimes painful, truth; nor can I desire for my readers any greater and more solid happiness than that which I felt (and still feel in retrospect) when I went up the stairs of the Vatican, and placed myself with all my cares—as I now desire to lay this little volume, with all its imperfections—at the feet of the Vicar of Jesus Christ.

LONDON, *June* 6, 1866.

WORKS PRINCIPALLY EMPLOYED IN THE COMPILATION OF THIS MANUAL.

Bouillet.—Dictionnaire d'Histoire; Ouvrage Approuvé par le Saint Siége.

Butler's Lives of the Saints. 12 vols.

Compendium Historiæ Ecclesiasticæ. Londini. 1778.

Döllinger.—History of the Church. 3 vols.

Drioux.—Précis Elémentaire d'Histoire Ecclésiastique.

Eusebius.—Historia Ecclesiastica.

Fleury.—Histoire Ecclésiastique. 40 vols.

Henrion.—Histoire de l'Eglise. 25 vols.

Manual of Church History. Burns. 1860.

Ranke.—Lives of the Popes of Rome during the Sixteenth and Seventeenth Centuries. 3 vols.

MANUAL

OF THE

LIVES OF THE POPES.

The object of the biographical notices in this series is to present a summary account of the principal events in each Pontificate, so far as they can be gathered from history; to draw as faithful a portrait as possible of each Pontiff; to trace the rise and fall of the several heresies which have assailed the Catholic faith; to mark the progress of civilisation under the fostering influence of Christianity;* and to invite constant attention to the wonderful and special providence of God in preserving the Popes from the promulgation of any theological error, illustrating them, on the whole, with exalted talents and resplendent virtues, and enabling them to wage ceaseless and successful

---

* I have treated this branch of the subject more at length in an article entitled "Rome, the Civiliser of Nations," in the *Dublin Review* of April 1866.

warfare with unbelief and misbelief in their subtlest as well as their most palpable forms. It is hoped, therefore, that the series, taken as a whole, will serve not merely as a manual of the lives of the Popes, but as an outline of Church history, and, in some sort, a book of evidences of the truth of Catholicism. Historical facts cannot, of course, be always equally interesting. Striking events cannot be created, nor sameness always avoided, in matter concerning 258 rulers, who have all (the Avignon Popes excepted) resided in the same spot, and have all, under different circumstances, had immutable duties to fulfil; yet no effort has been spared to make these sketches as entertaining and profitable to readers in general as their extreme brevity will permit, and by strict accuracy to render them useful to students in the way of reference. The want of such a manual has long been felt; for the Papacy is, to use the words of one of its bitterest enemies, "a spiritual and temporal monarchy, which, of all human institutions, perhaps most merits the attention of man, whether we consider its nature, its progress, or its prodigious consequences." (Russell's *History of Modern Europe*, vol. i.) Of several of the earlier Bishops of Rome nothing but the names remain on record; but even these are precious and worthy of honour. There are sometimes slight discrepancies amongst historians in regard to their respective dates; but in such cases I have selected those which appeared to me the best.

1. St Peter, a.d. 33-38.

On the rude shores of the Sea of Galilee—" Galilee of the Gentiles"—Simon, son of Jonas, exercised the humble trade of a fisherman. His brother Andrew had listened to the preaching of the Baptist, bore witness of the Messiah to Simon, and brought him to the Saviour's feet. (St John i. 40-42.) That voice which was persuasion's self called him, in the midst of his toils, to follow the Christ—he knew not whither—and promised to make him a fisher of men. (St Matt. iv. 18, 19.) His lowly dwelling, a fisher's hut, was honored by the presence of Jesus, who there miraculously healed his mother-in-law, sick of a fever, (St Matt. viii. 14, 15,) which fled at His divine touch. In the enumeration given by St Matthew of the twelve Apostles of our Lord, a distinct priority is assigned to that one whom the Church honours as their prince. The first, "Simon, who is called Peter." (St Matt. x. 2.) Simon was not known by this name of Peter in his earlier days. It was a new and mystical name which he received from Christ himself. Lest any should defraud him of this incommunicable honour and glory, it was given him in two languages—in Hebrew and in Greek; he was called Cephas, a rock; and Peter, a rock; that Jew and Gentile alike might learn and recognise his title, and ponder its deep import. From the moment when this distinction was conferred on him by our Lord, Simon Peter became of necessity an object of peculiar interest and veneration in the eyes of the disciples, and the more so because the language which our Saviour had employed on this solemn occasion was luminous and emphatic in the highest degree: "I say unto thee, Thou art Peter; and upon this Rock I will build my Church, and the gates of hell shall not prevail against it. And I will give to thee the keys of the Kingdom of Heaven: and whatsoever thou shalt bind upon earth, it shall be bound also in heaven: and whatsoever thou shalt loose on earth, it shall be loosed also in heaven." (St Matt. xvi. 18, 19.) The Catholic Church has always regarded this august promise as being fulfilled in St Peter, and his successors in the See of Rome. There he was destined to sit as Patriarch and Pope, in the city which was the world's metropolis then, and has been that of Christendom ever since. Many of our Lord's words addressed to Simon Peter, like those which have just been cited, had a deeper signification than appeared on the surface, and referred not to him only, but also to his successors, and many of His actions in regard to Simon were symbolical of His future dealing with the Catholic Church. He sustained him by His omnipotent hand when sinking, and empowered him to walk on the rolling waves. (Matt. xiv. 28-31.) He led him up the mount, and was transfigured before him, giving him a vision and foretaste of His future coming in glory. (Matt. xvii. 1-5; 2 Peter i. 16-18.) He caused him to find a piece of money in a fish's mouth, wherewith to pay tribute at Capharnaum. (Matt. xvii. 24-27.) He enjoined him to forgive, not seven times only, but seventy times seven. (Matt. xviii. 21, 22.) He promised him that in the regeneration, when the Son of Man shall sit on the throne of His glory, he also, with his co-apostles, shall sit enthroned and judge the twelve tribes of Israel. (Matt. xix. 27-29.) He taught the mysteries of His Kingdom to the people out of Peter's ship, and, in the miraculous draught of fishes, so manifested forth His glory, that Simon, in the depths of humiliation and self-abhorrence, exclaimed, "Depart from me; for I am a sinful man, O Lord." (St Luke v. 8-9.) On several occasions, He who spoke as never man spake, administered a gentle rebuke to His chief Apostle. "Thou savourest not divine things, but human," He said, when Peter would blindly have dissuaded Him from accomplishing His decease and passion at Jerusalem. (St Matt. xvi. 21-23.) In the midst of His bitter agony in the Garden of Gethsemani, He returned thrice to Peter, whom He had left with James and John to pass the time in prayer, and finding them asleep, He asked, "What! could ye not watch one hour with Me?" (St Matt. xxvi. 40.) On the night before his Saviour's crucifixion, St Peter had vowed to Him, saying, "Though all men should deny Thee, yet will I never deny Thee." He knew not himself. Lukewarm devotion and overweening self-confidence were followed by reiterated denials of his Master, his Friend, his Redeemer, his Lord, and his God. In his hasty zeal he had cut off the ear of the high-priest's servant; but soon after forsook the captured Jesus and fled; then followed Him afar off into the palace of the high-priest, and there, sitting with the servants, and warming himself at the fire, according to Christ's prediction, before the cock crew, denied Him thrice —denied Him with oaths. (St Mark xiv.) The Lord, however, in mercy, turned and looked upon Peter; that look subdued him; he went out and wept bitterly. (St Matt. xxvi. 75.) On the morning of the Resurrection, St Peter came to visit the holy sepulchre, and the same day at even received the Holy Ghost with the other Apostles from his risen Lord, and commission to bind and to loose the sins of mankind. (St John xx. 22,

23.) Again, ere He ascended into heaven, Jesus Christ encouraged and fortified the faith of His future Vicar by a miraculous draught of fishes, demanding of him three times, "Simon, son of Jona, lovest thou Me?" and three times commended the Christian flock to his pastoral care, (John xxi,) and promised to be with him and the Apostolic College always, even to the end of the world. (St Matt. xxviii. 20.) Thus Peter fell; and thus was he restored—thus reinstated in more than all his former pre-eminence, through the grace of Him who had said, "Simon, Simon, behold Satan hath desired to have you, that he may sift you as wheat; but I have prayed for thee, that thy faith fail not; and thou being once converted, confirm thy brethren." (St Luke xxii. 31, 32.)

A new era in St Peter's history was now about to commence. His Lord had departed; and the widowed Church, with Peter at its head, was waiting for the promised descent of the Holy Ghost to supply his place. Then stood he up in the midst of the disciples as their chief, and proposed the election of an Apostle in the stead of the fallen Judas. On the Feast of Pentecost the Paraclete came, and Peter again first and foremost proclaimed the glorious Gospel of the New Law to Jews and proselytes assembled from all nations. The Holy Ghost inspired his lips, and sat like a cloven tongue of fire on his head, and three thousand were converted and baptized. (Acts ii. 41.) Again he preached, and five thousand were added to the Church. (Acts iv. 4.) Then Christians had all things in common; and they who had lands or houses sold them, and laid the proceeds at the Apostles' feet. Ananias and Saphira, keeping back a part of the price of their possessions, made a false return; and the head of the Church straightway fulminated upon them the sentence of death which God had decreed. Great fear came upon the entire Church. (Acts v. 11.) All saw in Peter the Vicar of Christ. Multitudes were added to the Lord, and brought their sick on beds and couches, and laid them in the streets, that the shadow of Peter passing by might overshadow and heal them. (Acts v. 15, 16.) In the year 38 St Peter raised the palsied Eneas at Lydda, and in Joppa restored Dorcas to life. In 41 the destined conversion of the Gentiles was revealed to him in a vision, and he commanded that they should be baptised on whom the Holy Ghost had fallen, though they came not of the stock of Israel. (Acts x.) In 44 Herod Agrippa, to please the Jews, arrested and imprisoned Peter, intending to bring him forth to the People after the Passover. Prayer was made ceaselessly by the Church unto God for him, as the chief and centre of the Christian community.

The prayers were heard. While sleeping, bound with two chains, between two soldiers, the Angel of the Lord, effulgent with celestial brightness, smote his chains, and led him forth through the self-opening gates. (Acts xii.) Already, in the year 42, he had transferred the Pontifical See to Rome; and it is from this period that the twenty-five years of Roman Pontificate, assigned him in the chronicle of Eusebius, begin. Seven years he had sat as supreme pastor in the Church of Antioch—the first Gentile Church. Yet he made no place his continual residence; he travelled from shore to shore, that his successors might have an abiding city. In the year 52 the Prince of the Apostles presided in the Council of Jerusalem. He proposed the question. He first delivered his opinion, to which all assented; and the Council formerly declared that the Gentiles were not bound to the observance of the Mosaic law. (Acts xv.) St Peter was accompanied in his labours and travels by St Mark, whom, in his first epistle, written from Babylon, that is (according to Eusebius) Rome, he calls his son. At the solicitation of the Christians in Rome, St Mark wrote the Gospel which bears his name, which was approved, and probably, in part at least, dictated by St Peter. St Mark was subsequently sent from Rome by the Chief Pastor to evangelise Egypt, where he founded churches, and provided for an apostolic succession in his patriarchal see of Alexandria. On one occasion, St Peter, having at Antioch withdrawn from the table of the Gentiles for fear of giving offence to the Jews, was gravely reprehended by St Paul, his inferior in jurisdiction. (Gal. ii. 11, 12.) Some of the Apostles, and among them St Peter, were married before they were called to the Apostleship; but we do not find that they had any commerce with their wives after they were called by Christ. St Jerome expressly affirms (Epist. 50) that they had not. And this seems to be clear from St Matthew xix. 27, where St Peter says to our Lord, "Behold, we have left all things, and have followed Thee;" for that amongst the *all* which they had foresaken, wives also were comprehended, is gathered from the enumeration made by our Saviour in ver. 29, where He expressly mentions *wives*. It is true that St Paul asks, "Have we not power to carry about a woman, a sister, as well as the rest of the Apostles and the brethren of the Lord and Cephas?" (1 Cor. ix. 5.) But the Protestant translation has in this place misrepresented the original, ἀδελφὴν γυναῖκα. The Apostle here speaks not of wives, but of such pious women as, according to the custom of the Hebrew nation, waited on the Apostles and other teachers, serving them in necessaries, as they had done also upon our Lord in the time of His mortal life. (St Luke. viii. 2, 3; St Matt. xxvii. 55, 56.)

The latter part of St Peter's career was passed in the continual prospect of martyrdom. His Saviour had predicted that such should be his end, (St John xxi. 18, 19;) and to this St Peter refers in his second Catholic Epistle, (chap. i. 14,) which, as well as the former, he wrote under the plenary inspiration of the Holy Ghost. It is related that St Peter confounded Simon Magus, the old wizard of Samaria, at Rome, in the presence of Nero. The flying magician, falling, broke his legs; and then, filled with shame, threw himself from a window and died. The power of magic fell before the power of prayer. The imperial monster's hatred of the Christian name was now excited to frenzy. He caused the Apostles Peter and Paul to be seized and thrown into the Mammertine prison. Here, at the foot of the Capitol, they lingered nine months. St Peter was persuaded to escape. Between Rome and the Alban hills our Lord is said to have met him. "Lord, whither goest Thou?" asked Peter. "I go," replied our Saviour, "to Rome, to be crucified again." St Peter understood by these words that his Divine Master was to suffer anew in the person of His servant. He therefore returned to the imperial city, and was crucified with his head downwards on the summit of Mount Janiculum, in the Jews' quarter, on the 29th of June, the same day on which his brother Apostle Paul was beheaded. His body was deposited on the Vatican Hill; and over the tombs of the blessed Apostles Peter and Paul now rises the glorious dome of the Church of St Peter. His pontificate lasted for a longer period than any of his successors has hitherto attained. His Martyrdom took place, according to some chronologists, in the year 68; or, as is more generally maintained by recent writers, in 66.

Every Pontiff has fulfilled a special divine purpose in the history of the Church. That of St Peter was to set an example to all who should succeed him of deep repentance, unwearied zeal, profound humility, and heroic suffering. There is no second Peter, and no "Peter II." No Pope has been willing to retain or assume that august and hallowed name. All have owned St Peter as their model; but even the best and wisest have followed him at a distance in their pontifical career.

2. St Linus, a.d. 68–78.

St Linus is mentioned by Tertullian, as having been St Peter's successor in the See of Rome. He was born at Volterra in Tuscany, and suffered martyrdom in the year 78. His remains were interred in the Mons Vaticanus, near the tomb of St Peter.

3. St Cletus, a.d. 78–91.

St Cletus (who is also called Anacletus) is believed to have suffered martyrdom in the year 91. He had been a disciple of St Peter, and succeeded St Linus, beside whom he rested in death. He is mentioned as a martyr in the very ancient Canon of the Roman Mass.

I scrupulously avoid all that is legendary in reference to these early Popes. It was said by Cervantes, wittily enough, that history is the mother of truth. She is so too often; but in these lives, truth, on the contrary, will be the mother of history. Religion has no communion with any manner of error.

One of the principal sources of information respecting the early Church and its rulers is Eusebius, Bishop of Cæsarea. His ecclesiastical history is in ten books, and embraces more than three centuries—from Christ to the defeat of Licinius.

4. St Clement, a.d. 91–100.

St Clement, a Roman of Jewish extraction, is mentioned by St Paul in his Epistle to the Philippians, (iv. 3,) as one of his fellow-labourers whose names are in the book of life. He succeeded St Cletus in the Roman See, and is believed to have suffered martyrdom by decapitation. He was the author of two Epistles to the Corinthians, of which one has come down to us almost entire; while of the other only a fragment, remains. These for a long while were read publicly in the churches, and are regarded as among the most venerable monuments of Christian antiquity. When appealed to by the Corinthians, in reference to their doctrinal differences, St Clement sent legates to them to set matters right: their names, as we learn from Eusebius, were Ephebus, Valerius, Veto, and Fortunatus.

5. St Evaristus, A.D. 100–109.

"St Evaristus," says Cardinal Wiseman, "multiplied the churches of Rome with circumstances peculiarly interesting. First, he enacted that from thenceforward no altars should be erected except of stone, and that they should be blessed; and, secondly, he distributed the titles—that is, he divided Rome into parishes, to the churches of which he gave the name of title."

6. St Alexander I., A.D. 109–119.

This Pope is to be numbered among those already spoken of, whose names and martyrdom only remain on record. His tomb has been discovered lately in the Via Nomentana, where a church was raised over his remains.

7. St Sixtus I., a.d. 119–127.

He suffered martyrdom. The succession of the early Popes as here given is certain, but as Fleury remarks, the dates of their election and death cannot be so exactly ascertained.

8. St Telesphorus, a.d. 127–139.

St Telesphorus, a Greek by birth, was certainly martyred in the reign of the Emperor Antoninus, after a pontificate of ten or eleven years. St Irenæus reckons him as the first martyred Pope after St Peter; and this gives extreme probability to the opinion of some critics, that the title of "martyr," accorded to some others by authors of less weight than this Father, ought to be understood as denoting only that martyrdom which they were continually disposed to suffer; or of tortures which they really endured, without actual death.*

9. St Higinus, a.d. 139–142.

St Higinus condemned and excommunicated two heresiarchs,—Cerdon, a Syrian, and Valentine, an Egyptian Gnostic. Poverty and perse-

---

* Henrion. lib. iii. nn. 101.

cution did not deter the Roman Pontiffs at this early period from exercising the power with which Christ had invested them, of denouncing and suppressing, with a high hand, the first risings of error in the Church. The Gnostics boasted that they alone had the true knowledge of the Divinity and things divine. These oriental mystics developed, in the second and third centuries, into a crowd of sects.

10. St Pius I., a.d. 142–157.

St Pius I., so named for his piety, combated the heresies of Valentine and Marcion. Some of his letters are extant. The succession of the Bishops of Rome at this early epoch is found in the chronicles of Eusebius.

11. St Anicetus, a.d. 157–168.

St Anicetus suffered martyrdom in the reign of Marcus Aurelius.

12. St Soter, a.d. 168–177.

A letter is extant addressed to him as ruler of the Roman Church, by St Denis, Bishop of Corinth. In this, the Pope's pious care for the brethren and for distant churches is specially commended.

13. St Eleutherius, A.D. 177–193.

In very primitive times the election of the Pope was vested in the clergy and people conjointly; but the clergy soon obtained the principal voice in the selection. St Eleutherius, a Greek, was elected to the chair of St Peter in the year 177, and governed the Church during the reigns of Marcus Aurelius and Commodus. He guarded the treasure of the faith against the attacks of Valentinian; and it is to this Pontiff that the British Islands owe the first dawnings of Christian light. We are informed by Bede, in his Ecclesiastical History, that during the reign of Marcus Antoninus Aurelius, and his brother, Annius Lucius Verus, one Lucius, a British prince, sent Elvanus and Medwinus as envoys to Rome, to learn the Christian doctrine. They were instructed by Eleutherius, then Bishop of Rome, who sent SS. Fugatius and Damianus as his deputies to baptize converted Britons. They received the king and his household into the Church, and a great number of his subjects.

14. St Victor I., A.D. 193–202.

St Victor was an African by birth. He condemned and excommunicated Theodore of Byzantium, who denied the divinity of Jesus Christ; and in a council, held at Rome in 196, fixed the

Feast of Easter for the Sunday after the 14th day of the moon of March. He suffered martyrdom under Severus. St Victor threatened the Asiatic Church with excommunication for observing Easter after the Jewish custom, on the 14th of the March moon; but was energetically dissuaded by St Irenæus and other prelates. Moderation triumphed, and each church preserved her ancient customs.

The example thus set by St Victor has been followed by his successors in every age; and although the supreme pastors have uniformly endeavoured to promote unity of discipline in all parts of Christendom, they have not pressed this laudable effort beyond certain limits. Thus Oriental churches to this day retain the Mass in their respective dialects, a modified rule respecting the celibacy of the clergy, and other peculiarities to which they are strongly attached.

15. St Zephyrinus, A.D. 202–219.

It was during the reign of this Pope that the general persecution of the Christians by the Emperor Severus burst forth. Zephyrinus issued a "peremptory decree," as it is called by Tertullian, on the ground of his authority as St Peter's successor. The fact is important, as bearing on the doctrine of the Papal supremacy.

16. St Calixtus I., a.d. 219–223.

St Calixtus was a martyr to the faith. Being imprisoned, he was made to endure hunger. His persecutors beat him severely several days following, and then threw him into a well, where he died, after a pontificate of less than four years. It is thought that the catacombs which exist at Rome under the title of St Sebastian and St Calixtus, near the Appian way, were constructed by this Bishop.

From this period we are able to state the days of the martyrdom of those Popes who sealed the faith with their blood, and that with even more precision than the years, respecting which slight variations are often found in chronological tables. St Calixtus suffered on the 14th of October, on which day he is commemorated by the Church.

17. St Urban I., a.d. 223–230.

It was about the time of his election that Minucius Felix wrote at Rome his dialogue called "Octavius," in defence of the Christian religion. Urban suffered martyrdom on the 25th of May, while Heliogabalus, a monster of sensuality, sat on the imperial throne.

18. St Pontian, a.d. 230–235.

He was elected on the 22d of July, and was exiled to Sardinia in the first year of the Emperor Maximin, together with a priest named Hippolytus. In this island he renounced the pontificate on the 28th of September, and died soon after. The churches of Rome were burned during his reign.

19. St Anterus, a.d. 235–236.

St Anterus, elected on the 21st of November, died on the 3d of January in the following year. It is probable that he fell a victim to the persecution of Maximin.

20. St Fabian, a.d. 236–250.

The election of Fabian, which took place eight days after the death of his predecessor, was attended with circumstances which were regarded at the time as miraculous. He had a little while before come from the country with some other persons. When the Christians were assembled for the election of their chief pastor, different names of deserving and well-known persons were proposed. No one thought of Fabian, who mingled unnoticed with the crowd; but at a time when God was often pleased to manifest His designs to the people by signs and prodigies, a dove, which was suddenly seen flying in the air, and then lighting and resting on the head of Fabian, attracted the attention of every one. In times of heavy persecution Christians are more than ever wont to look out for Divine interposition, and to believe in miracles. The multitude cried with a unanimous voice that Fabian was worthy of the episcopate. They carried him away and placed him in the pontifical chair. He filled his high office during fourteen years in a manner which confirmed the idea of his miraculous election.

After the Christian Church had enjoyed thirty-eight years of peace—the longest period of tranquility which had been allowed her—the Pope was desirous of procuring for her advantages proportioned to this blessing. He ordained seven bishops, associated with them a large number of inferior ministers, and sent them into the provinces of Gaul to succor the old churches and establish new. The seven Bishops, according to Gregory of Tours, were, Trophimus of Arles, Paul of Narbonne, Denis of Paris, Gatian of Tours, Saturninus of Toulouse, Martial of Limoges, and Austramoine of Auvergne. Their labours were attended with wonderful success; and France treasures their memories with constant veneration and love. Fabian did not long survive this glorious epoch. The crown of martyrdom awaited him. He was one of the first and principal victims of the fury of Decius in the year 250, and suffered on the 20th of January, after a reign distinguished for zeal and goodness.

The Holy See was vacant nearly two years after the death of this Pope, owing to violent persecutions. The Roman Church at this time consisted of forty-six priests, seven deacons, seven sub-deacons, forty-two acolytes, and fifty-two exorcists, readers, and doorkeepers.

21. St Cornelius, a.d. 251–252.

St Cornelius, elected on the 4th of June by the people and clergy and sixteen bishops, was exiled by the Emperor Gallus to Centum Cellæ, now called Civita Vecchia, where he expired on the 14th of September, after a short pontificate of one year and three months. This period, moreover, was disturbed by the pretentions of an ambitious priest named Novatian, who, jealous of the reputation of Cornelius, caused himself to be elected Bishop of Rome by some of his partisans. He affected an extraordinary zeal, and denied that the Church had power to absolve those lapsed but repentant Christians who had sacrificed to the gods. He thus became the first antipope.

Three bishops proclaimed his election; but it was rejected by St Cyprian, and utterly repudiated by the Councils of Carthage and Antioch.

22. St Lucius I., A.D. 252–253.

Lucius had been a confessor, and in exile with St Cornelius. After his election, his persecutors banished him again, and St Cyprian had no sooner heard of it, than he wrote* to congratulate the Pope on having the double honour of priesthood and suffering for the faith. His pontificate lasted only five months. He was elected on the 25th of September, and died on the 4th or 5th of March in the following year.

23. St Stephen I., A.D. 253–257.

St Stephen combated the Novatians and Martial. In a council held in 257 he maintained the validity of heretical baptism in opposition to St Cyprian the Bishop of Carthage. St Stephen was martyred in the reign of Valerian, on the 2d of August. Some fragments only of his Epistles have come down to us. In resisting the practice of rebaptizing those who had received heretical baptism, St Stephen acted with equal firmness and moderation. He abstained from imposing ecclesiastical censures on those who rebaptized.

* Epist. 61.

It is not known precisely at what period the dispute terminated, but the Pope's decree triumphed in the end over the resistance which it ought never to have encountered. The Africans reformed their custom. The Orientals likewise retracted it; and the usage of rebaptizing was generally abolished in the Catholic Church by the Council of Arles, fifty years after St Cyprian, or, at the latest, by the Œcumenical Council of Nice. However this may have been, the Holy Father had not the consolation of seeing the end of these troubles. He had been especially set for the defence of the Church in her merciful and liberal character, in claiming pardon for the lapsed who repented, in opposition to the Novatians, and in ascribing the privileges of the gospel to those who, without their own fault, had received heretical baptism, but afterwards submitted to the Church.

24. St Sixtus II., A.D. 257–258.

He was an Athenian and a philosopher of the Academy before his conversion, was elected on the 24th of August, and, like his predecessor, suffered martyrdom by decapitation in Valerian's reign. St Laurence was his archdeacon. He wrought incalculable good for the provinces of Gaul, by means of a new company of evangelical labourers whom he sent there. St Pérégrin, the first Bishop of Auxerre, and a martyr, St Memmie of Châlons-sur-Marne, St Sixtus of Rheims, and Cinicus his disciple, were but a part of this fervent and apostolic colony.

A short time before his decease on the 29th of June, Sixtus transferred the bodies of the Apostles Peter and Paul to the Catacombs. These vast galleries, which extend for many miles under Rome and its suburbs, answered the threefold purpose of secret habitations in the time of furious persecutions; of churches, where the divine mysteries might be celebrated without fear of disturbance by the heathen; and, lastly, of burial-places for all Christian brethren, and especially those who had died as martyrs for the faith. St Laurence, whose intrepid sufferings are so famous, was one of those who with tears followed Pope Sixtus to the place of his execution. On his way thither, the venerable martyr predicted to Laurence that in three days he would himself enjoy the same happiness.

25. St Dionysius, a.d. 259–269.

He was a Calabrian by birth, and, when Pope, held a council at Rome (263) against the errors of Sabellius, who saw in the Trinity only the threefold action of one person or principle, which creates, saves, and sanctifies. The date of his election was July 22nd; that of his death December 20th. His charity as well as his vigilance extended over the whole Christian world. He sent alms to the faithful of Asia who had been pillaged by the barbarians, and bestowed his bounty upon those also who had been led captive. It has been said that he divided the churches and oratories of Rome among the priests of that city, and that he instituted parishes and even dioceses immediately dependent on him: but the fact is, that he merely rendered to the pastors those churches which they had lost through the misfortunes of their times, and regulated the bounds of their exertions in a more fixed and exact manner than before.

26. St Felix I., A.D. 269–275.

Felix was a native of Rome. The peace of the Church during his pontificate was disturbed by Paul of Samosata, Bishop of that see, and afterwards Patriarch of Antioch. He denied the doctrine of the Holy Trinity and the divinity of Jesus Christ. At the same time, the Christians were bitterly persecuted by the Emperor Aurelian. St Felix encouraged them in the support of their fearful trials, and exhorted them to suffer boldly for the faith of Christ. He celebrated

Masses in memory of the martyrs, and was ready to lay down his own life for the Christian cause, but died in prison on the 22d of December. He had been elected on the 29th of that month, in 269, three days after the death of St Dionysius. An epistle written by him to Maximus, Bishop of Alexandria, respecting Paul of Samosata, is extant.

27. St Eutychian, a.d. 275-283.

He had been Bishop of Luna, was elected on the 6th of January, and died on the 7th or 8th of December. Nothing further appears to be known respecting him.

28. St Caius, a.d. 283-296.

He was elected on the 17th of December, and died on the 22d of April. Some authors describe him as a martyr; but more ancient records lead us to believe that he was a confessor only. He is said to have been a relative of the Emperor Diocletian, and to have encouraged in their martyrdom Gabinius, the emperor's nephew, and Susanna, the daughter of Gabinius.

29. St Marcellinus, a.d. 296-304.

The persecution of Dioclesian took place under his pontificate. The Church honours him as a martyr. His fall into idolatry, and appearance before the Council of Sinuessa, seem to be fables invented by the Donatists.* St Augustine distinctly maintains the falsity of the charge, in opposition to the Donatist Petilian. On the other hand, the incident is recorded in the Breviary.†

The Decretals, or Epistles of the Popes of the three first centuries, collected by Isidore in the eighth, are rejected by the best critics as spurious; excepting, however, those which are cited by ancient fathers—Athanasius, Hilary, Cyprian, Theodoret, &c.

St Marcellinus was elected on the 30th of June, and died on the 24th of October, in a manner worthy of a saint, as all historians, heterodox as well as orthodox, allow.

After his decease the Holy See was vacant more than three years and a half, so perilous was it to occupy the chair of the Apostle, on account of the implacable cruelty of the pagan persecutors. Should that chair ever be vacant again for so long a period, we shall look back to this and similar historical precedents for encouragement and consolation in our doubts and fears. The line of Vicars will never fail till Christ shall return.

---

* Henrion, lib. vi. an. 305. See also *Lamp*, May 16, 1863.
† See Newman's *Present Position of English Catholics*, p. 323.

30. St Marcellus, a.d. 308–310.

He was banished by the Emperor Maxentius, under pretext of his causing disturbances by his undue severity towards the lapsed. He certainly obliged those who had fallen into idolatry during persecution to do penance for their sin, and this just discipline produced division and serious disorders.

He was ordained to the pontificate on the 19th of May, and died on the 16th of January.

31. St Eusebius, a.d. 310–311.

He was elected on the 20th of May, and died on the 26th of September. Nothing remarkable is known concerning him.

32. St Milchiades, a.d. 311–314.

He was of African origin, and combated the Donatist heresy, and excommunicated Donatus, Bishop of Cellæ Negræ in Numidia, who denied absolution to the "betrayers," as they called those who had given up the sacred books to the heathen. When the Donatists appealed to the Emperor Constantine to obtain his support against the African Catholics, he rebuked them for seeking the aid of temporal authority, and at once referred them to the Pope, Milchiades. "But because," says St Augustine, "Constantine dared not judge the bishops' cause, he appointed it to be discussed and terminated by bishops, which also was done at Rome, under the presidency of Milchiades."

The Pope chose fifteen bishops out of Italy to sit with him; and by them the too-rigorous Donatists were condemned (A.D. 313.)

Milchiades was elected on the 2d of July, and died on the 10th of January.

33. St Silvester, A.D. 314-336.

St Silvester was a native of Rome, and enjoyed the favour of the Emperor Constantine. He was elected on the 31st of January. His pontificate was marked by the happy close of the pagan persecutions, by the first Œcumenical Council, held at Nice in the year 325 for the suppression of the Arian heresy, and by the prevalence of the Donatist schism. To this reign is assigned the donation attributed to Constantine,* which is said to have been the origin of the temporal power of the Popes. The advantages of this power will be pointed out under Leo III.

The following allusion to the emperor's gift deserves a passing notice:

* Gibbon, *Decline and Fall*, chap. lxix.

> "Ahi, Costantin, di quanto mal fu madre,
> Non la tua conversione, ma quella dote
> Che da te prese il primo ricco padre!"*

These lines of the great poet, which are so often quoted, glance at the subject in one aspect only: and are not even intended to take a comprehensive view of it. Incidental evils have befallen what was a good on the whole.

The Council of Nice was summoned by the authority of St Silvester in conjunction with the emperor; he presided over it in the person of his legates, Vito and Vicentius; and the decrees of the council were referred to him for confirmation.

The wooden altar used by St Peter, and kept till this time in the church of St Prudentiana, was transferred by St Silvester to the Lateran basilica, of which it forms the high altar. Constantine conferred on the sovereign pontiffs, hitherto the objects of persecution, the Lateran palace, and of an adjoining palace he made the basilica just referred to, which was then called the basilica of Constantine, and now the church of St John Lateran.

The baptistry in which, according to some writers, he was received into the Church of

---

* Dante, *L'Inferno*, canto xix.:
> "Ah Constantine, of how much ill was cause,
> Not thy conversion, but th' endowment, which
> From thee the first rich father then received!"

Christ by St Silvester, in the imperial city, was afterwards magnificently restored by Gregory XIII. and Urban VIII.

St Silvester died on the 31st of December. In order to elucidate the history of the Popes, I will give, each in its proper place, a brief sketch of the lives of the principal heresiarchs, whose errors have, through the providence of God, been the occasion of calling forth the judgments of the Universal Church in council, and rendering the faith of Catholics purer, because more clearly defined.

Arius.

Arius was born about the year 270, in Cyrenaica or Alexandria. He was ordained priest at an advanced age; and having settled in the city just named, he began in 312 to teach a new doctrine, which rapidly gained ground. He opposed the Trinity, denied the consubstantiality of the Word with the Father, and consequently His divinity, and made Him a creature very inferior to God, though divine in a subordinate sense. He affirmed that the Son of God was of *like* essence with the Father ($\dot{\iota}\mu\epsilon\iota\acute{\nu}\sigma\iota\varsigma$) but not of the *same* essence ($\dot{\iota}\mu\epsilon\iota\acute{\nu}\sigma\iota\varsigma$). He was opposed successively by St Alexander and St Athanasius, Bishops of Alexandria, condemned by several councils, especially that of Nice in 325, and anathematised and exiled during many years. Yet he persisted in his errors, unsoftened by the solicitations, and unawed by the censures of the Church. Being supported by Eusebius, Bishop of Nicomedia, one of his party, he was absolved by some petty cabal councils, and even succeeded in deceiving Constantine, who recalled him from exile, and re-established him at Alexandria. His return, however, having excited some disturbances in this city, he retired to Constantinople, and, in spite of the opposition of St Alexander, who had become its Patriarch, he was about to enter the church in triumph, when he died suddenly of a violent colic, in 336. The faithful regarded his death as a Divine judgment, while his partisans affirmed he had been poisoned.

After the death of Arius, his heresy made great progress. It was openly protected by the Emperor Constantius and by several of his successors, approved by many conventicles, and supported for a long time by very numerous adherents, though steadily and strongly resisted by every Pontiff from St Silvester to Vitalian.

The Emperor Theodosius succeeded in stifling the heresy almost entirely in the heart of his dominions; but it was embraced by most of the barbarous people who had invaded the Roman empire, and lasted several centuries among the Goths, the Vandals, the Teutonic Burgundi, and the Lombards. It was extinguished, about the year 660, by the abjuration of Anibert, the last Arian king of the Lombards.

34. St Mark, A.D. 336–337.

He was elected on the 18th of January, and died on the 7th of October. Little mention is made of him in the histories of his time.

35. St Julius I., A.D. 337–352.

He was born in Rome. St Athanasius, having been deposed from his patriarchate of Alexandria by a cabal council of Arians at Tyre in 335, was summoned by St Julius to the Apostolic See, pronounced innocent, and reinstated by the councils of Rome and Sardica, (in 347,) to which last St Julius sent his legates. The Church of Alexandria, the second patriarchal see, having thus, in censuring their bishop, proceeded on their own authority, instead of obtaining a just sentence from Rome, the Pope, in his "Apology to Constantine concerning St Athanasius," stigmatised this as "a novel practice." He was elected on the 6th of February, and died on the 12th of April.

36. Liberius, A.D. 352–365.

Marcellinus Felix Liberius assembled several councils to decide between Athanasius and the

Arians, and was exiled from Rome by the Emperor Constantius because he would not subscribe to the condemnation of the great doctor of the mystery of the Incarnation. It is generally objected to Liberius by innovators that he lapsed into the Arian heresy in order to be recalled from exile; but Catholic writers vindicate him from this charge, and show that the first *formula fidei* of the first council of Sirmium, which he subscribed in obedience to his persecutors, was not Arian in its terms, but might be construed in an orthodox sense.* Others regard the whole matter as a fabrication of the Arians. † Felix II., a Roman archdeacon, was ordained Pope by the emperor and the Arian party in 355, and expelled on Liberius's return in 358. After having suffered much from the Arians, Liberius was crowned with martyrdom on the 26th of September, 365.

37. Felix II., a.d. 355–358.

The name of Felix II. occurs in some lists of the Popes, while in others it is omitted for obvious reasons.

38. St Damasus, a.d. 366–384.

He was born in Portugal, and was sixty years of age at the time of his elevation. His father

---

* See J. de Maistre, Du Pape, pp. 99, 100.
† *Manual of Church History*, (Burns and Lambert,) p. 57.

had been admitted as priest in the Roman Church. When a deacon, he vowed never to make terms with the schismatical successors of the exiled Liberius. When he became Pope (October 1st) he laboured for the preservation of morals and ecclesiastical discipline, especially among the monastic orders. He held several councils against the Arians, and anathematised Ursacius, Valens, Anxentius, Vitalis, and Timothy, all heretics or schismatics. He was resisted by the Anti-pope Ursinus, who was elected by seditious men, and expelled by the Emperor Valentinian. Some of his Christian poems and theological writings are extant. Under his authority, and that of Theodosius the Great, the second œcumenical council was held at Constantinople in 381. It condemned the Macedonians, who made the Holy Ghost a mere creature, and it added a clause to the symbol of Nicæa.

St Damasus availed himself of the pen and counsels of St Jerome, whose reputation for wisdom and learning was now universal. When he came to Rome, for the second time, the Pope chose him as his secretary, and induced him to correct the Latin version of the Holy Bible. We have in Theodoret a letter signed by St Damasus and ninety bishops from Italy and Gaul, which says, "As soon as the Arian heresy began to reach that pitch which the blasphemy has now attained, 218 of our Fathers, with legates from the Bishop of Rome, deliberated on the subject at Nice." About the time of the anti-popes above mentioned, the pontificate began to be surrounded by a degree of splendour sufficient to excite cupidity and ambition. "I am not surprised," says Ammianus Marcellinus, in recalling the history of this schism, "that those who aspire to the pontificate of the Christians use their greatest efforts in order to arrive at it; since it establishes them in a fixed position of honour and of fortune, in which the offerings of Roman ladies procure for them inexhaustible funds. When they go out it is in magnificent equipages; when they appear abroad they are superbly attired, and the daintiness of their table would vie with that of kings."* One perceives by this bitter tone that this pagan writer was much more careful to indulge his own malignity and prejudice than to record the truth. In the same spirit, Pretextatus, consul elect, said to Pope Damasus, who exhorted him to be converted, "Give me your place, and I will be a Christian immediately." All that can be reasonably concluded from this irony is, that at that period the Papacy was invested with a certain degree of magnificence, the necessary consequence of the extension of the Christian kingdom.

*Amm. xxvii. c. 3.

How greatly the Catholic religion had advanced by this time, and how important was the influence which it was attaining, may be inferred from the celebrated law of the Emperor Theodosius in favour of the Roman Church, which was published throughout his vast empire. The date of this enactment is February 28, 380. "It is our will," he says, "that all the people of our obedience follow the religion which the Prince of the Apostles taught the Romans, and which is followed at present by the Pontiff Damasus, and by Peter, Bishop of Alexandria; so that according to the teaching of the Apostles, and the doctrine of the Gospel, we believe in one only divinity of the Father, the Son, and the Holy Ghost, under an equal majesty and sacred Trinity. We order that those who hold this pure faith shall bear the name of Catholics; and that the others, whose rash and insensate impiety we reprove, shall be called by the infamous name of heretics, and that their assemblies shall not arrogate to themselves the quality of churches."* St Damasus died on the 10th or 11th of December, 384, after a pontificate of more than eighteen years, and in the eightieth year of his age.

He was endowed with one of the finest and most cultivated intellects of his time. Among other writings which he has left, we have his

---

* Code of Theodosius, lib. ii, De Fid. Cath. lib. xvi.

own epitaph and that of his sister, the virgin Irene, by whose side he desired his body might repose after death.

39. St Siricius, a.d. 384–398.

A Roman by birth, and priest of the title of the Pastor, he was elevated on the 1st of January. He combated the Novatians and Donatians, and aided Theodosius in repressing the Manicheans. Several of his letters remain. They contain important evidence as to the supremacy of the see of St Peter. He replied to Hymerus, Bishop of Taragona, who had consulted the Holy See on various points of discipline, and censured the marriage of the clergy in the Western Church. He died on the 25th of November, 398.

40. St Anastasius I., a.d. 398–401.

Rome was his native city. He distinguished himself by his piety, which St Jerome extols; reconciled the Orientals with the Roman Church, and condemned the Origenists, who believed in the pre-existence of souls in a higher sphere, whence they came to animate human bodies. They maintained that the soul had sinned before it became imprisoned in the body, and that it suffers here the penalty of its former offences; that the pains of hell will not be everlasting, and that Christ was the Son of God only by adoption. How grotesque and various are the forms of heresy; how subtle and suited to the nations and times in which they arise; and how incapable is their finest plausibility of eluding the discriminating eye of that Church of whom it is said, "Every voice that riseth up against thee in judgment thou shalt condemn!"

The following tables will probably be found useful to students, as epitomising the history of the Church under different aspects:

THE ŒCUMENICAL COUNCILS.

No.	Date.	Bishops present.	Place.	Popes presiding in Person or by Legates.	Character of the Council in barbarous words, to aid the memory.
I.	325	318	Nicæa	St Silvester	Anti-Arian.
II.	381	150	Constantinople (1st)	St Damasus	Anti-Macedonian.
III.	431	200	Ephesus	St Celestine	Anti-Nestorian.
IV.	451	600	Chalcedon	St Leo	Anti-Eutychian and Anti-Monophysite.
V.	553	165	Constantinople (2d)	Vigilius	Anti-Triacapitula.
VI.	680	289	Constantinople (3d)	St Agatho	Anti-Monothelite.
VII.	787	360	Nicæa (2d)	Adrian I	Anti-Iconoclast.
VIII.	869	102	Constantinople (4th)	Adrian II	Anti-Photian.
IX.	1123	300, & 600 abbots	1st Lateran	Calixtus II	Anti-Investiture.
X.	1139	1000	2d Lateran	Innocent II	Anti-Arnaldist.
XI.	1179	302	3d Lateran	Alexander III	Anti-Albigensian.
XII.	1215	412	4th Lateran	Innocent III	"
XIII.	1245	140	1st Lyons	Innocent IV	Anti-Fredericum secundum.
XIV.	1274	500	2d Lyons	Gregory X	Pro-Græco-Latino reunion.
XV.	1311	300	Vienne	Clement V	Anti-Templar.
XVI.	1414 to 1418	300	Constance	John XXIII and Martin V	Anti-Wickliff, Huss, and Avignon Anti-Popes.
XVII.	1438 1439	141	Florence	Eugenius IV	Pro-Græco-Latino reunion.
XVIII.	1545 to 1563	270	Trent	Paul III, Julius III, Marcellus II, Paul IV, Pius IV	Anti-Protestant.

SECULA ECCLESIASTICA.

1. Seculum	Apostolicum.	10. Seculum	Obscurum.
2. "	Gnosticum.	11. "	Hildebrandicum.
3. "	Novatianum.	12. "	Waldensicum.
4. "	Arianum.	13. "	Scholasticum.
5. "	Nestorianum.	14. "	Wicklevianum.
6. "	Eutychianum.	15. "	Synodalicum.
7. "	Monotheleticum.	16. "	Protestanticum.
8. "	Iconoclasticum.	17. "	Jansenisticum.
9. "	Photianum.	18. "	Scepticum.

41. St Innocent I., A.D. 402–417.

He obtained from the Emperor Honorius some severe laws against the Donatists; urged him to treat for peace with Alaric; and when the city of Rome had been taken and devastated, he applied himself to the utmost to repair the losses. He condemned the doctrines of Pelagius, who denied the necessity of divine grace, and the existence of original sin; and he checked the progress of the Novatians. He replied at length to various questions on points of discipline proposed to him by St Victrice of Rouen, and St Exuperius of Toulouse. His letters and decretals, which have been collected and published by Constant, show that he claimed and exercised the Papal power as fully and decidedly as it was claimed and exercised by his successors in later ages. He died on the 12th of March.

St John Chrysostom having been unjustly deposed from the see of Constantinople, and cruelly exiled by Arcadius, the emperor of the East, the Pope warmly espoused the cause of this Demosthenes of Christian orators, and interceded in his behalf with Honorius, the emperor of the West, and brother of the persecutor. These glorious efforts, however, could not prevent the death of St Chrysostom in exile, after the endurance of long and various sufferings. The Popes have been in all ages the defenders of the oppressed, and the consolation of the afflicted; and to each of them, in his official capacity, may be applied the words of the prophet, "A man shall be as a hiding-place from the wind and a covert from the tempest, and as the shadow of a rock that standeth out in a desert land."

42. St Zozimus, a.d. 417–418.

St Zozimus, a Greek, was elected on the 18th of March. Celestius, a deciple of Pelagius, came to Rome and endeavoured to deceive this Pope by an artful exposition of his master's doctrines. But Zozimus soon recognised the heresy and condemned it. Eighteen Bishops appealed from his judgment to an œcumenical council; but his condemnation was renewed in the Council of Ephesus. The denial of original sin disordered and enfeebled the whole fabric of Christianity.

By making men less fallen, it made grace, baptism, and the atonement less needful. "All through Church history from the first," says Dr Newman, "how slow is authority in interfering! . . . . Zozimus treated Pelagius and Celestius with extreme forbearance; St Gregory VII. was equally indulgent with Berengarius. By reason of the very power of the Popes, they have commonly been slow and moderate in their use of it." Thirteen letters of St Zozimus are extant, and also a fragment of his "Constitution against Pelagius." In his letter to the Council of Carthage he says, "No one may dare to doubt of the decisions of the Apostolic See," and "no one may dare to recede from our judgment." He died on the 20th of December.

43. St Boniface I., A.D. 418–422.

His election took place on the 28th of December. He was disquieted by an antipope, Eulalius the archdeacon, who, after obstinate resistance, was banished from Rome by the Emperor Honorius. St Augustine, who held the Pontiff in the highest estimation, dedicated to him his four books against the Pelagians. In the second of these, the holy doctor formally attests that neither the teaching of Pelagius nor of Celestius were ever approved at Rome; though Zozimus, during a certain time, exercised indulgence towards the latter.* The following remarkable passage occurs in the Epistles of St Boniface: "It never was allowed to agitate a question which has once been settled by the Apostolic See."† "The government of the Universal Church, at its commencement, derived its origin from the dignity of the blessed Peter, in whom its rule and management abide. . . . . It is certain, then, that this (the Roman Church) is as the head of its members over all other churches; from which, if any cut himself off, he becomes an alien from the Christian religion, since he has ceased to be in that unity."‡ St Boniface died on the 4th of September, 422; according to another chronology, on the 25th of October.

We learn from an ancient epitaph, that Boniface came to the pontificate at a very advanced age, but that from the time of his youth he had rendered useful services to the Apostolic See, and had solaced the city of Rome in a year of sterility. His character was distinguished by clemency, gentleness, and modesty; engaging virtues, which served much better than severity to extinguish the schism which his election occasioned, but which did not hinder him from powerfully sustaining the dignity of his position.

* Cap. ii.   † Ep. xiii. Constant. p. 1036.   ‡ Ep. xiv. Constant. p. 1037.

44. St Celestine I., a.d. 422–432.

He was a Roman, and elected on the 10th of September. He sent missionaries to Ireland, and deputed St Cyril of Alexandria to preside in his name, with Arcadius and Projectus, at the third œcumenical council of Ephesus in 431, in the reign of Theodosius the younger. This synod, in opposition to Nestorius, declared that in Christ there is but one person, and that St Mary is the mother of God. It also proscribed Pelagianism. This Pope's epistles are forcible and conclusive on the supremacy of the Holy See. St Celestine was another Pope for whom St Augustine had the highest reverence, and to whom he appealed in the humblest manner under the perplexities of the African Church; and on the other hand, it was Celestine who assigned to the marvellous writings of Augustine that high authority and consideration they have in the Church. To this Pope the British nation is mainly indebted for the preservation of the pure faith. Pelagianism had been making rapid strides there, when St Germanus and St Palladius came, the former to England, and the latter to the Scots, or Irish, invested by St Celestine with the authority of the Holy See; and chiefly by the miracles which it pleased Almighty God to work by their hands, the heresy was completely extinguished. The great work of St Celestine's reign was the conflict with Nestorianism. He did not long survive its consumation. He was succeeded by Sixtus III., a native of Rome, a priest of the Roman Church, the same to whom St Augustine had addressed his famous letter on Divine grace. It is to the zealous Pope Celestine that Ireland owes the faith which she has retained with so much constancy during ages of persecution, oppression, and bribery. St Patrick, whose birthplace has long been matter of debate, is said to have travelled into Gaul and Italy, and to have seen St Celestine. From this pontiff he is supposed to have received his mission and the apostolical blessing.* A good deal of uncertainty hangs over his earlier history; and his own writings, which are the best authority, state that he was made bishop in his own country. But however this may have been, his zeal, supported by miraculous gifts, produced such abundant fruits that he has always been regarded as the Apostle of Ireland, where he founded three monasteries, and the metropolitan church of Armagh. St Celestine died on the 6th of April, 432.

45. Sixtus III., A.D. 432–440.

He was ordained on the 26th of April. He aided St Cyril in uniting the Churches of the

---

* See Butler's *Lives*, vol. iii. p. 213.

East, and left five thousand marks of silver to be expended in religious decorations. He had, indeed, an extraordinary zeal for the honour of God's house, and one is astonished at the prodigious gifts with which he enriched in less than eight years most of the churches of Rome. In his epistle to St Cyril he is firm and clear on the Roman supremacy. He died on the 10th of August.

The persecution of Genseric had been violent, from the beginning of his conquest under the pontificate of St Celestine; but it was still more so, and lasted much longer, under that of his successor; for Sixtus III. died the year after the capture of Carthage by the Vandals.

Nestorius.

Nestorius was a native of Germanica in Syria, and was nominated Patriarch of Constantinople in 420 by Theodosius the younger. He persecuted the Arians and Novatians, while he preached himself a new heresy: he denied the hypostatic union of the Word with the human nature, and affirmed that in Jesus Christ we ought to distinguish *two persons* as well as two natures. According to Nestorius, St Mary was not θεοτόκος, mother of God. The national council of Alexandria (430) and general council of Ephesus (431) condemned these errors, and the latter deposed Nestorius, who was banished, and died in an oasis of Libya about 439. His writings were burnt by order of Theodosius II. Some of his homilies and letters are still extant.

EUTYCHES.

Eutyches was archimandrite of a monastery near Constantinople when the heresy of Nestorius started up. He quitted his retreat to defend the faith, but fell himself into a new heresy which began to spread in 448. He taught that there existed but *one nature* in Jesus Christ, the Divine nature, which absorbed the human, as the sea absorbs a drop of water. Eutyches was accused by Eusebius of Dorylæum, and Flavian, Patriarch of Constantinople, and obliged to appear in a council held at Ephesus, which, on account of the violence it committed, is called the Brigand Council of Ephesus. Eutyches, being secretly supported by the Emperor Theodosius II. was absolved; but after the death of this prince he was condemned by the Council of Chalcedon in 451. Soon after this he died, aged seventy-five. His heresy made great progress after his decease, and engendered a crowd of new sects, some of which exist still in the East. His partisans were called Monophysites.

46. St Leo the Great, a.d. 440–461.

The epithet "great," though it has often been bestowed on those who had no real greatness, invariably indicates a man who has made an impression on the age in which he lived. This was eminently the case with St Leo: he was great in his connexion with political events, great in his ecclesiastical influence and decrees, and great in his writings. The place of his birth is not precisely known; it was either Rome or Tuscany. His family was certainly Tuscan; but it is thought that he was born in Rome, which he always calls his country. He had been the Archdeacon of Sixtus III., whom he aided by his counsels. His merits had been developing daily, and marked him as the most suitable person to fill the vacant see. He was elected on the 29th of September, when absent on a mission in Gaul, whither he had been sent to reconcile Aëtius and Albin, the two chief captains of the West, whose dissensions were equally pernicious to the Church and to the empire. It was therefore necessary to wait about fourteen days before their choice could be announced to him; and this in itself was a testimony of esteem without example up to that time. Moreover, a public deputation was appointed to carry to Leo the news of his election. Scarcely had he mounted the chair of St Peter when the brilliancy of his genius became evident to all. His labours and his vigilance as head of the Church knew no bounds. In every corner of Italy, in Campania, in Tuscany, in the Marsh of Ancona, in Sicily, and in Africa, as well as in the other parts of the East—in Egypt, and even in the deserts of Mauritania—his letters and decretals shed abundant light. Through his instructions and exhortations the priesthood in Italy acquired new dignity and lustre. He multiplied the disqualifications for the sacred ministry, excluding slaves, those engaged in illicit or unsuitable business, and those who had been married to a widow or had wedded twice.

The invasion of Italy by Alaric during the pontificate of St Innocent I. was followed by that of Attila, king of the Huns. This barbarian, like Alaric, conceiving that a providential mission was intrusted to him, called himself *the scourge of God*. His aspect and bearing were anything but distinguished and commanding. He was small in stature, with a broad chest, and a head large even to deformity; he had eyes of fire; his hair and beard were short; he had a flat nose, a bronzed complexion, and withal a proud menacing walk. Peaceful kings, his vassals, trembled in his presence. He was on the point of sacking and destroying Rome, when St

Leo, armed with invisible might, appeared before him with an air of perfect confidence and composure. Addressing him with respect, but with energy and force, he advocated the cause of afflicted Italy. The firmness and eloquence of the prelate astonished the ferocious invader; and he said to those who surrounded him: "The words of this priest have touched me, and I know not why." Having become more tractable, he listened to the proposals which were made him by the Emperor of the West, caused hostilities to cease, and (in 452) withdrew his army from Italy. St Leo was not equally happy in the result of his interview with Genseric, king of the vandals, who, three years later, (455,) presented himself at the gates of the imperial city. He was, indeed, unable to prevent his penetrating within the gates; but he persuaded the rapacious barbarian to content himself with despoiling Rome, without destroying either the inhabitants or the edifices.

This Pontiff condemned in several Councils the sects which troubled the Church, particularly the Eutychians and Manichees. Being unable to take a journey to the East, Paschasinus and Lucentius presided in his name at the fourth Œcumenical Council held at Chalcedon, in the reign of Marcian and Pulcheria, (451.) The holy Gospels were, as at the Council of Ephesus, placed upon a throne in the midst of the assembly. The Eutychians were condemned; and St Leo's letter maintaining the doctrine of two natures in the person of Christ without separation and without confusion or change, was approved without a dissenting voice, and regarded as a rule of faith. "This we all believe," cried the Bishops; "this is the faith of the Apostles; it is Peter himself who has spoken by the mouth of Leo. This doctrine must be held as orthodox; anathema to him who believes it not."

The Pope, however, refused to ratify those decrees of the Council which attributed certain prerogatives to the see of Constantinople. The Eutychians agitated for a new council; Leo firmly resisted. Losing all hope of success in the attempt, they demanded at least a conference, in which they might state their difficulties. The Pope was inflexible. "To accede," he said,* "to this artful request of restless sectarians is impossible. Let them never hope to obtain my consent to it. In seeking to dispute anew concerning the faith, they would have it believed that nothing has yet been settled on the point in question. The snare is too manifest; Leo will never be taken by it."

St Leo is justly regarded as one of the great lights and doctors of the Church. His works,

* Epist. 70.

many of which are extant, abound in the most lucid and explicit testimony to the supremacy of St Peter's See. St Leo did not long survive the commencement of the calm which he had procured for the Church. He died on the 4th or 5th of November, 461. His pontificate had lasted twenty-one years, during which period the greatness of his mind and soul had never ceased to shine forth. His knowledge and genius were no less eminent than his virtues. His mode of writing is noble and pure for the age in which he lived; and the eloquence which glows in most of his sermons is extremely touching and pathetic, and worthy of any era. Of these sermons ninety-six remain. They were preached on the principal festivals; and in them he treats of the mysteries with a clearness and an unction which can never fail to interest just and pious minds. We have also one hundred and forty-one letters of this illustrious Pontiff.

He is the first of the Popes who have left a collection of works, and to whom has been given by general consent the epithet of Great. He was zealous for the decency and magnificence of divine worship; for the foundation, and still more, for the restoration of churches, which he adorned with a taste which bore the impress of his noble soul and exalted genius. After the ravages of the Vandals he renewed the silver vessels and ornaments in all the churches of Rome. For this purpose he melted down six large vases of a hundred pounds weight each, formerly given by Constantine the Great. At the tombs of the holy Apostles Peter and Paul he appointed guardians or chaplains, who were then called chamberlains, from *camera*, a chamber or chapel.

47. ST HILARY, A.D. 461–468.

A Sardinian and archdeacon, who was elected November 10, and died February 21, 468; or, as Henrion says,* on the 20th of September, 467. Twelve years before he had acquitted himself worthily, as legate of St Leo, at the false and Eutychian Council of Ephesus. He gave to different churches 84 lbs. of gold and 152 lbs. of silver in sacred vessels, besides many other equally munificent gifts. We may judge by this fact of the opulence of the Roman Church, even in untoward times.

48. ST SIMPLICIUS, A.D. 468–483.

He established in the East the authority of the Council of Chalcedon, and reinstated the lawful Bishops in the sees of Antioch and Alexandria; but he did not quiet so promptly the troubles in

* Lib. xvii. A.D. 474.

the West. This Pope was elected on the 25th of February, 468; or, according to Henrion, the 20th of September, 467. Nothing is more difficult than to reconcile the chronological discrepancies which we find in different writers in respect to the dates of the elections of the early Popes. In the history of the Church by Henrion, they are often given differently in the body of the work and in the tables at the end of each volume.

Simplicius died on the 27th of February, when on the point of condemning the *Henoticon* of Zeno. Several of his letters remain. His piety and prudence made him worthy of his predecessors in the Holy See.

49. St Felix III., a.d. 483–492.

He was a native of Rome, and ancestor of St Gregory the Great. His election took place on the 2d of March. He rejected the edict for the union of the two Churches published by Zeno, emperor of the East; and condemned its chief promoter, Acacius, Bishop of Constantinople, an Eutychian, and many other heretics. In his letter to Acacius, the Pope reproaches this irreligious and political patriarch with his tergiversations and culpable silence on subjects with regard to which it was so necessary for the edification of the Church that he should clearly explain himself. Returning again to the strange conduct of the emperor, so contrary to what they had reason to hope from him, he says: "It was your duty to represent to this prince all that has been done in opposition to Peter of Alexandria and in favour of the Catholic Timothy; for it is well known how much influence you have with Zeno. Why did you not employ it to deter the emperor from re-establishing the heresy which he had overthrown? Without this, of what avail will be the zeal which you manifest against him who first fostered the impiety, that is, against the tyrant Basilicus (a usurper and rival of Zeno?) Will you lose its eternal reward? Will you lose yourself for ever, for having abandoned the Lord's flock to devouring wolves, or at least for having taken flight like a cowardly hireling? You could not even screen yourself under the shameful pretext of fear and cowardice, since it is well known that you have nothing to risk for this world: but fear for eternity; it is for you that I tremble, considering the promises of Jesus Christ. I have no disquietude as to the fate of the Church, which depends neither on your efforts nor on mine; but let us fear the fate of the guilty pilot who lets go the helm during the tempest. The vessel of the Church will be preserved; but those who abandon her, like those who keep aloof from

4*

her, will infallibly perish, and not to provide for her security is in effect to forsake her." Acacius had taken his side, and all the eloquence of the Pope was unable to change his resolution. His excommunication followed. St Felix assembled a council in Rome in 487, and died on the 24th or 25th of February, 492.

50. St Gelasius, a.d. 492–496.

He was a native of Rome, elected on the 1st of March. He approved what his predecessor had done against Acacius; and refused to admit to communion Euphemius, patriarch of Constantinople, who would not condemn the memory of this fosterer of heresy. He combated the errors of the Eutychians, and convened a council of seventy Bishops at Rome in 494, in which the existing canon of the sacred Scriptures was fixed, precisely as in Catholic Bibles of our day, and various apocryphal writings were censured. It is through the Catholic Church only that we can ever know what is, and what is not, a portion of the Word of God. She is the witness, as well as the keeper, of Holy Writ. This Pope, Gelasius, composed prayers for the administration of the Sacraments and for the Sacrifice of the Mass, several prefaces and hymns, in imitation of St Ambrose. He also enjoined communion in both kinds, in opposition to a heresy then current. The Manicheans condemned the use of wine; and some of the clergy and laity, infected with their tenets, wished to disuse it even in the Holy Eucharist. It was to combat this that Gelasius issued the order in question.* He was a man of rare piety, and gave himself especially to prayer and intercourse with the servants of God. When raised to the highest dignity, he regarded it as the heaviest burden, as a servitude for which he was accountable to all men. He fed all the poor whom he could discover; lived himself as a poor man, and in the practice of the most rigorous austerities. His death was as holy as his life, and took place on the 19th of November, 496. He is the first Pope who fixed the Ember weeks as the periods of Ordination.

51. St Anastasius II., A.D. 496–498.

Anastasius II. also was a Roman. He was elected on the 24th of November. He addressed a letter in favour of the Catholic religion to the Greek emperor Anastasius I., by whom Catholics were persecuted and Eutychians favoured. When Clovis, King of France, had embraced Christianity at the instance of his wife Clotilda, and received baptism at Rheims from the hands of

* See *Lamp*, May, 1863, p. 318.

St Remigius, the Pope wrote him a letter of congratulation on his happy change. He died on the 17th of November.

52. Symmachus, a.d. 498–514.

Cælius Symmachus was a deacon, and by birth a Sardinian. He was elected on the 22d of November. He triumphed over the antipope Laurentius, (a *protégé* of the patrician Festus and supporter of the *Henoticon*,) through the decision of Theodoric, king of the Goths. Laurentius and Symmachus—the false and the true Pope—were elected on the same day, the former in the basilica of St Mary, the latter in that of Constantine, by a majority of votes. The adherents of his rival, who had filled Rome with slaughter, accused him of horrible crimes; but he was absolved by the Council of Palma, so called from the name of a door of the basilica of St Peter.

He displayed much zeal against Eutychianism and Nestorianism, as also against the famous *Henoticon*, or edict for the union of the Eutychians and Catholics, published by the Emperor Zeno. He allowed the intetest of ecclesiastical possessions to be paid to worthy clergymen and monasteries under the title of *beneficia;* and in a council held in 504 it was forbidden to alienate such revenues. This appears to be the origin of church-benefices, which a little after were confirmed by the Council of Aurelia, (538,) in which glebes are granted to the clergy for life.

Symmachus wrote an apology for himself in answer to a libel which had been published against him by the Emperor Anastasius, who, furious at seeing his stratagems and duplicity exposed, went so far as to treat the Pope as a Manichean. Anastasius himself was a low-born man, who had married the widow of the Emperor Zeno, and followed in his steps in favouring the Eutychians and persecuting the Catholics, while he made himself detested for his violence and avarice. The Pontiff troubled himself but little about the imputation, which fell to the ground of itself. His own conduct sufficiently justified him, since, when he had discovered at Rome the presence of some of these wretched disciples of Manes, he had caused them to be banished with disgrace and had condemned their books to the flames. He replied with more earnestness to the complaints which Anastasius made of the Pope's having concerted measures with the senate for his excommunication. Symmachus showed that this excommunication was not a judgment pronounced against the emperor in person, but a simple cessation of intercourse in accordance with the usage of the times. "It is not you, my Lord," he said to him, "whom we excommunicate; it is Acacius, (the Eutychian patriarch of Constantinople.) What is Acacius to me? you say. Abandon him, then, and you will from that moment be released from an excommunication due only to him; if you act otherwise, it is not we, it is you who excommunicate yourself." He then complains of the persecution which Anastasius urged forward against the Catholics, forbidding them only the free exercise of their religion, while he allowed it to sects without number who infested the East.

In the year 512, the bishops of the East, groaning over their separation from the communion of Rome, wrote to Symmachus supplicating him to reunite them to the Apostolic See. The division, however, subsisted some time longer, in spite of these good dispositions on their part.

The Pope Symmachus died on the 19th of July, after a pontificate of nearly sixteen years. It is said that he was the first who ordered the *Gloria in excelsis* to be sung in churches on Sundays and the feasts of martyrs. He conferred valuable gifts on churches; in several he placed *ciboria*, and tabernacles of silver weighing 120 lbs. each, the workmanship of which was on a par with the richness of the material.

One of these *chefs-d'œuvre* is particularly highly spoken of, on account of the figures of our Saviour and the twelve apostles which it bears upon it.

53. Hormisdas, a.d. 514–523.

He was a native of Campagnia, and remarkable for his virtues and zeal against the Eutychians. He was elected on the 26th of July. Some monks, (Scythæ,) the chief of whom was Joannes Maxentius, excited serious disorders by putting forth the following extraordinary proposition, "one of the Trinity was crucified;" by which they intended to affirm that the Divine nature had suffered. Hormisdas condemned these irreverent affirmations. He died on the 6th of August.

54. John I., a.d. 523–526.

He was a native of Tuscany, and succeeded Hormisdas on the 12th of August. No Roman Pontiff as yet had been seen in the new Rome; but the Emperor Justin, wishing to constrain the Arians to be converted, took from them their churches, to make them over to the Catholics. Theodoric, therefore, the Arian King of Italy, obliged the Pope to go as an ambassador to Constantinople in order to inspire the emperor with greater moderation. The royal Goth was the more shocked at the violence of Justin, because he himself had never dreamed but of governing his subjects in peace, without regard to their differences in religion. He even dismissed one of his officers, with whom in other respects he was highly satisfied, because he had renounced the Roman faith to embrace Arianism, with a view to pleasing the king. "How will he be faithful to me," said this prince, "if he is not faithful to his God?" He joined with the Pope four ambassadors of senatorial rank, and earnestly recommended them all to acquit themselves well of their commission, and threatened to treat the Catholics of Italy in the same manner as the Arians should be treated in the East.

The Pope John appeared at Constantinople as a holy and sovereign Pontiff. It is said that on entering the city he healed a blind man, in the presence of all, by laying a hand upon his eyes, and that the citizens preceded him with crosses and lighted tapers in a cortege twelve miles in length. The emperor prostrated himself at his feet, and would be crowned by him, though he had been already crowned by Epiphanius the patriarch. This prelate then, in honour of the Pope, invited his Holiness to officiate in the great church. This he did in Latin on Easter-day, amid the greatest pomp and solemnity, and sat in the first place, a mark of deference which was paid to no other bishop, however distinguished he might be. John communicated with all those of the Oriental Bishops who respected the Council of Chalcedon, and persons remarked none other than Timothy of Alexandria as being excluded from this communion. Without annoying the emperor in an unsuitable manner in the measures which he took for the prosperity of the Eastern Church, the Pontiff nevertheless zealously executed his diplomatic function in accordance with the wishes of the King Theodoric, and the interests of the faithful of the West, who were menaced with the most grievous reprisals. By representing in a lively manner to Justin the danger in which he placed the adherents of the Catholic faith in Italy, he obtained from him that the Arians in the empire should remain unmolested.

This is not the only instance of a Pope espousing the cause of religious toleration. Thus Innocent XI., though he approved the revocation of the Edict of Nantes,* loudly reprobated the subsequent persecution of the Huguenots by Louis XIV. But whatever toleration the Church may exercise in particular cases, she can never in the abstract recognise men's right to profess what is theologically wrong.

55. Felix IV., A.D. 526–530.

He was a native of Beneventum, and chosen by the favour of Theodoric. He governed wisely.

---

* See *Dublin Review*, Jan. 1865, p. 89.

During this pontificate, Athalaric, or rather his regent-mother, Amalassonte, in confirmation of the ancient custom, ordered that if any one wanted to bring an action against a clergyman of Rome, he should address himself first to the Pope, and not have recourse to the secular judge till he had been denied justice on the part of the Church.

56. BONIFACE II., A.D. 530–532.

He was a Goth by descent, a Roman by birth. His letter to St Césaire d'Arles is extant. He was resisted by Dioscorus, the antipope. His election, which took place on the 15th of October, a month or two after the death of Felix IV., did not obtain universal assent; but the antipope dying a month after the double election put an end to the schism. It is urged against Boniface that he caused his rival to be condemned and his memory to be anathematised after his death.* This was regarded by some of his contemporaries as a resentment more consistent with the harshness of his barbarous origin than with the gentleness becoming the Vicar of the Saviour of men; it may be pleaded in his defence that his rival was an antipope, and guilty therefore of a pretension presumptuous above all others. Feeling acutely the troubles which had attended his

---

* Fleury, *Histoire Ecclesiastique*, xxxii. 21.

accession, and fearing lest similar turmoils should take place after his death, he obliged the bishops assembled in council in the basilica of St Peter to authorise him to choose a successor, and accordingly he appointed the deacon Vigilius. This novel proceeding, at variance with the sacred canons, and contrary to civil law, was revoked in another council. Providence did not permit this Pope to remain long at the head of His Church. He died in the month of October or November, and his clergy long remembered his charities to them and their flocks during a season of scarcity.

57. JOHN II., (CALLED MERCURIUS,) A.D. 533–535.

He was a Roman, and priest of the title of St Clement. He was elected on the 22d of January by the clergy and people, was confirmed in his place by King Athalaric, and died on the 27th of May. The prince who confirmed his appointment required by edict a certain payment to be made for such recognition. Little further is known respecting him.

58. AGAPETUS, A.D. 535–536.

He reigned only ten months. Having been Archdeacon of the Roman Church, he succeeded John Mercurius on the 3d of June. He was obliged by the King Theodat to undertake a political embassy to Constantinople. The Emperor Justinian and the Empress Theodora endeavoured, first by bribes and then by menaces, to induce the conscientious Agapetus to recognise the patriarch Anthimus as a fellow-Christian. "Let him be brought before me," said the Pontiff, "and ask him if he will own the existence of two natures in Christ." Anthimus was called; and by his refusal to acknowledge that our Lord had both a human and a divine nature, proved himself to be a Eutychian. The emperor was convinced of his heresy, and countenanced Agapetus in consecrating in his place Mennas, who had been duly elected, and was the first who was made Bishop in the East by the hands of the Pope. Some beautiful verses are put into the mouth of Justinian by Dante, (*Parad.* canto vi.,) in reference to his being thus converted to the orthodox faith.

While Agapetus was preparing to return to Italy he fell ill, and died on the 22d of April, and was succeeded by Silverius on the 8th of the following June.

59. St Silverius, a.d. 536–538.

He refused to replace the Eutychian Anthimus in the see of Constantinople; and thus braved the anger and resentment of Belisarius, who had just taken Rome. At the instigation and through the bribery of the Empress Theodora, who favoured the Eutychians, he was accused unjustly of a treacherous understanding with the Goths; sent to Patara in Lycia; replaced by Vigilius, a Roman deacon, (who had been unlawfully elected on the 22d of November, 537,) and at last conducted by servants of Vigilius* to the island Palmaria, where he died of hunger on the 20th of June, 538.

60. Vigilius, a.d. 537–555.

Vigilius, canonically elected, so far from being the enemy of the Council of Chalcedon, was changed into another man. Hitherto he had truckled to imperial power; but henceforth the grace of the Popedom, if I may so speak, came upon him, and he proved a Confessor for the Faith. His history, as well as that of Boniface II. and Silverius, is full of interest, and may be found at length in Henrion and also in Fleury, who, except when Gallican tendencies are concerned, may be trusted as a most learned and able ecclesiastical historian. In the present Manual I am often obliged to be more concise than I could wish, and can give only the more

---

* Fleury, *Histoire Ecclesiastique*, xxxii. 57.

prominent features in the life of each Pontiff. Though he seemed at first to favour the doctrine of Anthimus and the Acephali, (a name given to the Eutychians,) Vigilius soon condemned them strongly, and thus drew on himself the resentment of Theodora, who caused him to be dragged, with a halter round his neck, through the streets of Constantinople, (whither he had been invited by the Emperor,) and immured him in a dungeon, (547.) In the affair of the "Three Chapters," or three theological works of Mopsueste, Theodoret and Ibas, which were tinged with the Eutychian heresy of the fusion of two natures in Christ, Vigilius at first refused to condemn these writings. But when the second Œcumenical Council of Constantinople had formally pronounced itself against them under the reign of Justinian in 553, Vigilius adhered to the decrees of the council, sparing only the persons of the heterodox authors. This reservation gave rise to a momentary division in some of the Oriental churches.

Vigilius died at Syracuse on the 10th of January, when on his way back to Rome. The horrible pains of the stone brought his troubled career to its close not far from that very island where he had banished his holy predecessor.* His firmness, however, in withstanding the fury

---

* Henrion, lib. xix. an. 555.

of the emperor, and the artifices of Eutychian and semi-Eutychian theologians in the East, is a striking proof of the special providence which, even under the most adverse circumstances, watches over and controls the decisions of the supreme head of the Church.

61. Pelagus I., a.d. 555–560.

He began the church of St Philip and St James at Rome, which his successor completed. He had been a deacon, was a native of Rome, and a son of a prefect of the prætorium. He was ordained on the 16th of April. The vacancies of the Holy See, since the last revolution of Italy, became longer than before, owing to the influence which the emperors began to assume over the election, or at least the exaltation, of the Popes. The Gothic kings of Rome laid claim to the right of confirming these pontiffs, a pretension to which the masters of the world had not aspired even in the most flourishing days of the empire, and which was viewed with jealousy by their successors in the empire's decline.

In his endeavours to repress the turbulent and schismatical opponents of the fifth council, Pelagus was seconded by the authority of the eunuch Narses, the victorious general of Justinian in Italy. In answer to inquiries proposed by Chil debert, Pelagus assured the king and bishops of France that the fifth council had concluded nothing contrary to the Faith; and the sovereign having requested some relics, the Pope charged a sub-deacon to convey them to France. He died on the 1st of March.

62. JOHN III., A.D. 560-573.

He succeeded Pelagus on the 18th of July. He was surnamed Catelin, and was son of Anastasius, a great man in his day and sphere. He was confirmed in his seat by the exarch of Ravenna, in the name of the Emperor Justinian.

John III. is said to have died on the 13th of July, 573.

He had acquired the title of the Illustrious. He was active in the erection and repair of churches, and restored the cemeteries of the martyrs. Owing to the ravages of the Lombards, the Holy See remained vacant six months after his death.

63. BENEDICT I., (SURNAMED BONOSUS,) A.D. 574-578.

The ravages of the barbarians delayed the election of this Roman till the 3d of June. His death took place on the 30th of July.

He consented very unwillingly to St Gregory's going, as he ardently desired, to evangelise the distant isle of Britain; but the Roman people, whose attachment to the Archdeacon Gregory was prodigious, lined the streets when the Pope was on his way to St Peter's, and cried aloud, "You offend the Prince of the Apostles; you cause the ruin of Rome in allowing Gregory to depart." Benedict in consequence sent couriers to overtake the Archdeacon, who stopped him when advanced three days on his journey.

64. Pelagus II., a.d. 578–590.

He strove, without great success, to stifle in Istria the schism of the "Three Chapters." He had succeeded Benedict I. on the 30th of November, and was consecrated without waiting for the consent of the emperor, because the Lombards were besieging Rome. These barbarians were partly pagans, and practised against the Christians many horrible cruelties.

Gregory, afterwards the Great, and one of the seven deacons of the Roman Church, was the legate of Pelagus at Constantinople. This Pontiff died on the 8th of February of a contagious disease. Such was his charity, that he had converted his house into an hospital for the aged poor.

The Ecclesiastical History of Socrates will be found of great use to the student, as a continuation of that of Eusebius. It reaches from A.D. 305 to 439. After him, we have Sozomen's, 324 to 440; Theodoret's, 322 to 428; and Evagrius's, 431 to 594. Their works have been translated into English.

65. St Gregory the Great, A.D. 590-604.

He was born at Rome about 540, and embraced a religious life, after having been prætor of his native city. Illustrious birth, a pious life, and great talent for the administration of affairs, caused him to be chosen, in spite of his intense reluctance, to succeed Pelagus. He was consecrated in the Church of St Peter, on the 3d of September. He supported the pontificate as a burden, and complained sorely to his friends of its weight. At the time of the invasion of the Lombards in Italy, he concluded an honourable treaty with the barbarians. He made great efforts to introduce pure Christianity among the conquerors; aided and directed Theodelind, wife of Agilulf, the Lombard Duke of Turin, in her zeal for the true faith; laboured for the abolition of slavery, and extinction of paganism in Italy; founded monasteries; greatly encouraged the Order of St Benedict; and caused strict discipline and reformation of abuses to be observed among the clergy.

Before Gregory the Great was elected Pope, he was walking one day in the forum at Rome, and saw some boys standing in the market to be sold for slaves. They were very fair, with large blue eyes, and long, curling, yellow hair. He asked who they were, and was told they were Angles. "Justly are they so named," said he, "for their face is angelic, and they ought to be co-heirs with the angels in heaven. And how is their province named?" The boys answered, "Deira," which was the name of Northumberland. "De ira Dei," (from the wrath of God,) he replied; "they must indeed be delivered from His wrath, and called to His mercy. What is the name of the king of their country?" The boys answered, "Ælla." "Then," said Gregory, "Alleluia, in praise of God, shall be surely hymned in that portion of the earth.

When raised to the Popedom, St Gregory remembered the Saxon boys; and he sent Augustine, and several others, as missionaries to England. They landed in the isle of Thanet, in Kent, in 596, and asked leave to preach before King Ethelbert; promising him, as a reward, a lasting kingdom, whose joys should never decay. Ethelbert himself, influenced by the persuasions of his wife Bertha, a Christian princess, embraced the faith, and ten thousand of his subjects followed his example; and by degrees other kings were converted, and all the southern parts of England were restored to the Church.

The conversion of the Arian Goths is due also to St Gregory. Some have accused this Pope of having, through excess of zeal, burnt the profane authors, and destroyed the monuments of pagan art; but this accusation has been triumphantly refuted. He established "the Gregorian rite," with a view to liturgical uniformity.

St Gregory shed lustre on the Church, not only by his virtues, but also by his miracles; and his writings, which are more numerous than those of any other Pope, rank him among the doctors of the Church. He was well versed in Latin literature, and is said to have supported the hall of the Apostolic See upon the columns of the seven liberal arts. He died on the 12th of March, and was interred in St Peter's, with his pallium, girdle, and reliquary which he wore. The Holy See had in his time large landed properties in Italy, Sardinia, Sicily, and even Africa; in the administration of which, and appropriation of the revenues to the poor, St Gregory assiduously concerned himself, studying carefully the account of the Church patrimonies drawn up by Pope Gelasius. Far from enjoying robust health for his great and various avocations, St Gregory laboured under perpetual infirmities. For several years before his death, disease and pain made his existence a long martyrdom. "I expect and desire death," he wrote, in the year 600, "as my only remedy."

Considerable stress is laid by some Protestants on the fact of St Gregory's having repudiated the title of Universal Bishop; but there is in his Epistles abundant evidence to prove that he exercised supremacy over all Bishops; and that, though he and his predecessors disclaimed the title in question, which had frequently been offered to them, they did so merely because it sounded too ambitious, and seemed to derogate unduly from the character of their episcopal brethren.*

66. Sabinian, A.D. 604-606.

He ordered, it is said, that the faithful should be called to church by the sound of bells. He was a native of Volterra, had been ordained deacon, and succeeded St Gregory on the 1st or 13th of September. His charity to the people during a famine is on record. He died on the 22d of February.

67. Boniface III., A.D. 607-608.

Nearly a year elapsed between the death of Sabinian and the choice of Boniface. He was a

* See Epist., lib, v., 18, 19.

Roman deacon, and died nine months after his election. He obtained from the Greek emperor Phocas that the Patriarch of Constantinople should be prevented from bearing the title of Universal Bishop, which he had usurped, and that it should be used only by the Bishop of Rome.

68. Boniface IV., A.D. 608-614.

He was the son of a physician in Valeria. The Emperor Phocas having accorded the Pantheon to him, he consecrated it to St Mary and all Saints under the name of St Mary of the Rotunda, on the 1st of November, which from that time became the feast of All Saints.

He converted his paternal house, in the country of the Marsi, into a monastery, and richly endowed it. He was buried in St Peter's, and his memory is honoured on the 25th of May.

69. St Deusdedit, A.D. 614-617.

He was a Roman, and son of Stephen, a subdeacon. His love for the clergy is particularly mentioned, and also his zeal for the restoration of ancient discipline. He was ordained on the 13th of November in the year Boniface died, and was the first who affixed leaden seals to the bulls.

70. BONIFACE V., A.D. 617–625.

This Pope was a Neapolitan, and evinced his zeal for the conversion of our pagan forefathers by writing to Edwin, king of Northumbria, and to his queen Ethelburga. He forbade the judges to prosecute those who fled to churches for refuge. This merciful provision was much abused in later times. The Holy See was vacant nearly seven months after his decease, which took place on the 25th of October.

71. HONORIUS I., A.D. 626–638.

He was born near Rome, and was the son of the consul Petronius. He ruled with zeal; and we find in Bede repeated notices of his care for the churches of Great Britain. He has been charged with having inclined to Monothelitism in a private letter to Sergius, Patriarch of Constantinople; and the letters which passed between that prelate, the Pope, and Cyrus, Patriarch of Alexander, may be seen in Fleury.*
It is evident that much artifice was employed to deceive the Pontiff; "and if," says the *Manual of Church History*, "Honorius failed in any way, it was in too readily crediting the good faith of the artful Sergius, and not making strict inquiry

---
* Vol. viii. pp. 304–330; Döllinger, *Ch. Hist.* vol. ii. pp. 112, 196, 197.

before committing himself to a reply. As for his orthodoxy on the point in question, it was abundantly vindicated by Pope John IV. and by St Maximus, the holy abbot of Constantinople, who bears special testimony to his zeal against Monothelitism." The same writer adds that the acts of the sixth œcumenical council, in which he was supposed to be condemned, were falsified by those who had an interest in doing so, and believes that this has been satisfactorily established by recent research.* Bartoli, in his "Apologia pro Honorio," Baronius, and others, have written likewise in refutation of the charges brought against this Pope.

Honorius was extremely active in promoting the repairs and construction of churches, and he enriched them with costly presents. He also reunited to the Church the countries of Aquileia and Istria, which had been drawn into schism by the "Three Chapters" seventy years before. After his death the see of Rome remained vacant about a year and eight months.

72. SEVERINUS, A.D. 640.

His pontificate was very short, but his virtues were highly prized. Faithful to the solemn

---

* *Manual of Church History*, p. 111; *Annales de la Philosophie Chrétienne*, vol. viii. série iv. pp. 54–60, 415–438.

duties of his office, he condemned the formidable heresy of his day, and the imperial edict which favoured it. After his decease the Holy See was vacant five months.

73. John IV., A.D. 640-642.

He was a native of Dalmatia; and in a Roman council he condemned the famous edict of the Emperor Heraclius in favour of Monothelitism called the Ecthesis. It was an exposition pretending to be of the Catholic faith, drawn up by the Patriarch Sergius in the emperor's name. John IV. sent large sums of money into Dalmatia and Istria to redeem captives; and was buried in the Church of St Peter, October 12th, 642.

74. Theodorus I., A.D. 642-649.

Theodorus was a native of Jerusalem, and of Greek parentage. He vigorously opposed the Monothelite doctrine of one will only in Christ; condemned and deposed the Eastern prelates Paul and Pyrrhus, who maintained it; and subscribed the document in the Church of St Peter with a pen dipped in the consecrated chalice.*
He built several churches, and his kindness and charity towards the poor are specially recorded.

* Fleury, vol. viii. p. 394.

75. St Martin, a.d. 649–654.

He condemned the Monothelite heresy and hereby incurred the anger of Constantius II., who issued a second edict in its favour. The emperor had him removed from Rome to Constantinople, and then sent him into exile, after his having been put in chains and treated with barbarity and contempt. His death, which took place within two years, was consequent on the hardships he suffered in his captivity; these he endured without a murmur, and never remitted his pastoral exertions.

Sectarians at this period strove as hard to be recognised by Papal authority as they are now eager to escape from it.

76. Eugenius I., a.d. 654–657.

Eugenius was intruded during the lifetime of Martin I., whom Constantius II. had deposed; but after the death of Martin in what is now called the Crimea, in 655, he was regarded by all as the lawful Pope; and his goodness and liberality are specially praised. He was interred in St Peter's.

77. Vitalian, a.d. 657–672.

He was a native of Signia in Campania. He maintained ecclesiastical discipline, sent missionaries to England, and died in the odour of sanctity. Our forefathers were indebted to him for the choice of Theodore of Tarsus and Adrian, an African, as respectively Archbishop and Abbot of Canterbury. They founded schools of secular and sacred learning through the south of the island, and St Bede testifies to the proficiency of the scholars.

78. Adeodatus, A.D. 672–676.

He was the first Pope who dated by the years of his pontificate. In his time the Saracens landed in Sicily and pillaged Syracuse. The number of Bishops consecrated by each Pope of this period is found in all extended histories of the Church. In four ordinations Adeodatus is recorded to have ordained ninety-seven Bishops, twenty-two priests, and one deacon. The priests were probably for the diocese of Rome, and the bishops for the world.

79. Domnus, A.D. 676–678.

Little is known of him, except that he also shared in the controversy and suppression of Monothelitism. He adorned St Peter's with rich marbles, and repaired other churches. Ravenna, which had fallen into schism, submitted to his rule.

80. St Agatho, A.D. 678–682.

Under this Pope, who presided by his legates, the sixth œcumenical council was held at Constantinople, in the reign of the Emperor Pogonatus. It condemned the Monothelite errors. This blow was fatal to the heresy, and all agitation henceforward gradually subsided. St Agatho was highly esteemed for the sweetness of his disposition, and was the first Pope who ceased to pay the customary tribute to the emperor at his election.

"The heads of the Church," says Dr Newman, in speaking of the ravages of the Lombards, "bewailed a universal ignorance which they could not remedy; it was a great thing that schools remained sufficient for clerical education, and this education was only sufficient, as Pope Agatho informs us, to enable them to hand on the traditions of the fathers, without scientific exposition or polemical defence." *

81. St Leo II., A.D. 682–684.

This Pope was a Sicilian. His consecration was delayed till the emperor's consent to his election should be obtained. He instituted the kiss of peace and the aspersion with holy water;

---

* *Office and Work of Universities,* p. 171.

was remarkable for his knowledge of Holy Scripture; cultivated church music; and practised poverty for love of the poor. He received and confirmed the acts of the sixth general council, and sent a careful abstract of them to Spain.* In a letter to King Erwig, he severely censures Honorius, nor will this fact present any difficulty to the Catholic who remembers that Honorius's doctrinal pronouncement was only disciplinary, and as such might be reversed.† The second council of Nice also mentions his fault, in speaking of the sixth general council. ‡ His reign lasted only one year and seven months.

82. Benedict II., A.D. 684–685.

He was a native of Rome. He desired that the Pontiff chosen by the clergy and people of Rome should be consecrated without the confirmation of the emperor. Constantine consented to this arrangement, but Justinian IV. appears to have repealed it. Benedict II.'s reign was short. He had long been in general repute for the gravity of his character and the simplicity of his habits. He repaired and adorned many churches, and was buried in St Peter's on the 8th of May.

* Fleury, vol. ix., pp. 65, 66.
† See *Dublin Review*, Jan. 1865, p. 49, in a series of articles by Dr Ward on the Extent of the Church's Infallibility.
‡ Fleury, an. 778.

83. John V., a.d. 685-686.

He had been legate of Pope Agatho in the sixth general council. He and the six following Pontiffs were Greeks or Syrians. He was learned and moderate in all his ways. A long and painful illness impeded him greatly in the exercise of his functions, which lasted a twelvemonth only.

84. Conon, a.d. 686-687.

Conon was very old at the time of his election, which was contested by Peter and Theodore. His habits were simple and peaceful, and he was little skilled in worldly affairs. Like his predecessor, he suffered long and painfully, so that he could scarcely ordain priests and bishops. He was buried in St Peter's after a short reign.

85. Sergius I., a.d. 687-701.

His pontificate was troubled by the antipopes Theodore and Pascal. It appears from his epitaph that he remained seven years absent from Rome on account of persecutions directed against him. He rejected the canons of the Trullan Synod in 694, and the Emperor Justinian sought therefore to have him conveyed as a prisoner to Constantinople. By a singular spirit of insubordination the Archbishop of Aquileia and his suffragans refused to admit the fifth general council; but Sergius happily brought them back to the unity of the Church. He appointed several new ceremonies; raised a tomb to the memory of St Leo; and was buried in his turn in St Peter's, the common resting-place of the Popes at this period.

86. JOHN VI., A.D. 701–705.

He acted with firmness and wisdom under trying circumstances, and sent large sums of money to redeem the captives taken by the marauding Gisulf Lombard, Duke of Benevento. In a council held at Rome, he acquitted Wilfred, Archbishop of York, of charges brought against him by some of the English clergy.

87. JOHN VII., A.D. 705–707.

The Trullan decrees having been sent to him for his approval by Justinian, he returned them without alteration. Fleury speaks of this middle course as a *faiblesse humaine;* but in reading Fleury, his Gallican spirit must always be borne in mind. John VII. adorned many churches with images, and placed his own portrait among them.

88. Sisinnius, a.d. 708.

He reigned twenty days only, and during this time was so afflicted with the gout, that he could not even raise his hands to his mouth. His patience and affection for his people are particularly recorded.

89. Constantine, a.d. 708–715.

He was a native of Syria, and combated what remained of the Monothelite faction. He undertook a journey to Constantinople by the emperor's desire, and was received there with great honour. He ordained twelve Bishops during his absence; returned to Rome within the year; and died there after a reign of seven years, esteemed for his piety and gentle behaviour.

90. St Gregory II., a.d. 715–731.

He was a native of Rome, had accompanied Pope Constantine to Constantinople, and was highly in repute for his strict life and ability in explaining the Scriptures. He convened a council in 729 against the Iconoclasts, and sent Boniface to preach the Gospel in Germany. This Apostle was English by birth, and manifested from his infancy signs of the high destiny for which God reserved him. He entered early one of the most flourishing monasteries of England at Exeter, and subsequently went to Rome to ask of Pope Gregory II. a mission to evangelise the heathen. It was after he had obtained great success in Bavaria and Thuringia that the Pope recalled him to Rome, consecrated him Bishop, and gave him jurisdiction in Germany. The oath which he took to Gregory is preserved, and may be found in Lingard.*

St Gregory II. earnestly opposed the revolt of the Italians against the Greek emperor, and died on the 13th of February, on which day the Church honours him as a saint.

91. Gregory III., a.d. 731–741.

This Pope was a native of Syria, learned, pious, and an effective preacher. He knew the Psalms by heart, and studied the hidden sense of Scripture. He was placed by the people on the pontifical throne during the funeral of Gregory II. He laboured, like his predecessor, against the Iconoclasts, but died ere he could extirpate the error. He had to contend against the Lombards when they invaded Italy, and by his charity he merited the title of "the friend of the poor." Both Gregory III. and his predecessor Gregory II. excommunicated the Greek emperor, Leo the Isaurian, who was an ardent Iconoclast.

* *History of the Anglo-Saxon Church*, vol. ii. p. 478.

The emperor equipped a fleet with a view of taking vengeance on the Pope, but it suffered shipwreck in the Adriatic Sea. St Boniface, having been favoured with the powerful protection of Charles Martel, king of France, converted to Christianity almost all the inhabitants of Hesse and Thuringia. He applied himself especially to founding convents; and after fifteen years' labour, he betook himself to Rome for the third time, and received from Gregory III. the archbishop's pall as a token of his jurisdiction over all Germany. Subsequently he gained the crown of martyrdom. "The temporal power," says Bouillet, "dates from the pontificate of Gregory III., who rendered himself independent in Rome when it had been abandoned by the emperors of the East." It was most desirable that, in freeing themselves from the Greek sovereigns, the Popes should not fall a prey to the kings of Italy.

History has left us a long account of the churches which Gregory III. adorned and built at Rome during his reign. He died November 10th, 741, having filled the Holy See nearly eleven years.

92. St Zacharias, A.D. 741–752.

He was a Greek by birth, and of a most peaceful and forgiving disposition. He decided Luitprand, the Lombard king, on making peace.

Taking advantage of dissensions between the Emperor Leo the Isaurian and Gregory II., Luitprand had in 728 taken from the Greeks Ravenna, Pentapolis, and all they possessed north of Rome; but he now restored to the Holy See many possessions which had been wrested from it.

Rachis also, his successor, having invaded the Roman dukedom, was implored by Zacharias to desist with so much fervour, that he abandoned his enterprise, and retiring to Monte Casino, took the habit of St Benedict. Zacharias approved the elevation of Pepin le Bref to the throne of France, (751,) saying in reply to a question submitted to him by that prince, "It is better that he who had the power, should also have the title of king." He held several councils for the restoration of discipline; showed such devotion to the people that he more than once exposed his life to save them; distinguished himself by almsgiving and public works; and commenced the Vatican Library. It has been erroneously stated that Pope Zacharias condemned the Bishop Virgil for maintaining the existence of the Antipodes; though even if he had done so it would not have been without reason, if Virgil's theory involved the idea of two worlds, in one of which the inhabitants were not of the race of Adam, nor redeemed by Christ.*

*Barthélemy, *Erreurs Historiques*, pp. 269-286.

Zacharias translated St Gregory's Dialogues into Greek, and the Church has numbered him also among the Saints.

93. Stephen II., A.D. 752.

He was elected, but never consecrated, since he died four days after his election; hence he is omitted in many lists of the Popes, and his successor is in these catalogues called Stephen II. instead of Stephen III. It is needful to pay attention to this circumstance, otherwise confusion will arise.

94. Stephen III., A.D. 752–757.

He was a Roman deacon. Finding Rome besieged by Astolph, king of the Lombards, he went into Gaul, and on his knees* implored Pepin to help and deliver the Roman people. His suit was granted; and in gratitude he crowned Pepin and his two sons a second time in the basilica of St Denis, near Paris; annointed him with holy oil; and released him and his nobles from the oath of fidelity which they had taken to Childeric III., lately deceased, (754.)

The king made two expeditions into Italy, defeated the Lombards, (754–756,) re-conquered Æmilia and Pentapolis, confirmed the Roman Church in her possessions, and ceded to the

---

* Fleury, vol. ix. p. 329.

Popes forever the exarchate of Ravenna. The grant was ratified by Charlemagne, and formed the nucleus of the Papal States. The temporal power of the popedom thus arose under the protection of France, and has, with occasional interruptions, continued under it to this day.

Stephen III. often assembled his clergy in the Lateran Palace, exhorted them to the study of the Scriptures and other spiritual reading. He was buried in St Peter's.

95. Paul I., A.D. 757–767.

He was the brother of Stephen III. He has left twenty-two letters, most of which were addressed to King Pepin, to ask his aid against the Greeks or Lombards, and King Didier, and to enlist his services on the side of religion. Paul I. was in the habit of visiting the sick and poor at night, carrying them provisions, paying their debts, or consoling them if in prison. He was interred in St Paul's, but three months afterwards was transported up the Tiber to St Peter's.

96. Stephen IV., A.D. 768–772.

He was a Sicilian, cultivated sacred literature, and strictly observed ecclesiastical tradition. He was elected after a vacancy of thirteen months, and his authority was resisted by the antipope

Constantine, whose history presents a sad picture of the violence and disorder of the times. He caused Constantine to be condemned in a council of Bishops held at Rome, and died on the 1st of February, 772. The antipope was driven from Rome, and his eyes were put out through the cruelty of Longobard, Duke of Spoleto, and others. He was then confined in a monastery, where he ended his days.

97. ADRIAN I., A.D. 772–795.

He was born of a noble family in Rome. After having been attacked by Didier, king of the Lombards, he was avenged by Charlemagne, Didier's son-in-law, whom Adrian had called to his assistance. This most worthy Pontiff reigned twenty-three years; and during his pontificate was held the second Council of Nice, being the seventh œcumenical council of the Church. Adrian presided by his legates. It assembled in the year 787, in the reign of Constantine and his mother, Irene. Three hundred and sixty bishops were present. The council condemned the Iconoclasts, and defended the proper use of sacred images and pictures.

The authority of this synod was impugned by the council of Frankfort, (794,) at which more than a hundred bishops of the West were present. The œcumenical character of the seventh council was not yet known in all parts, and the Frankfort fathers were led into error by an inaccurate translation of the council into Latin, and thought that it allowed to sacred images the worship of *latria*. They were right in doctrine; wrong only in a matter of fact.

The Church has ever defended the outworks, no less than the citadel, of the faith. They are, in fact, one. The former demolished, the latter falls. The Church ignores the distinction, so hackneyed among her adversaries, between essential and non-essential points of faith. The faith, in her eyes, is one compact and indivisible body of doctrine, of which each part is essential to the whole. She condemned the Iconoclasts as emphatically as the Arians. They erred alike in resisting her authority. The right use of hallowed images was a matter of great practical importance, and it behoved the Church, as the exponent of Divine law, to rule it distinctly. Adrian's charities were prodigious; and the number of churches and monasteries he built or restored was but an outward sign of his zeal for the Church's spiritual edification.

98. Leo III., A.D. 795–816.

This Pope was a native of Rome. He was the victim of a conspiracy framed by two of his competitors, and was assailed by a troop of assassins, who, after having subjected him to horrible treatment, shut him up in a monastery. He found means to escape, and fled to Charlemagne in France. This prince sent him back to Italy, and re-established him on his throne. Leo in return placed the imperial crown on the head of Charlemagne (800) at Rome.

The illustrious conqueror was worthily rewarded for having turned all his glorious exploits to the advantage of religion. It was when troubles had arisen at Rome that he repaired to that city to appease them, and lighted on the festivities of Christmas. He was praying devoutly before the tomb of the Apostles, when the Pope approached him with the effulgent diadem, and the people cried with transports of joy, "Life and victory to Charles the Great, the pacific Roman Emperor, crowned by the will of God!" All the West ratified this promotion, and recognised Charlemagne as its sovereign chief. The Caliph of the East, "the good Haroun Alraschid," solicited his friendship, and Charlemagne took advantage of this circumstance to obtain some alleviating enactments in favour of Christians in the Holy Land. Before leaving Rome, Charlemagne confirmed the donation of States, which his father Pepin had made from feelings of homage to the Holy See. These States formed the temporal domain of the

Popes. This domain rendered them independent sovereigns in Europe, and enabled them to exercise their influence in a salutary manner over all Christian kingdoms. By making the Head of the Church a prince among princes, it brought him into diplomatic relations with them, and gave him that degree of worldly equality without which his authority would have been diminished, and often despised; and it placed at his disposal a variety of means, secondary indeed, yet indispensable for the evangelisation and instruction of barbarous nations. It helped to exalt the Pope's spiritual authority over the heads of kings, inducing and urging them to wholesome measures, restraining them from acts of violence and injustice, and visiting them often with heavy retribution when they persisted in an evil cause. It put power into his hands, which, if sometimes misused, was exerted on the whole for the glory of God, and the extension of His Church, and vindication of the cause of the oppressed. It was suited to the exigencies of half-civilised ages, in which rulers, unrestrained, as in our day, by the power of the people, required a mightier one to keep them in check. It was necessary then, as it is now, for the security and independence of the Holy See. Without it the Pope would be a subject, his acts would be liable to human constraint and the Church would inevitably suffer a variety of vexations and serious disadvantages.

By combining the offices of priest and king, the Popes became the antitypes of Simon and Hyrcanus, the high priest kings of Judah; in their supremacy they represent Moses, who led the people of Israel, and came from the Mount with the Tables of the Law in his hands; while in their pontifical capacity they realise the figure of Aaron, with the Urim and Thummim beaming oracular responses on his breast.*

Leo III. made many rich offerings to the Roman churches. The Romans reckoned him among the saints.

99. STEPHEN V., A.D. 816–817.

He was born at Rome of a noble family, and had long been given to spiritual studies. He took, as Duke of Rome, an oath of fidelity to Louis I., and crowned him at Rheims. His reign lasted only seven months.

100. PASCAL I., A.D. 817–824.

He was a native of Rome. He had been director of the monastery of St Stephen; to which post Stephen V. had appointed him, in

---
* Leviticus viii. 8.

consequence of his holy and ascetic habits. Louis le Débonnaire bestowed on him the islands of Corsica and Sardinia. He crowned Lothaire (Louis's son) emperor in 823, and opened at Rome a refuge for the Greeks, whom the Iconoclast persecution obliged to leave the East. He adorned and rebuilt many churches, and died May the 11th, 824.

101. Eugene II., a.d. 824–827.

In the time of Louis le Débonnaire he held a council at Rome for the reform of the clergy, and was called, for his loving kindness and charities, "the father of the afflicted." Trial by cold water is ascribed to him. Few particulars are preserved respecting him. He died on the 27th of August.

102. Valentine, a.d. 827.

He had been attached to the service of Popes Pascal and Eugene, and was highly esteemed by them. His pontificate lasted only forty days. The Popes at this time were the actual sovereigns of Rome and its territory, although the emperor, as guardian of the Roman Church, exercised a degree of jurisdiction rather advantageous than otherwise.

103. GREGORY IV., A.D. 827–844.

He was the son of a Roman patrician. In the time of the troubles between Louis le Débonnaire and his sons he went to France to effect peace, but without success. He gave his voice against Louis, returned to Rome, where he enjoyed a high reputation, and died January the 8th, 844.

104. SERGIUS II., A.D. 844–847.

Sergius had received many marks of esteem from four of the preceding Pontiffs. He was elected without the authorisation of the Emperor Lothaire, who disputed his election, but it was confirmed in an assembly of Bishops. He crowned Louis, son of Lothaire I., King of the Lombards. The Arabs in this reign pillaged the environs of Rome and the churches outside the walls. Sergius II. died suddenly, after having held the Holy See three years.

105. LEO IV., A.D. 847–855.

He was a native of Rome. He repaired St Peter's, embellished his capital, protected the States of the Church from the Saracens, and raised near Rome a city, which he named Leopolis, now included in Rome itself. He also restored the town of Porto, near the mouth of the Tiber, and there settled some thousands of Corsicans who had been forced to fly from their native island in consequence of a Saracen invasion. He caused towers to be built on both sides of the river; and chains were drawn across to prevent Moslem galleys from sailing up to Rome itself. He died on the 17th of July.

Even Voltaire, in his *Essai sur les Mœurs*, speaks of him, Adrian IV., and Alexander III., in terms of admiration and respect.

The ridiculous fable of Pope Joan belongs to this period. According to the fiction, on the death of Leo IV. in 855, and before the accession of Benedict III., the papal throne was occupied by a woman, under the name of John VIII. She was, it is said, a native of Mayence, who having come to Rome, concealed her sex, gave herself to theological studies, became proficient in them, was admitted into the order of priesthood under the name of John of England, elected Pope, and reigned for two years, until, being pregnant, she gave birth to a child during a public religious procession at Rome. This imposture is rejected by all learned men, whether Catholic or Protestant; and it has been clearly shown that no interval elapsed between the decease of Leo IV. and the election of Benedict III. The story is supposed to have taken rise from the fact of John

VIII. having had the weakness to recognise Photius as the Patriarch of Constantinople; in this he was thought to have acted like a woman, and gained the surname of Joanna Papissa, (Pope Joan)* The fable was, it seems, first promulgated by a Cistercian monk named Martinus, who wrote a *Chronicon Summorum Pontificum*, which is full of absurdities.

106. BENEDICT III., A.D. 855–858.

He was a Roman by birth, and was elected in spite of the opposition of the Emperor Lothaire and Louis. Anastasius the antipope resisted him. When informed of his election, he was found on his knees, and he entreated with tears that he might not be obliged to accept so serious a responsibility. During his pontificate, he constantly attended the funerals of bishops, priests, and deacons, and desired that his successors should continue the like practice.

107. NICOLAS I., CALLED THE GREAT, A.D. 858–867.

He was a deacon at the time of his election, and hid himself in St Peter's, saying that he was unworthy of being raised to so high an

---
* *Erreurs et Mensonges Historiques*, p. 35.

eminence. Two days after he visited the Emperor Louis, who walked before him on foot, and held his horse's bridle. He showed great firmness in his dogmatic decisions. He anathematised in council (860) Photius, pseudo Patriarch of Constantinople, author of the Greek schism, who denied the possession of the Holy Ghost from the Son. He launched various censures on the bishops of France, and had the satisfaction of seeing Bogoris, king of the Bulgarians, embrace Christianity with his subjects, and recognise the supremacy of the Holy See, (861.)

It was to the East that this people owed the boon of the faith. In a war which they had to sustain against the Greek emperor Theophilus, they had lost a considerable battle, and among the captives was the sister of their king. This princess was brought to Constantinople with the other prisoners of war, and detained there thirty-eight years. In this long period she was instructed in the Christian religion, and received baptism. The liberty wherewith Christ had made her free inspired her with zeal. On her return to her brother she never ceased to speak to him of the faith of the gospel, and to exhort him to embrace it. These discourses shook the king, and Heaven seemed to act in concert with the princess. A contagious malady having spread through Bulgaria, the king had recourse to the God of his sister, and the plague was almost immediately removed. Convinced by this portent, he was baptized by a bishop. The Bulgarians, knowing this, revolted and attacked the palace of their sovereign; but he, full of confidence in the Divine assistance, went forth at the head of his servants, and scattered the seditious multitude. He then pardoned the rebels, who became penetrated with juster ideas of his religion, and embraced it themselves. Then it was that the king sent ambassadors to the Pope, as head of the Church, to ask of him evangelical ministers, and to propose many questions regarding faith and morals. Nicolas I. looked with tender affection on these neophytes come from afar to seek instruction from the Holy See. After having welcomed them as a father, he replied to their questions, and sent them away full of joy, accompanied by two bishops remarkable for their wisdom and virtue.

In the establishment of these new churches we see how all missionaries rendered homage to the primacy of the Roman Church. All the Anglo-Saxon and Frank apostles solicited their missions from the See of St Peter, and placed the people whom they converted to the faith under its immediate jurisdiction. The missionaries who came from the East addressed themselves in like manner to Rome in all grave and difficult questions, and conformed to her decisions. It seems as if Providence decreed that the Greek Church should, by the submission of Bogoris to the centre of unity, pronounce her own condemnation in the face of the whole world only a few years before her schism.

A remarkable divorce case occurred during this pontificate; and Nicolas, like all his successors in similar instances, showed great firmness in refusing to sanction a divorce between Lothaire, king of Lorraine, and his wife Teutberge, though it was desired by both parties. No infidelity on either side is allowed by the Church to cancel a valid marriage. Pope Nicolas abounded in works of charity; and kept a list of all the blind, lame, and bedridden poor in Rome, to whom he regularly sent alms. He was consulted by persons from all parts of the known world, both by correspondence and in person. About a hundred of his letters are still extant. He died on the 13th of November, and was buried in St Peter's.

108. Adrian II., A.D. 867–872.

He was a native of Rome, son of Talarus, who afterwards became bishop, and was elected after having twice refused the pontificate, at the age of seventy-six. He withdrew the excommunication pronounced against Lothaire, king of Lorraine, who had repudiated his wife.

He sent legates to the eighth œcumenical council, the fourth held at Constantinople, in the reign of the emperor Basil, (869.) St Ignatius, unjustly expelled in 857 from the See of Constantinople, was restored by the council; and Photius, the intruder, thrust into the see with violence though a layman, was excommunicated and deposed.

Adrian had been married when a deacon, but had separated from his wife Stephana on entering priest's orders. Both she and his daughter were living when he ascended the papal throne.* Several pious persons had long predicted his elevation, and it is even said that on one occasion loaves multiplied in his hands while he distributed them to the poor. He died in November, 872, aged eighty-one.

109. John VIII., A.D. 872–882.

He was, before his elevation, Archdeacon of Rome. Being attacked by the Saracens, he implored the aid of Charles le Chauve, King of France; who died (877) before he could succour him. John VIII. had placed the imperial crown

* Fleury, vol. xl. p. 102.

on the head of Charles in 875, and Charles in return had ceded to the Pope the sovereignty of Rome.

Imprisoned by Lambert, Duke of Spoleto, who desired to possess himself of Rome, he escaped to France and took refuge with Louis le Bègue, who gave him the means of repairing his losses; but being pressed by the Saracens, he had recourse to Basil, Emperor of Constantinople, and at his request consented to recognise Photius (who had managed to deceive him) as Patriarch—a circumstance already alluded to under Leo IV. The letter written by John VIII. on the subject to the emperor is extant;* and though he consents to the restoration of Photius on condition of his asking pardon of the episcopal synod, his epistle was afterwards altered by Photius, and made to subserve the heresiarch's purpose in a way never contemplated.

This Pope crowned three emperors; Charles le Chauve, 875; Louis le Bègue, 878; Charles le Gros, 881. He presided at, or convoked, eleven councils.

From about this period the history of the pontifical line becomes more and more intimately blended with that of Europe in general, increasing at the same time in political importance.

* Epist. 199; Fleury, vol. xl. pp. 401, 402.

The conversion of so many nations to the Christian faith brings their rulers into immediate relation with the Holy See, and renders their laws and edicts liable to the spiritual supervision of the Supreme Pastor.

John VIII. has left 320 letters, in which we observe that he was much occupied with the temporal concerns of Italy and France, and had occasion to pronounce numerous excommunications. He ordered the life of St Gregory the Great to be written by the deacon John, and commuted some severe penances into a pilgrimage to Rome. He died on the 15th of December.

Photius.

Photius, Patriarch of Constantinople and native of the same city, had already been ambassador in Persia, and chief secretary of the Emperor Michel, where he was installed, though a layman, in the patriarchate of Constantinople in place of Ignatius, who had just been deposed in 857. Odious violence marked his intrusion, which Pope Nicolas I. opposed. Photius, having been anathematised and condemned by the Pope in council, assembled some Bishops, anathematised the Pope in turn, (858,) and thus gave birth to the Greek schism, which has already saddened Christendom a thousand years. Basil the Macedonian re-established Ignatius in his see, and Photius did not return to his functions till after the Patriarch's decease; but he again quarrelled with the Pope, who excommunicated him anew. Photius, however, held his seat till the accession of Leo the philosopher, who exiled him. In exile, like Nestorius, he died, in a retired convent of Armenia, in 891. He united vast erudition with great subtlety and craft, and a singularly penetrating intellect. His *Myriabiblon* is a very valuable compilation containing a multitude of extracts from various authors, which are known only through this work. He has left also some letters; the Nomocanon, or argument of imperial laws and canons; a Greek Lexicon; and divers theological writings, amongst others, *Adversos Latinos, de Processione Spiritus Sancti.*

110. MARINUS, OR MARTIN II., A.D. 882–884.

He was the first Pope who before his elevation, had received episcopal consecration.* He had been legate at Constantinople and in Bulgaria. As Bishop, he was not attached to any particular see, but ordained missionaries to labor among the Sclavonians. He absolved Formosus, Bishop of Porto, (afterwards Pope,) from the

---

* Döllinger's *History of the Church*, vol. iii. p. 133.

censures pronounced on him by John VIII., but forbid his ever entering Rome; and he condemned Photius, the author of the Greek schism.

111. Adrian III., a.d. 884–885.

He firmly maintained all that had been done against the archschismatic Photius; and died on a journey to Worms, undertaken to attend the imperial diet at the desire of the Emperor Charles. He was buried in the Abbey of Nonantule, and honoured there as a saint.

112. Stephen VI., a.d. 885–891.

He was a native of Rome, and of a noble family. He solaced the people during a cruel famine, while drought and locusts afflicted the land. Orphans had constantly a place at his table; and he spent his patrimony in providing for the poor. He wrote with great energy to the Emperor Basil in defence of Pope Marinus; and stigmatised Photius as a prevaricator and intruder. A letter written by him to Stylian, Bishop of Neocesaræa, concludes thus: "As we cannot pronounce any judgment without exact information, both parties must send their Bishops to us, that we may speak what God shall dictate; for the Roman Church is the model of other churches, and her decrees must abide for ever."

Many other good works are recorded of Stephen VI; and he is believed to have died on the 7th of August.

113. Formosus, A.D. 891–896.

He had been Papal legate in Bulgaria, where he laboured successfully, but was afterwards severely censured by John VIII. for political offences,* and absolved, as we have seen, by Marinus. Public affairs, at that time, were in great confusion; and it is very doubtful whether the charges brought against him were well founded. He was opposed by the antipope Sergius. He condemned Photius, the scourge of the East, who, as already mentioned, died in exile in 891. He crowned Lambert, Duke of Spoleto, emperor; and then put Arnoul, king of Germany, in his place, (896.) His remains, outraged by Stephen VII., were restored to honour by John IX.

Auxilius, a priest, wrote a defence of Formosus, in which he highly extolled his abstemious and virtuous habits. This was during the popedom of Sergius III.

114. Boniface VI., A.D. 896

He was a native of Rome. He died of the gout fifteen days after his election, which was affected

* Fleury, vol. xi. p. 345.

by a popular commotion, and is regarded as irregular. He had, in fact, been already deposed; first from his subdeaconship, and afterwards from the priesthood.

115. Stephen VII., a.d. 896–897.

Hitherto, as we have seen, most of the Popes have been men of distinguished piety; many of them sainted by common consent, and many crowned with martyrdom. But we have now arrived at a period when various sinister influences acted on the Holy See, and two or three Pontiffs arose, respecting whose ill-fame all historians are agreed. In speaking of them I shall not attempt, on the one hand, to suppress the witness of history, nor, on the other, shall I record anything to their discredit which is not well attested. The divine institution of the Papacy is so august and holy, that it is with sincere regret I am compelled to notice some spots which dim its brightness. The accounts of this period of Papal history which have come down to us are derived chiefly from the works of Luitprand, Bishop of Cremona, ambassador at Constantinople in the tenth century, and Flodoard, Canon of Rheims, his contemporary. In reading such records it is important to expect neither too little nor too much. The human element will ever be found blended with the divine. He who expects to see stainless lives in *all* the Pontiffs will be sadly disappointed; but he who does not discover a merciful Providence watching over all their doctrinal decisions, and guarding them from every taint of error, will be still more gravely at fault.

Stephen VII. was the first great scandal of the Holy See. He exhumed the corpse of his predecessor, Formosus. He presented it in a council, still arrayed in the pontifical vestments. He accused the lifeless Formosus of having usurped the See of Rome, beheaded him by the hand of an executioner, and caused his body to be hurled into the Tiber, after having stripped it of its robes, and mutilated it by cutting off three of the fingers. All who had been ordained by the Pope, to whom he and his party were so hostile, were suspended from their functions. His judgment lingered not. The people rose against him, and loaded him with chains. He died, strangled in prison, after a reign of fourteen months.*

116. Romanus, a.d. 897–898.

His family name was Gallesin. He took the name Romanus, and wore the tiara ten (some historians say five) months.

* Fleury, vol. xi. p. 543; Luitprand, l. i. c. 8.

117. Theodore II., A.D. 898.

He reigned only twenty days; but during that time he ordered the body of Formosus to be drawn from the Tiber, where some fishermen had found it; and those ordained by him to be restored to their functions. He was beloved by the clergy, kind to the poor, grave and pacific in disposition.

118. John IX., A.D. 898–900.

His election was contested, and, after it, he was opposed by the antipope Sergius, who withdrew into Tuscany, where he remained seven years, and subsequently became Sergius III. John IX. strenuously upheld all that his predecessors had done against Photius; and about forty years had elapsed from the commencement of the schism, when the ninth century closed with this Pontiff's death.

119. Benedict IV., A.D. 900–903.

He was a Roman by birth, and is reported to have governed with much wisdom during a short reign. He was bountiful to the poor; and history calls him "a great Pope." He assembled a council in the Lateran Palace, and confirmed to Argrim, Bishop of Langres, the pallium he had received from Pope Formosus. He also crowned Louis emperor and king of Italy, after the extinction of the Carlovingian dynasty.

120. Leo V., a.d. 903.

He was born at Ardea; and little is recorded of him, but that he died of grief in prison forty days after his election. Christopher, the intruder, by whom he had been imprisoned, was himself incarcerated six months after.*

121. Christopher, a.d. 903.

He wore the tiara little more than half a year, and was compelled to give way to Sergius III., who, as he belonged to the anti-Formosian party, confirmed all the acts of Stephen VII. against Formosus, and regarded John IX and the two following Popes as usurpers.†

122. Sergius III., a.d. 904–911.

Sergius has already been mentioned under John IX. He was elevated to the papal throne by the intrigues of the notorious Marozia, who, by her personal charms, gained to her side a

---

* Fleury, vol. xi., p. 565. † Fleury, vol. xi., p. 570.

large number of the chief men of Rome, became mistress of the city, and for many years was able to nominate and displace the Popes at her pleasure. She secured, it is said, the elevation of Anastasius III., (911,) and Landon, (913,) who reigned only six months; and the deposition in 928 of John X., who had been chosen in 914 by the influence of her sister and rival Theodora. With the help of her second husband, Guy, Duke of Tuscany, she put an end to John X., and caused one of her sons, at the age of twenty-five years,[*] to be thrust into the Holy See under the name of John XI., (931.) By the providence of God, none of the ill-famed Popes of this dismal period published any definitions of faith. Evil Pontiffs, though few in number, have been the severest trial of the Church; but she has triumphed over all obstacles, and will triumph even to the end. "The historical research of our days," says Father Gallwey, "is gradually clearing the injured memories of the Popes. Already so much has been effected that, in the judgment of sound historians, there are but three," (he refers, probably, to Stephen VII., John XII., and Benedict IX.,) "in the long line of two hundred and fifty Popes and more, to whom the reproach attaches that they were not better men than the average of princes are. How far future research

---

[*] Bouillet, *Dictionnaire d'Histoire*—Marosie; Fleury, vol. xii., p. 10.

will succeed in vindicating the fair fame of these three we know not."* Sergius caused the body of Stephen VII. to be transferred to a decent place of sepulture, ten years after Stephen's death, and placed over it an honourable epitaph. In speaking of an irregularity ascribed to Sergius, Fleury says: "He is the first Pope I find charged with a like reproach." This incidental testimony to the purity of the Popes' lives during nine centuries is worthy of note.

123. ANASTASIUS III., A.D. 911-913.

Anastasius was a Roman; and we learn that his government was mild and praiseworthy.

124. LANDON, A.D. 913.

He reigned only six months and two days. No other record of him remains, except that he ordained John, afterwards his successor, Archbishop of Ravenna.

125. JOHN X., A.D. 914-928.

He had been a clerk at Ravenna, and afterwards its Archbishop. He was elected, as stated above, through the influence of Maro-

---
* *Lamp,* May 30, 1863.

zia's younger sister, Theodora.* He marched with the Marquis Alberic, Marozia's son, against the Saracens, and drove them from their ground in 915. He then crowned Berenger emperor anew in 916, because, though he had been crowned already by Stephen VII., the coronation had been declared null by John IX. The history of Rome during the tenth century is extremely obscure; but it is evident, by all concurrent testimony, that it was a most corrupt age.

John X. sent a legate to Compostella, in Spain, to pay special honour to the relics of St James, and secure his intercession for the Holy See.

Marozia and her husband, Guy of Tuscany, resolved to put an end to Pope John, being jealous of the power he permitted his brother Peter to exercise in Rome. Their soldiers therefore entered the Papal palace, slew Peter before the Pope's eyes, and threw him into prison, where he died, stifled, it is said, by pillows.

126. Leo VI., A.D. 928.

He was a Roman. He reigned only eight months; and no further account of him which can be relied on remains.

* Luitprand, l. ii. c. 13; Fleury, vol. xi. p. 589.

127. STEPHEN VIII., A.D. 929–931.

This Pope was a native of Rome. In some catalogues of the Popes he is called Stephen VII., for a reason given under Stephen II. We have no historical records respecting the particulars of his pontificate.

128. JOHN XI., A.D. 931–933.

John XI. was, with several important disqualifications, thrust into the Holy See, at the early age of twenty-five, by his mother Marozia. Her second husband, Guy, being dead, she married Hugh, King of Lombardy, who, through this alliance, became master of Rome. Having, however, struck Alberic, Marozia's son, the latter excited the Romans against him and his own mother. Alberic then drove Hugh from Rome, and imprisoned Marozia, and the Pope his brother, in the fortress of St Angelo. Here he remained till his death in 933; after which the Chair of St Peter was vacant during three years.*

129. LEO VII., A.D. 936–939.

It is pleasing to turn to such a Pope at this period. Far from seeking the pontifical dignity,

---

* Flodoart, Chron. 936; Fleury, vol. xii. pp. 10-20.

Leo VII. did all he could to avoid it. He was truly a servant of God, given to prayer, meditation, and good works. Flodoart, who describes him, had conversed with him, and sat at his table. By inviting St Odo, Abbot of Cluny, to Rome, he brought about a reconciliation between Hugh and Alberic, to whom the king gave his daughter in marriage. Leo VII. died in 939.

130. STEPHEN IX., A.D. 939-942.

He was a relation of the Emperor Otho, and raised to the Holy See by the influence of Hugh, King of Italy. In consequence of his German origin, the Romans took such a dislike to him, that they cut and disfigured his face till he could no longer appear in public. He reigned, however, three years and four months.

131. MARTIN III., A.D. 942-946.

He was a Pontiff of blameless character, who applied himself assiduously to the duties of religion, the relief of the poor, and repair of churches.

132. AGAPETUS II., A.D. 946-956.

He invited the Emperor Otho the Great to Rome to oppose Berenger, (who had revolted against him, desiring to make himself independent sovereign of Italy,) and by his moderation he calmed the troubled waters.

133. John XII., A.D. 956–963.

Octavian was the first who changed his name at his consecration. He was a son of Alberic, a Roman patrician, and elected at the age of eighteen. Being disquieted by Berenger, who had made himself King of Italy in 950, he appealed to Otho, (961,) gave him the title of King of Italy, and crowned him emperor in 962. He then betrayed Otho, and leagued with Adelbert, son of Berenger, against him. The irritated emperor had him deposed by a council, which declared him guilty of all sorts of sacrilege; and Leo VIII. was chosen in his place, and ordained contrary to the canons, being a layman. John, however, succeeded in returning to Rome, and there exercised cruel vengeance against those who had taken Leo's part. This unworthy Pontiff died three months after of a short illness; or, as others say, was assassinated. The discrepancy of these accounts is reconciled by the continuator of Luitprand, who reports him to have died of a wound received in a night of dissipation. A more dismal end, for one filling so high and holy an office, can scarcely be imagined; but all Church histories concur in the account here given. The Viaticum was not administered.

134. Leo VIII., a.d. 963–965.

He is regarded as an intruder, having been elected in the lifetime of John XII. by the authority of Otho. Benedict V., chosen by some cardinals after John's death, disputed the tiara with him, but was unable to maintain his ground as Pontiff. Leo VIII. deprived him even of the priesthood, and allowed him to continue deacon only on condition of his going into exile. Leo himself died in 965.

135. Benedict V., a.d. 964–965.

This Pope was born at Rome. Otho the Great, irritated at his election, had him detained at Hamburg, where he died on the 5th of July, 965. He was a learned and virtuous man, and would have been worthy of the popedom if his election had been more regular. He edified the Saxons by his instructions and good example; and the emperor was ready to restore him to the Romans, when death intervened. In the year 1000 his remains were carried to Rome, according to a prediction he had uttered.*

* Dithmar, Chron. lib. iv. p. 47.

136. John XIII., A.D. 965-972.

He was Bishop of Narni, and a Roman by birth. A faction of powerful Romans seized and held him in captivity in the Castle of St Angelo, and afterwards in Campania. It is said that he had treated them with disdain, and thus provoked their enmity; but this is a weak reason to assign for revolting against a lawful ruler and Pope. After remaining in exile eleven months, he was recalled, and his enemies were disgraced. In 968 he sent legates to Constantinople with letters to the emperor Nicephorus; but they were treated with great disrespect through jealousy of Otho, whom the Pope crowned and styled Emperor of the Romans.

137. Benedict VI., A.D. 972-974.

He was a native of Rome. He was overthrown and imprisoned by Centius, who supported Francon, the antipope, under the name of Boniface VII. He died in prison, poisoned or strangled: and his rival, driven from power, fled to Constantinople.

138. Domnus II, A.D. 974.

He reigned only three months. History is almost silent respecting him, and his place in the list of Popes is matter of dispute.

139. Benedict VII., a.d. 975-983.

He was Bishop of Sutri, and a relation of Alberic, a Roman noble. He was opposed by the antipope Boniface VII., who, though in exile, had not resigned his pretentions to the Papal Chair, but returned to Rome on hearing of Benedict's death.

Notwithstanding the disorders prevailing at Rome during this century, many distant nations were evangelised by saintly missionaries and hermits, bishops and kings. But it would be foreign to the purpose of this Manual to do more than glance at such names as St Wolfang, St Dunstan, St Edward, St Romuald, and St Nilus, whose virtues and labours are amply recorded in Church history. Each of them was living in the time of Benedict VII. It often happens, as Dr Coleridge observes,* that such dark periods are most prolific of the noblest fruits of the interior life.

140. John XIV., a.d. 984-985.

His name was Peter, which he changed when elected Pope, after having been Bishop of Pavia and chancellor to Otho II. He likewise was resisted by the antipope called Boniface VII.,

* *Month*, May 1865.

who cast him into prison in the Castle of St Angelo, where, at the end of four months, he died of hunger. No one of the Romans could or would oppose the usurper; but the populace avenged themselves by the indignities they offered to his corpse when, after a few months, he fell by death from his ill-gotten power. They dragged it through the streets, pierced and mangled, and left it bare before the statue of Constantine's horse.

141. John XV., a.d. 985.

He was elected, but not consecrated. He held the Holy See four months, but is not reckoned among the true Popes. The disturbances caused by Crescentius began during his pontificate, but he remained at Rome, and kept on good terms with that powerful patrician. He died in 996.

142. John XVI., a.d. 986-996.

Little is known of this Pontiff that deserves to be recorded. Fleury says that he was not what he should have been, but loved gain, and was ready to sell everything.*

The century in which he flourished is the least brilliant and interesting of Christian eras. The

---
* Tome xii. p. 307.

Popes of this period succeeded each other very rapidly, insomuch that from A.D. 896 to 996 twenty-nine occupied the Papal chair. In some catalogues of the Popes he is called John XV., and hence a little confusion arises, as in the case of the Stephens. He died in April of a violent fever.

143. Gregory V., A.D. 996–999.

His family name was Bruno, and he was a nephew of the Emperor Otho III., who caused him to be elected, though he was only twenty-four years of age. He was soon driven from Rome by Crescentius, a powerful senator, and took refuge in Lombardy. His cause was espoused the same year by his imperial uncle, with the help of whose soldiers he drove from Rome an antipope calling himself John XVI. (*bis*) in 997. This miserable man was pursued by some of the emperor's servants, and taken. They cut out his eyes and tongue, mutilated his nose, and cast him into prison in this state. To what lengths will not a vindictive spirit carry those who yield to its impulse! Robert le Pieux having married his cousin Bertha, contrary to ecclesiastical law, Gregory excommunicated him, and put France under an interdict. After a struggle of three years Robert yielded, and repudiated Bertha. The Pope imposed on him seven years' penance. Even in those cases where ecclesiastical dispensations may be obtained, the Catholic Church visits with her severest censures those who marry within the prohibited degrees without her consent. Gregory V. was the first German who sat on a Papal throne. He was well skilled in letters, and spoke three languages. Young as he was, he died in less than three years after his elevation.

144. Silvester II., A.D. 999–1003.

He was born at Aurillac in Auvergne, of an obscure family named Gerbert, about 930. He received a learned education in a monastery of Aurillac, and went to perfect himself in Spain under the erudite Hatton, Bishop of Vich. He then entered the Order of the Benedictines, and attached himself to the emperor Otho I., who intrusted to him the education of his son, afterwards Otho II., and gave him the Abbey of Bobbio, near Geneva. He afterwards returned to France, where Hugh Capet appointed him preceptor to his son Robert, and raised him to the archbishopric of Rheims, after having deposed Arnoul, (992.) This nomination displeasing Pope John XV., Gerbert went back to Germany. Otho III., Lord of Italy, made him

Archbishop of Ravenna, (997,) and caused him to be elected Pope, (999.) He ruled with great wisdom, aided in the development of intellect, surrounded himself with brilliant disciples, and died in 1003. He possessed prodigious knowledge for his time in geometry, mechanics, and astronomy. He united indeed in himself all the ecclesiastical and all the profane learning of the epoch in which he flourished. The introduction of the Arabic figures into Europe is attributed to him, and also that of pendulum clocks. Some of his letters and discourses are extant, and published by Duchesne in 1636. The occasional reigns of such Popes refreshed the spirits and reassured the faith of those who were saddened by the disorders of the times. Silvester II. was very old at the time of his election, and died after a pontificate of four years. He was buried in St John Lateran; and when the marble coffin in which he lay was opened in 1648, his body emitted a grateful odour, and then, at the touch of light and air,

"Slipt into ashes, and was found no more."

145. JOHN XVII., A.D. 1003.

His reign lasted only five months. He died in October, and the Holy See remained vacant four months and a half.

146. John XVIII., A.D. 1003–1009.

In his time the Church of Constantinople was united to that of Rome, and the name of this Pope was recited there in the Mass together with that of the other Patriarchs. Three months elapsed after his death before a successor was named.

147. Sergius IV., A.D. 1009–1012.

His family name was Pietro Bocca-di-Porco, (Pig's-snout.) He was Bishop of Albano, and a Roman by birth. He died on the 13th of July.

148. Benedict VIII., A.D. 1012–1024.

He had been Bishop of Porto, and had for competitor a certain Gregory, who compelled him to leave Rome; but he induced Henry II., Emperor of Germany, to reinstate him, and crowned the emperor and empress in St Peter's with great pomp, on February the 22d, 1014. The Saracens coming in 1016 to invade his States, he put himself at the head of the Christian troops, and exterminated the foe. In 1020, he visited the emperor at Bamberg, and it was probably on this occasion that Henry confirmed to him the temporal possession of Rome, the exarchate of

Ravenna, and other Italian domains. He died in 1024, and was succeeded by his brother, John XIX. They were of the family of the Counts of Tusculum, who were now all-powerful at Rome.

149. JOHN XIX., A.D., 1024–1033.

He was son of Count Gregory of Tuscany. He and his predecessor Benedict VIII. were desirous of making the Holy See an inheritance in their family. He was layman and Pope in the same day; and historians say that bribery was employed to secure his elevation. In 1033, some of the Romans conspired against him during an eclipse of the sun, and drove him from the See. But he was restored by the emperor Conrad, at the head of his army, and died in November of the same year.

150. BENEDICT IX., A.D. 1033–1048.

He was the nephew of John XIX., and son of Alberic, Count of Tusculum. He is one of those few Popes, of whom I have spoken already, whose history is painful to record.

The accounts of him which have come down to us, rest principally on the authority of the monk Glaber, and have, I believe, never been disputed. He was raised to the Papal throne at the age of twelve years by means of large bribes,* and gave himself up to all kinds of disorderly living. His violence made him odious to the Romans, who rose against him and drove him from Rome, in 1044; but he succeeded in getting himself reinstated. Silvester III., as he was called, who had been appointed in his place, was dethroned; and Benedict might have held his ground, had he been willing to reform his life. He continued, however, to cause the greatest scandal; and being despised by the clergy and people, he consented to accept a large sum of money, and retire from government. Gregory VI. was chosen in his stead. Glaber speaks of him as a very pious man, whose virtues were well known.

After the death of Clement II., Benedict took possession of the Holy See for the third time, and held it more than eight months. He again ceased to rule in 1048, retired to Grotto Ferrati, near Frascati, and when near his death in 1065, sent for the holy Abbot Bartholomew, and confessed his sins. The abbot reminded him that he was unable to give absolution to one who, though deprived of sacerdotal functions, still pretended to be Pope; and on this Benedict renounced all such claim, and strove to make his peace with God.†

* Glaber, vol. iv. c. 5; Fleury, vol. xii. p. 505.
† See Fleury, vol. xii. p. 545, and the authorities there quoted.

During his time simony became extremely prevalent, and great efforts were soon afterwards made to suppress it.

151. GREGORY VI., A.D. 1044–1046.

As a priest, he was known under the name of John Gratian. He was elected Pope in 1044; while three others, Benedict IX., Silvester, and John XX., disputed the Holy See, and all the patrimony of St Peter was pillaged. He contrived by means of gold to send away the antipopes, and used all his efforts to put an end to disorder; but some ambitious cardinals, and the Emperor Henry III., named the Black, impeded him in his wise reforms, and in his discouragement he abdicated, (1046.) The emperor insured the election of three succeeding Pontiffs; for at this period the sovereigns of Germany exerted over the Church and Bishops of Rome an influence similar to that of the Emperors of the East, and, in earlier times, those of the West. They were by turns friends and foes, nursing fathers and cruel oppressors. Nothing can exceed the deplorable state of society in Italy at this time. The roads were beset with robbers; the cities swarmed with thieves and assassins; swords were often drawn in church. The revenues of the Pontiff scarcely sufficed for his subsistence, and his efforts to restrain and punish the vices of the people were rewarded with calumny and violence.

152. Clement II., a.d. 1046–1048.

He was a Saxon, and his family name was Suidger. He became Bishop of Bamburg, and was elected pope at the council of Sutri, convoked by Henry the Black. He held a council at Rome, and died in Germany in 1048. He was buried at Bamberg, and his tomb was to be seen there six hundred years after his death. In this year, Berengarius of Tours, Archdeacon of Angers, taught with impiety that the body of Christ is not really present in the Eucharist. He was refuted by Abbon and Lanfranc, and ten different councils (such was the Church's zeal) condemned his doctrine. He was obliged to abjure his errors, and burn his books; but soon returned to heresy. At last, however, he came to a better mind; and after a cordial renunciation, retired into the island of St Côme, near Tours, where he died at the age of ninety.

153. Damasus II., a.d. 1048.

He had been Bishop of Brixen, in the Tyrol. He died, twenty-three days after his election, at Preneste.

154. St Leo IX., A.D. 1049-1055.

Bruno, Bishop of Toul, was a kinsman of the Emperor Henry III., and a very learned man. His pleasing manners and appearance made him generally liked. He was extremely fond of music, and composed himself. Every year he visited Rome, through devotion to St Peter; and sometimes a suit of five hundred persons followed him. It was long before he would consent to be made ruler of the Church; but when he became Pope he set himself earnestly to reform ecclesiastical discipline, and held several councils for the suppression of two monster evils—simony and incontinence. For the same purpose he undertook several journeys into France and Germany. The Greek schism became confirmed during his pontificate by the calumnious writings of Michael Cerularius, Patriarch of Constantinople, and by his closing the Latin churches. Leo IX. excommunicated him; and the Greeks added heresy to their schism. Having accompanied, in 1053, the troops, which the emperor had sent to his aid against the Normans, he was beaten and taken captive. He was set at liberty in ten months, and brought back to Rome, where he died soon after, aged fifty.*
The details of his saintly life are varied and highly interesting. Unfeigned piety marked his

* *Vies des Saints*, 19 avril.

career throughout; and, though raised to the highest dignity, he lived in the constant practice of austerity and recitation of the Psalter, which he preferred to any other devotional book. Marriage within the prohibited degrees had, in his time, become very prevalent, and he laboured hard to rectify the corrupt usage.

155. Victor II., A.D. 1055-1057.

His family name was Gebhard. He was Bishop of Erichstedt, and counsellor of the Emperor Henry III., who, in concert with Hildebrand, assured him of the tiara. Gebhard deserved this honour, though he did not desire it. He used every effort to uproot simony, and thus prepared the way for Gregory VII.

Lambert, a German chronicler and Benedictine, relates that a subdeacon attempted to poison the Pope by mixing some deadly substance with the wine in the chalice. Victor could not raise it after the consecration, fell on his knees, and prayed that the cause might be made known. The subdeacon forthwith became possessed, and his intention being at once suspected, the chalice, with its contents, was enclosed in an altar by Pope Victor's order. He then continued in prayer with the people till the poisoner was exorcised.*

* *Histoire de l'Allemagne*, an. 1054.

Victor II. died in Tuscany, on his way from Ratisbone to Rome.

156. Stephen X., a.d. 1057–1058.

He was abbot of the vast and wealthy Benedictine monastery of Monte Cassino, and brother of Godfroi le Barbu, Duke of Lorraine. He was a reformer of public morals, and died at Florence in the odour of sanctity. He held several councils with a view of suppressing irregularities among the clergy and unlawful marriages among the laity. The antipope Benedict X. held forcible possession of the Holy See during ten months after his decease, and contrary to his express decree.

157. Nicolas II., a.d. 1058–1061.

Gerard de Bourgogne was so called because he was born in Savoy, which then belonged to the kings of Bourgogne; he was Bishop of Florence, and elected Pope through the support of the Empress Agnes, mother of Henry IV., and the choice of Hildebrand, with the consent of the Roman clergy and people. By means of the Bishops of Tuscany and Lombardy, he effected the deposition of his rival, John of Velletri, called Benedict X. He invested the Normans, Richard and Robert Guiscard; the first with the principality of Capua, the second with that of Apulia and Calabria, (1059.) These princes thus became vassals of the Church. He regulated in council the formalities to be observed in the election of the Popes, and died in Florence in June, 1061. He had retained possession of that see during his pontificate, and he was buried in the Church of Santa Reparata. St Peter Damien relates, on the testimony of Bishop Mainard, that Nicolas II. never passed a day without washing the feet of twelve poor persons. It was before this Pope that Berengarius appeared and abjured his errors in these terms: "I protest with my heart and lips that I hold the faith which the Pope and the council (of Paris) have prescribed me, according to the authority of the Gospels and of the Apostle, viz., that the bread and the wine which are offered on the altar are, after the consecration, the true body and the true blood of Jesus Christ."

158. ALEXANDER II., A.D. 1061-1073.

Anselm de Bagio was born at Milan, and became Bishop of Lucca. His election was rejected by the imperial court, because it had taken place without its sanction; but it was defended by St Peter Damien and Hildebrand, being unquestionably valid. Alexander obliged the Normans to render up the land they had wrested from the Holy See, and opposed the persecutions inflicted by the Christians on the Jews. He was resisted by the antipope Cadolous, called Honorius II., a bishop who, with his chief supporters, lived with a wife or paramour, contrary to the canons, and practised simony. The constant recurrence of antipopes about this period is a melancholy feature in the state of the times, and shows how large an amount of ambition and violence reigned among the higher clergy. Christianity as yet had but half developed her civilising power; and there is much in the history of the Popes of the ninth, and two following centuries, which it is painful to record. Alexander II. died in April, 1073, and was buried in St Peter's. He is reported to have wrought two miracles of healing. Forty-five of his letters are extant, and throw considerable light on the usages of his time and the position of affairs.

159. St Gregory VII., A.D. 1073–1085.

The celebrated Hildebrand was the son of a carpenter of Soana, in Tuscany, and was born about 1013. He became a monk of Cluny. Being charged with a mission to Rome, he fell in with the priest Gratien, afterwards Gregory VI., and attached himself to him. By his advice

St Leo IX., who had been nominated by the Emperor, Henry III., secured his election by the Roman people, declaring that the emperor's nomination was worth nothing. Hildebrand acquired the greatest influence over Leo IX. and his successors, and brought about a decree, in a council held by Alexander II., to the effect that the nomination of the Popes should in future belong only to the people of Rome. Thus he prepared himself for his great and arduous struggle with imperial power. He was created cardinal by St Leo IX., and under the succeeding Popes his reputation steadily increased, and at the death of Alexander II. the people with shouts of applause proclaimed him Pope. He was sixty years old when he began his pontifical life, and many might have asked whether at so advanced an age it would be possible to achieve great works and acquire imperishable fame. He restored ecclesiastical celibacy to new vigour, stemmed the torrent of simony and incontinence among the clergy,* and boldly exerted his lawful authority to keep in check the temporal power of Christian princes. At this epoch, sovereigns, not content with distributing immense domains or fiefs to bishops, archbishops, and abbots, invested them themselves with ecclesiastical titles, giving them, at the same time, sceptre, sword, crosier,

* Reeve's *History of the Church*, vol. ii. p. 202.

and ring, the symbols of baronial and episcopal dignity. This was clearly an infraction of Papal privileges and Papal rights, and such as no Catholic sovereign in our day would dream of. It was exalting the State above the Church, and human power above Divine authority. It tended, above all things to secularise the Church, and to make the bishops and mitred abbots sworn vassals of the crown; and if the practice had continued unchecked, it could have issued in nothing but interminable schisms and national Churches, instead of one compact and Catholic Church. Gregory VII. resolved to emancipate the ecclesiastical power, and to recover for it the rights of investiture and canonical institution. He found in the Emperor Henry IV. a formidable adversary; and the terrible struggle which took place between them, and continued under Urban II., Pascal II., Gelasius II., and Calixtus II., is called "the investiture quarrel." The Pope was scrupulously circumspect in his first negotiations, especially with Henry IV., who, being King of Germany, was destined to wear the imperial crown. He therefore wrote to conjure him to put an end to the disorders which afflicted the Church and made his subjects groan. The letter was full of sweetness and charity; but Henry replied to it with promises which he forgot immediately after. Having employed several other means with no greater success, the Pontiff decided on convening a Synod at Rome, where he found bishops assembled from most of the nations of Europe. There he prohibited investitures under pain of an anathema. He then cited Henry to appear before his tribunal to justify himself from all the accusations brought against him. The monarch answered this citation by holding a cabal-council of his own, in which he dared to pass a sentence of deposition on the Pope, (1076.) This impious act induced St Gregory VII. to fulminate an excommunication against the schismatical sovereign. No sooner had the anathema been pronounced against Henry than every one abandoned him, and the nobles of his realm assembled to elect another in his place. The Pope, however, demanded a delay of one year, that Henry might have the opportunity of effecting a reconciliation with the Church. Before the expiration of this term, Henry sought the Pope at the Château of Canossa, not far from Modena, remained at the gate three days in the habit of a suppliant, and then received absolution. Such was the power of the Popes when public opinion was on their side. The faithless sovereign soon violated all his promises, and even endeavoured to get the Pope into his hands. The great men of the kingdom, becoming indignant, straightway declared him to be set aside, and appointed another king. But afterwards uniting with all who were discontented with the Pope on account of the severity with which he followed up all disorders, Henry kept up a struggle against Rodolph, who had been elected in his stead. Rodolph was slain in battle. Henry marched against Rome, and laid siege to it during three years, (1081–1084.) He also opposed to St Gregory VII. the antipope Guibert, under the name of Clement III. The Pope was at last delivered by Robert Guiscard, Duke of Calabria, who re-established him in his see and on his throne, but filled Rome with blood. The pious Pontiff, finding the city insecure, followed his liberators when they vacated the capital, and retired into the states of the Normans, at Salerno, where he died soon after, saying, "I have loved justice and hated iniquity; therefore I die in exile." (1085.) Many miracles are said to have been wrought at his tomb. Possessed of ardent zeal, which writers adverse to his memory describe as excessive, inflexible in his resolutions, and austere in his morals, this Pontiff was undoubtedly a great and holy man, and merited canonisation. Some letters of St Gregory VII. are extant, inserted in the collection of councils; some maxims concerning pontifical power, preserved in the work entitled *Dictatus Papæ;* and a commentary on the Penitential Psalms, which is ascribed also to Gregory the Great. It is evident from these works that Gregory VII. held, not merely that Christian princes ought to be subject as obedient children to the Holy See, but that all temporal power flows from the spiritual authority of the Pope, and depends on it for its existence. Numerous passages are quoted by Fleury * from Hildebrand's writings in illustration of this opinion, which, though held by many good and learned men, is not, in the view of that historian, to be considered binding on any one. Forty-five years after St Gregory VII.'s death, Canon Paul, a Bavarian, wrote his life; and Paul V., in 1609, allowed the Archbishop and Chapter of Salerno to honour him as a saint with a public office. Mr Bowden's life of him, (1840,) though written from an Anglican point of view, evinces great research, and is well worth consulting.

160. Victor III., A.D. 1086–1087.

He was of the ducal house of Capua, and his family name was Didier. He had been twenty-nine years abbot of Monte Cassino, in the kingdom of Naples, and had acted an important part under his friend St Gregory VII. When elected, he for a long time refused the tiara in spite

* Tome xiii. pp. 395–400.

of the most urgent entreaties. Consecrated in 1087, he reigned but four months. He preached against the Arabs of Africa, an expedition which proved disastrous to them, and had to combat the antipope Clement III., (Guibert of Ravenna,) whom the grand Countess Matilda drove from Rome. He continued to be abbot of Monte Cassino after his elevation; and he composed some works, of which the Dialogues on the miracles of St Benedict have come down to us. Indeed, he is known in the history of letters as "Desiderius, Abbot of Monte Cassino," for while in that convent he was a great collector of manuscripts, and employed persons to copy the works of the classics. Peregrinius, in his *series Abbatum Cassinensium*, gives a detailed account of him. On his deathbed, in September, 1087, he recommended the cardinals to choose Otho, Bishop of Ostia, as his successor, and his advice was taken.

161. Urban II., A.D. 1088–1099.

His family name was Eudes or Odon, and his birthplace, Lagery, near Châtilon-sur-Marne, in France. He was chosen from the Benedictine Abbey of Cluny to the See of Ostia by St Gregory VII., who also, when dying, designated him as a worthy successor. He vigorously sustained the Papal conflict with the empire, ruined the pretensions of the antipope Guibert, and espoused the cause of Anselm, Archbishop of Canterbury, in opposition to William Rufus.* Popes and primates, in former days, had to contend against princes, and they must now against parliaments, in defence of the Church's rights.

"It was at the council of Clermont, in November, 1095, that Pope Urban II, invited the Church and the chivalry of Europe to join in the perils and share the merits of a holy crusade. Pilgrims had returned from the far East with dreadful tales of the sufferings of the oriental Christians, the barbarity of the Mussulman tyrants, and the desecration of the sacred places, where man's redemption was accomplished. Peter the Hermit, a man of small stature but great soul, on his return from a pilgrimage, obtained the ear of the Pope, and, commissioned by him, journeyed with untiring zeal from village to village, from city to city, from court to court, exhorting prince and peasant, secular and religious, for the love of Christ and the love of Christians, to arm and recover Jerusalem. The multitude, therefore, that had assembled at Clermont was well prepared, at the conclusion of the Pope's address, to join as one man in the cry, '*Deus id vult, Deus id vult!*' 'Where two or three,' said Urban, 'are met together in the name of Christ, the Lord

* Butler's *Lives*, vol. iv. p. 214.

has kept his promise, and is present. Let every one, then, take on his breast the sign of the cross: as it is written, "He that taketh not up his cross cannot be my disciple."' The assembly, by the mouth of Cardinal Gregory, confessed their sins, and at the hands of St Peter's successor received absolution.

"Adhemas, Bishop of Puy, was the first to take the cross, and was appointed general of the expedition. Europe, in the year that followed, poured out her sons by thousands and by millions. The roads were too narrow for the immense multitudes. Lands and castles were mortgaged, cottages and fields sold; the knight went forth in all the glory of chivalry; the peasant shod his oxen like horses, and carried forth his family in the heavy farm-cart; and at each succeeding town, the inquiries were anxious, 'Is this Jerusalem?' Thus six millions—so say the chroniclers—obeyed the call of Urban, and fulfilled the injunctions of Clermont."* Jerusalem was taken just fifteen days before the death of Urban, which happened on the 29th of July, 1099. Guibert, Abbot of Nogent, relates that several miracles were wrought at his tomb.

* Neale's *Crusades*, Introd.

162. Pascal II., A.D. 1099–1118.

His family name was Rainieri; he was born at Bleda in Tuscany, and became a monk of Cluny. He was made by St Gregory VII. Abbot of St Paul *extra muros*. He supported Henry (V.) against his father Henry IV. He then fell out with this prince, who had broken his engagements, and refused to crown him.* Henry V. imprisoned him in Rome itself from February to April, 1111, and obtained from him by forcible means "the rights of investiture." Pascal was set free, but was blamed by the clergy for this concession, acknowledged his fault, and made all possible reparation. On two occasions, in full council, (A.D. 1112 and 1116,) he cleared himself from the charge of heresy, which was constantly brought against those who favoured imperial investiture. He founded many churches. He was opposed by the antipope Bourdin of Limoges, Albert, and Theodoric. It was during this pontificate that the Holy See received as a donation the states of Matilda, marchioness of Tuscany, (1102.) She had made a previous gift of the allodial "patrimony of St Peter" in 1077 to St Gregory VII., whom she aided strenuously against Henry IV., and received in her fortress of Canossa, near Reggio,

* *Concil. Lateran*, vol. x. pp. 767, 856.

when the emperor there submitted to a humiliating penance. The legacy of Eturia was subsequently invalidated.

A valuable history of the Papal States has been written by Dr Miley, in three volumes. As we descend the stream of Papal history, the lives of the several Pontiffs assume larger proportions, in consequence of the materials being more abundant. I shall not, on this account, be able to lengthen, in any great degree, my notices of them; but I shall endeavour to direct the student to those sources from which he may derive the best information.

Two years before Pascal's death, a sedition arose in the capital, the family of the Pope suffered ill-treatment, and a civil conflict ensued, which lasted till harvest time. He died in January, 1118.

163. Gelasius II., a.d. 1118–1119.

John of Gaeta was no sooner elected than Cincio Frangipani, consul of Rome, obliged him to leave the city; and in concert with Henry V. caused Maurice Bourdin, "Gregory VIII.," who had been Archbishop of Braga in Portugal, to be chosen in his place. Gelasius retired to Gaeta, where he excommunicated the antipope and his protectors. Shortly after he returned to

Rome, but was soon expelled again by Frangipani. He then took refuge in France, where he was received with honour, and ended his days in the Abbey of Cluny. According to monastic custom, he was laid on the bare floor, and thus died, after receiving the holy sacraments, on the 29th of January, 1119. The antipope was soon abandoned by Henry, and being besieged at Sutri by Calixtus II., the successor of Gelasius, he was taken captive and thrown into prison, where he died in 1122.

164. CALIXTUS II., A.D. 1119–1124.

He was named Gui, and was the son of William, count of Bourgogne, and archbishop of Vienna. He took and confined the antipope Bourdin, as mentioned above. He brought to a close the investiture quarrel in the Concordat of Worms, (1112,) recognising in the emperor Henry V. the right of giving the temporal investiture, regarding secular goods, and reserved to himself the spiritual investiture, or right of conferring ecclesiastical titles. The former was done by means of the sceptre; the latter, with the crosier and ring. The investiture quarrel broke out again in the following century, but was mixed up with the Guelph and Ghibelline conflict. It ended only with the death of Conradin in 1268. Under this Pontiff was held the first Lateran council in the Basilica of St John Lateran, founded by Constantine. This was the ninth œcumenical council of the Church. It was celebrated in the year 1123, in the presence of Calixtus II., during the reigns of the Emperor Henry V. and Charles le Gros in France. Three hundred bishops and six hundred abbots were present in this assembly. The principal objects of this council were to settle finally the investiture question, and to set on foot a crusade against the Saracens, either in Palestine or Spain. Calixtus consecrated Thurstan Archbishop of York at Rheims, on the 20th of October, 1119. During five years Thurstan had suffered from the opposition of Henry I. and Ralph, the Archbishop of Canterbury, to whom he refused to make a promise of obedience.

Calixtus II. died on the 12th of December, 1124, having in his lifetime made rich presents to the Church of St Peter, and promoted public works in Rome.

165. Honorius II., A.D. 1124-1130.

Before his elevation to the Popedom, he was known as Cardinal Lambert, bishop of Ostia. His reign was disturbed by Roger, Duke of Apulia, against whom he waged for a time unsuccessful war. Peace was then concluded between them, and Honorius granted Roger the investiture of the Duchies of Apulia and Calabria. He confirmed Lothaire in the imperial dignity, and condemned the abbots of Cluny and Monte Cassino for divers faults. Some of his letters are extant. He died in February, 1130, and was interred in the church of St John Lateran. St Bernard at this time acted a prominent part in the affairs of Europe.

166. INNOCENT II., A.D. 1130-1143.

His family name was Gregoire de Passis. He was forced by the preponderance of his rival Peter de Leo (Anacletus) to quit Rome and took refuge in France with Louis (VI.) le Gros, who endeavoured in vain to reinstate him. It was not till the death of Anacletus that he recovered his authority, (1138.) He was opposed also by the antipope Victor. He condemned the doctrine of the famous Abelard concerning the Trinity, and of his disciple Arnaud of Brescia, who with his followers pretended to restore the primitive purity of the Church, like the Waldenses, denied to the clergy the right to possess temporal goods, and taught erroneously respecting the Eucharist, and baptism of infants. Disagreements, which St Bernard strove to appease, arose between Innocent II. and Louis VII. of France, relative to the nomination of the Archbishop of Bourges. He held the second Lateran, or tenth œcumenical, Synod in 1139. About a thousand bishops were present. This council restored discipline, proscribed the Arnaudists and Petrobusians, who denied the sacrifice of the Mass, prayers for the dead, and baptism of infants; and condemned the schism of Peter de Leo, (Anacletus,) the antipope and monk of Cluny.

Innocent I. died in September, 1143, and, like his predecessor, was buried in the Lateran Church.

167. CELESTINE II., A.D. 1143-1144.

He was a Tuscan named Guido de Castel, and reigned only five months. He received a letter from Peter, Abbot of Cluny, in which the latter congratulated the Pope on his peaceful election, and said that no other Pontiff had been elevated with so little commotion since Alexander II., in 1061. He expressed great desire to see Celestine, and renew their former friendship; but this pleasure was not granted him, at least in this world.

168. LUCIUS II., A.D. 1144-1145.

This Pope, like his predecessor, reigned but a short time. He was born at Bologna, and had been made Cardinal and librarian of the Roman Church by Honorius II. Innocent II., also knowing his worth, gave him the chancellorship, and, when dying, entrusted him as chamberlain with the management of the Church's property. His pontificate lasted eleven months. He was wounded by a stone flung during a tumult of the Roman people, died soon after, and was buried, according to the usage of his time, in the Lateran Church.

169. Eugene III., A.D. 1145–1153.

He was a disciple of St Bernard and a monk of Clairvaux, the celebrated Benedictine monastery, of which St Bernard became the first abbot in 1115. Subsequently he became Abbot of St Anastasius in Rome; and when St Bernard heard of his elevation he wrote to the Cardinals and Bishops at Rome to express his deep regret at their having withdrawn from the shades of the cloister a man wholly unacquainted with mundane affairs, to seat him above princes and at the head of the Church. He speaks of him as "a little man covered with rags"—"a rustic whose hands have been holding the spade and hatchet."*
Arnaud of Brescia had already succeeded in driving Lucius II. from Rome. He had united

---
* Epistle 237.

projects of political with those of religious reform. He drove Eugenius III. also from the Holy City to Viterbo, established a republic, formed a senate, and remained master of Rome for ten years. Eugenius, driven from Rome a second time, took refuge in Paris, advocated a second crusade, and held a council to examine the errors of Gilbert de la Poirée, Bishop of Poitiers, professor of dialectics and theology in the capital, a realist and antinominalist. His statements concerning the Divine Essence were repudiated in four distinct propositions, which may be found in Fleury.* In 1148, Eugenius visited Clairvaux, edified all around him by his humility and simple habits, and soon after re-entered Rome, where he died on the 8th of July, 1153. He was regarded as a saint, and several miracles were wrought at his tomb.

170. Anastasius IV., a.d. 1153–1154.

He had been known as Cardinal Conrad, Bishop of Sabina. He distinguished himself by his charity during a great famine. He was an aged man, and one of great experience and ability, but his short reign was disturbed by the schism of Arnaud de Brescia and his followers.

---

* Tome xiv., an. 1148.

171. Adrian IV., A.D. 1154–1159.

Nicholas Breakspeare was the only Englishman who has become Pope; and his rise to that dignity was very remarkable. He was born at Abbots-Langley in Hertfordshire, was the son of a beggar, and for a long time himself subsisted on alms, for which he was compelled to beg. He hired himself as servant to the canons of St Ruf near Avignon, became a religious of that community, and soon after was made superior of the convent.* Eugene III. raised Breakspeare to the Bishopric of Albano, near Rome, and sent him as legate to Denmark and Norway, where he reformed the habits of the clergy. He was elected Pope in 1154, and had to contend with those who still sustained the pretensions and authority of Arnaud de Brescia. He had to struggle also with William of Sicily, whom he excommunicated, and the Emperor Frederic, who had made inroads on some of the possessions of the Church. Adrian IV. died in 1159. The Catholic Church is essentially opposed to distinctions of caste, and tends to abolish them. The fact of her priests, bishops, cardinals, and even Popes coming from all nations and all classes greatly contribute to this happy tendency. "At a time," says Lord Macaulay,

* Dr Miley's *Papal States*, vol. iii. p. 11.

"when the English name was a reproach, and when all the civil and military dignities of the kingdom were supposed to belong exclusively to the countrymen of the Conqueror, the despised race learned, with transports of delight, that one of themselves, Nicholas Breakspeare, had been elevated to the Papal throne, and had held out his feet to be kissed by ambassadors sprung from the noblest houses of Normandy." It must not, however, be supposed that the Pope became haughty in consequence of his rise. An account is preserved of his interviews with John of Salisbury, in Apulia, from which it appears that the Papal dignity brought him great increase of trouble. "All the pain," he said, "which he had suffered before seemed to him light and sweet in comparison with the burden of supreme government. Gladly would he fly from it if he could. The Lord, who had always kept him between the anvil and the hammer, could, if He pleased, put His hand under the weight which, without Him, would be utterly insupportable."

172. ALEXANDER III, A.D. 1159–1181.

His family name was Rolando Rainuce, and he was born at Sienna. During his pontificate the Waldenses and Albigenses, who were increasing in number, began to render an œcumenical council expedient. The Waldenses, who were called Cathares, (Puritans,) inveighed against the priests, and pretended to revive the primitive purity of the Church. The Albigenses were tainted with Manicheism. Alexander III. presided at the third Lateran council in which these sects were condemned. It was assembled in the year 1179, and three hundred and two bishops were present. Alexander governed the Church in a holy manner, and died at Rome in 1181, cherished by the Romans and respected by Europe. He combated slavery, reserved to the Popes the right of canonisation of saints, and introduced the use of monitories. While the Popes defended Christianity from the Islamite invasion from without, they watched also within over the interests of peoples, and protected them against the despotism of sovereigns. The great struggle between the priesthood and the empire which had begun under Gregory VII. was not yet concluded. The emperors were obstinately attached to their excessive pretensions, and the Church was obliged to resist them. Frederic Barbarossa appeared still more violent and more ambitious than his predecessors. He was, withal, a man of great genius, whose reign was one of the most brilliant in the history of Germany. After having re-established order in his empire and extended his sovereignty over Poland and

Hungary, he passed into Italy, and assumed the exercise of absolute power over the Lombard cities, which for a long time past had enjoyed almost complete independence, and over Rome itself. He had gained from the University of Bologna a kind of sanction to his pretensions, she having decided that in his quality of emperor he was master of the world. The most powerful of the Lombard Republics, Milan, took arms to resist the imperial despotism, but after a heroic struggle of two years, the inhabitants were compelled to surrender at discretion.

Frederic ordered the evacuation of the city in three days. He then demolished this opulent Guelph stronghold, and sowed salt on its ruins, (1162.) All the other cities, seized with terror, then submitted, and the emperor imposed on them, under the name of *podestas*, governors who oppressed them with horrible exactions. Frederic, intoxicated with pride, proceeded to declare himself in some sort the lord of religion itself, by appointing three antipopes who depended entirely on his will. These were Victor IV., Pascal III., and Calixtus III. Alexander III. was obliged to take refuge in France. At the moment when the courageous Pontiff was going into exile, he learned that the Archbishop of Canterbury was also compelled to leave England because he had defended the rights of the Church against the despotic pretensions of King

Henry II. Thomas à Becket had in the first place been a courtier, whom this prince had made his chancellor. The Archbishop of Canterbury, Thibaut, being dead, the king thought he should serve his ambition by placing his prime minister in the vacant see. Becket for a long time refused the dignity, because he knew that his conscience would not consent to the usurpations meditated by Henry, in opposition to the rights of the clergy. But the monarch still insisting, the Saxon Becket deposed the seals of office to assume the primate's crosier, (1162.) Suddenly an immense change took place in his life; he abandoned the pride of the court, with which he ostentatiously invested himself when chancellor, and embraced apostolic poverty. He became the father of the poor, and resolved to defend the rights of his Church. He demanded therefore of Henry all the ecclesiastical goods on which he had laid hands. The king replied by some statutes, commonly called constitutions, which he caused to be promulgated in a synod, held at Clarendon, (1164.) These statutes, which robbed the Church of England of all her liberty, and confiscated all ecclesiastical dignities, to the advantage of the royal authority, were signed by Thomas in the first moment of weakness. He was soon stung with remorse, and wrote to Alexander III., who disapproved what he had done, and condemned the statutes which he had subscribed. The illustrious archbishop then retracted, and Henry, furious, obliged him to quit the kingdom. He took refuge at St Omer, then at Pontigny, and excommunicated Henry II. at Vezelay in 1166. Louis VII. and Alexander III. openly declared themselves his protectors; and the King of England was fain to yield with regret, and to allow the noble exile to return to his Church, which was impatient to receive him. Scarcely had he arrived, when four courtiers, having heard the king utter these murderous words, "What! not one of these cowards whom I feed has the heart to relieve me of this priest!" went and slew him in his cathedral, at the foot of the altar, on the fifth day after Christmas, 1170. Alexander III. canonised this Christian hero, and the faithful from all countries performed pilgrimages to his tomb. Meanwhile Christendom at large cried out with indignation against the persecutor of the Sovereign Pontiff. Alexander III. was re-established in Rome in 1165, and Frederic, having undertaken a new expedition against the Holy City, saw his army destroyed by a contagious malady. While he himself was forced to retire into Germany in disguise, the Lombard cities drove out the podestats, and, recognising Alexander III. as their chief, they formed the league of which the first result was the reconstruction of Milan. At the same time they built

Alexandria, so called in honour of the Pope, for the defence of Lombardy. The strategic importance of this fortified town was seen in 1859. After having been detained a long time in Germany, by the revolts of the Welfs or Guelphs, Frederic returned into Italy in 1174, and signalised his arrival by the destruction of Susa, which he made a heap of ruins. He failed, however, in the siege of Alexandria, and was defeated soon after at Legnano, in 1176; after which he was obliged to recognise, by a treaty signed at Venice, the liberty of Italy and the rights of the Holy See, (1177.) His excommunication being rescinded, he accepted pardon, and kissed the Pontiff's feet.

Alexander III., after a reign of nearly twenty-two years, died in August at Citta di Castello. He was one of the most learned Popes that had filled the Papal chair for a hundred years; and his knowledge of Holy Scripture and Roman law is particularly recorded. Dr Miley, in his History of the Papal States, throws much light on the character of Alexander III., and the condition of Rome under Arnaud of Brescia.

173. Lucius III., A.D. 1181–1185.

He was a native of Lucca, and known before his elevation as Cardinal Ubaldo. He was elected to the vacant see by the cardinal (*i.e.*, principal parish) priests only, to the exclusion of the rest of the clergy and people, and in the midst of troubles. The Cardinals from this period obtained that pre-eminence which they now enjoy. The new Pontiff was obliged to leave Rome, in consequence of a revolt of the Romans. The cause of their rebellion appears to have been slight, and consisted merely in the Pope's refusal to observe some usages which he thought no longer desirable. The barbarous people avenged themselves by taking out the eyes of all the clerks, excepting one, who were closely attached to him.* He retired to Veletri, and afterwards to Verona, and there convened a council, which condemned the Patarins, a sect of the Albigenses, (1184,) who maintained, as did the Waldenses, that the "Pater" was the only prayer needful, and moreover that man and the world were made by the devil. Lucius died at Verona on the 24th of November, 1185, shortly after his having an interview with the Emperor Frederic Barbarossa in that city.

174. Urban III., a.d. 1185–1187.

Hubert Privelli, or Crivelli, had been made Archbishop of Milan, and Cardinal, by Lucius III. He died at Ferrara, after having striven

---

* Fleury, tome xv. pp. 454, 460.

without much success against Frederic I., (Barbarossa,) in defence of the Church's rights. The tidings brought him of the disasters of the Crusaders in Palestine contributed to his end, which took place in October, 1187. He was buried in the Cathedral of Ferrara. Muratori's *Annali d'Italia* contain a mass of interesting matter respecting the Popes of this period.

175. Gregory VIII., a.d. 1187.

His family name was Albert de Spinacchia. He reigned only two months. His life had been pure, and his zeal was fervent. Several letters of his are extant; in the first of which he endeavoured to animate the faithful with fresh courage for the recovery of the Holy Land. He must not be confounded with the antipope, Maurice Bourdon, who assumed the title of Gregory VIII. in 1118.

176. Clement III., a.d. 1187–1191.

Paulino Scolaro was a native of Rome, and was made Bishop of Preneste. He proclaimed the third crusade, (1189.) "Ninety years had elapsed since the Council of Clermont, as with the voice of one man, declared it to be the will of God that the Sepulchre should be rescued from the hands of the infidels. Urban II.

opened the spiritual treasures of the Vatican; Peter the Hermit stirred up the hearts of princes; France and Germany poured out thousands on thousands to become warriors of the Cross; God delivered Nicæa and Antioch into the hands of of His servants; and finally Jerusalem itself crowned their conquest. Godfrey of Bouillion, the holiest leader of the Crusade, mounted the throne; but where his Lord had worn the crown of thorns he refused the crown of gold. He was shortly called to his reward in the heavenly Jerusalem; and then his brother Baldwin succeeded—a man of a more worldly spirit. The strength of the Christians was much dispersed and wasted; the principality of Antioch demanded men for its defence that had been better employed in the preservation of the Holy Land. Still the arms of the Christians were successful. Cæsarea rewarded the courage of the king, Baldwin, and Europe was not slow to come to his assistance. Eighty thousand men marched to establish his empire; but of this great multitude a part perished in Cilicia, and a part were ingloriously routed near Jerusalem. The king drew down on him the wrath of God by his licentious life. He perished during a campaign in Egypt by a violent disease, and Baldwin II., his kinsman, at the election of the lords succeeded him on the throne. Then arose the noble

Order of the Templars, the first of those many bodies that united chivalry in a yet closer bond with the Church; and in the course of years the Hospitallers, that second prop of the kingdom of Jerusalem, emulated the valour of the older community. To Baldwin succeeded Fulk, and at his death began the decline of the empire. His son, Baldwin III., was but thirteen years of age at his accession to the throne. Edessa was retaken by the infidels; a schism broke out at Tyre; and had it not been for the seasonable assistance afforded by the remains of the second crusade, Jerusalem could not have held out for many years. But the miserable termination of that expedition left the Christians of the East in a condition worse than that in which it had found them. To Baldwin III. succeeded his younger brother Armaury; to Armaury his son Baldwin IV. The pride and ill-faith of the Templars lost more than their valour had gained: Saladin, the scourge of the Christians, arose in Egypt; Baldwin IV. was a leper; a civil war broke out in his wretched shadow of a kingdom; Guy de Lusignan, brother-in-law of the king, was appointed regent, and deprived for incapacity; Baldwin V., a child of five years old, was crowned, and the regency given to the Count of Tripoli; De Lusignan shut himself up in Ascalon and refused to obey the royal orders. This was the state of Palestine when Heraclius, the Latin Patriarch of the Holy City, came over into Europe to implore succor."*

Clement III. made a treaty with the Romans in reference to the city of Tusculum, which belonged to the Popes, and had been a cause of dispute between them and their people since the time of Alexander III. He died on the 28th March, 1191.

177. Celestine III., a.d. 1191–1198.

He was known before his elevation by the name Cardinal Hyacinth; and was elected at the advanced age of eighty-five. He crowned the Emperor Henry VI. with the Empress Constance, and gave Sicily to Frederic, Henry's son, on condition of his paying a tribute to the Holy See. Serious differences arose between Celestine and Leopold, Duke of Austria, and Alonso IX., King of Leon. He preached and encouraged crusades with great earnestness. Seventeen of his letters are extant. The valuable *Annals* of Cardinal Baronius terminate with his death.

178. Innocent III., a.d. 1198–1216.

His family name was Lothario Conti. He was only thirty-seven years old when raised to the

* Neale's *Crusades*, p. 28.

Papacy. He enlarged the domains of the Church, and made himself complete master of Rome. He put France under an interdict in consequence of Philip II.'s divorce from Ingelburge, (1199.) In the early part of Innocent's reign, John, King of England, had a serious dispute with the Roman Pontiff concerning the election of English bishops; John claiming the right of granting or refusing a *congé d'élire*. At the death of Hubert, Archbishop of Canterbury, in 1205, the monks, without asking the king's approbation, elected a new one. As soon as the transaction was known, another archbishop was chosen by the royal authority. The Pope, however, annulled both elections, and sent to ask John's consent to his electing at Rome a learned English cardinal named Langton. John made no answer, and Langton was chosen. As soon as the king was informed of it, he drove the monks of Canterbury from their convent, seized their lands, and declared that Langton should never set foot in England. The Pope, finding him implacable, laid his kingdom under an interdict. The churches were instantly closed, and all religious services forbidden, except the administration of the sacraments to infants and the dying. John, though he dreaded the consequences of it, affected to despise the interdict, and occupied himself alternately in hostilities against the Scots, the Irish, and the Welsh; who, profiting by his embarrassed situation, endeavoured to recover their independence, but without success. At length in 1209, the Pope, finding John still inexorable, issued a bull of excommunication against him. It was shortly followed by a sentence of deposition, absolving his subjects from their oath of allegiance, and calling upon all Christian princes to unite in deposing him. Philip II., to whom the Pope had offered the crown of England for his son Louis, immediately prepared an invasion, and John saw a fearful storm gathering round him. The Pope, however, sent a legate named Pandulph to endeavour to effect a reconciliation; and the king, seeing the danger of a refusal, yielded, consenting to receive Langton, to make full restitution to the clergy, and to liberate those who were in prison. Two days after, on the 15th of May, 1213, in the church of the Templars at Dover, John took the oath of fealty to the Pope, made a resignation of his dominions to the Holy See, consenting to hold them as a vassal and to pay a yearly tribute of 10,000 marks. The interdict was then taken off, and the legate forbade the invasion preparing by Philip, King of France.

Innocent III. presided at the twelfth œcumenical (fourth Lateran) in 1215, which devised means of opposition to the Saracens and Albigenses, and for correcting the laxity of public morals. It prohibited also—but without much effect—the use of the physics and metaphysics of Aristotle, which caused, at that time, a perfect rage for disputation. Zealous alike for orthodoxy and morality, Innocent caused a crusade to be preached against the Albigenses, and appointed the first Inquisitor, the celebrated St Dominic, 1215.

Innocent III. has left some discourses and homilies, as well as some letters, which are very curious and interesting, from the historical facts they contain. He was the first to approve the Order of St Francis,* and was the author of the beautiful hymn *Veni Sancte Spiritus;* and the *Stabat Mater*, claimed by the Franciscans, is also attributed to him.

A few more particulars respecting this Pontiff are necessary to fill up the outline of his career.

Being one of the illustrious family of the Conti, he had studied law and theology in the most celebrated universities—Paris, Rome, and Bologna. Being raised against his will to the pontifical throne, he immediately conceived the design of delivering Rome and Italy from foreign domination, and of making his authority everywhere respected and cherished, by establishing

* Dante, *Parad.* xi. pp. 91-93.

in all countries subject to his sway, a reign of gentleness and justice.

At the time of his accession, Germany was desolated by civil war, and all Christian kingdoms were a prey to serious disorders which nothing but the Pope's interference could quell. The genius of Innocent grasped the extent of his mission, and he wanted neither prudence nor courage to fulfil it. In the first place, he observed the strictest neutrality between Philip of Swabia and Otho of Brunswick, who disputed the crown of Germany after the death of Henry VI.

The claims of Otho, however, appearing to him the more just, he declared for this prince, and even took part in his election, when, after ten years of rivalry, Philip, his competitor, was assassinated at the very moment that his cause appeared to be triumphing, (1207.) Every one hoped that the new emperor, bound by gratitude to the Pope, would refrain from desolating Christendom by renewing the struggle of the empire against the Holy See, at least during the reign of his benefactor; but it was not so. Scarcely was Otho crowned by the Pope, when he exerted his efforts to revive all the pretensions of his predecessor in opposition to the liberty of Rome and Italy.

After having employed persuasions and gentleness to bring him over to better feelings, Innocent at last excommunicated and deposed him, in favour of Frederic II.

Otho, unintimidated, leagued with his vassals, the King of England, and some other princes, against Philip Augustus of France, who had taken the part of the Pope. He was vanquished at Bouvines, and died in obscurity not long after.

On the proposition of Innocent III., Germany recognized as emperor the young Frederic II.; and peace was for a while restored. Almost all the States of Europe were then subject to the Holy See, and there was not one who had not reason to rejoice in the influence that See exerted; while it hesitated not to depose any monarch who opposed with violence its rights and authority.

The Crusaders of the fourth crusade, having conquered Constantinople for themselves, and decreed the imperial crown to Baldwin, Count of Flanders, (1204,) Innocent thought of excommunicating those who had thus deposed Christian emperors instead of fighting against the unbelievers, and had shown themselves thereby more alive to their own interests than to the cause of the Church. He felt, however, that under the critical circumstances in which the Papacy was placed, it would be better to use moderation and indulgence. The conclusion of this crusade greatly disappointed the zealous Pope, who had commissioned Foulques, the curé of Neuilly, to take up the exciting theme of Peter the Hermit, and call Europe for the fourth time to unfurl in Palestine the Banner of the Cross.

By preaching a crusade against the Moors, Innocent saved Spain and Portugal from barbarism; and he caused the sanctity of marriage to be respected in these nations by obliging even kings to break off the culpable alliances which they had contracted. The Holy Father extended his vigilant solicitude also over Scandinavia and the Sclavonic States, and even wrote to the Russians to withdraw them from schism, and induce them to return to the unity of the Church.

His reign was long, and it would require a volume to do justice to its history.

179. HONORIUS III., A.D. 1216–1227.

He was a native of Rome, and his family name was Cencio Savelli.

He sanctioned the Dominican and Carmelite Orders. He preached with feeble results, a crusade to reconquer the Holy Land. He armed Louis VIII. against the Albigenses. He was the first to accord indulgences at the canonisation of saints. He forbade the teaching of civil law in Paris, (1220,) permitting only that of canon law. We have under his name a "*Conjuratio contra principem tenebrarum.*" His death took place on the 18th of March, 1227.

There are generally reckoned to have been eight crusades:

1. A.D. 1096 to 1100 under Urban II.
2. " 1147 " 1149 " Eugene III.
3. " 1189 " 1193 " Clement III.
4. " 1202 " 1204 " Innocent III.
5. " 1217 " Honorius III.
6. " 1228 " 1229 " Gregory IX.
7. " 1248 " 1254 " Innocent IV.
8. " 1268 " 1270 " Clement IV.

The Albigenses.

In the twelfth century this name comprised all the heretics of the south of France, who were most of them imbued with Manicheism. They spread throughout Languedoc and Provence, and occupied principally the cities of Albi, (whence their name,) Béziers, Carcassonne, Toulouse, Montauban, and Avignon. They were supported by Raymond, Count of Toulouse, and Roger, Viscount Béziers.

Pope Alexander III. excommunicated them in the third Lateran council in 1179.

Innocent III. preached a crusade against them, and placed Pierre de Castelnau at its head in 1204, and afterwards the legates Milon and

Arnaud Amalric, as well as Simon de Montfort. The Crusaders in 1209 obtained possession of Béziers, and there slew 60,000, among whom were some Catholics.

Carcassonne also soon fell into their hands. The legate ordered his troops to slaughter all in this city, without distinction of age or sex. Thirty thousand persons, including women and children, perished in one day; and when one of the crusading officers, fatigued with carnage, came to the legate to inquire by what signs he should distinguish heretics in the crowd, the legate replied, "Kill, kill; God will know which are His."

The principle of action in this war was identical with that of the crusade against the Turks. The Pontiffs of these times thought it right to exterminate by the sword the unbelievers whom they could not convert, whenever their presence became hostile and dangerous to the Church and to society. Heresy was then regarded as rebellion against the State no less than against the Church. It was a crime of the deepest dye, and worthy of the severest punishment. It was a pestilence that must not spread, an aggression that must be resisted, a conflagration that must be extinguished. It was a foe the more formidable because its attacks were directed immediately against the soul; it was the assassin of the spiritual life; it imperilled the salvation of man. It was impossible to exaggerate the nature of the evil, or to devise means too rigorous for its suppression.

In 1215 the Count de Toulouse was despoiled of his states, which were given to Simon de Montfort. In 1219 a new crusade was undertaken against the Albigenses, which was commanded by Louis, son of Philip Augustus, (Louis VIII.) This prince took Avignon in 1226.

The Albigenses were almost entirely destroyed in these wars; all that remained were confounded with the Vaudois.

180. Gregory IX., A.D. 1227–1241.

He was the nephew of Innocent III.; he became a Cardinal and Bishop of Ostia. He preached a new crusade. He saw, no less than preceding Popes, that the very existence of Christian society and of general civilisation depended on keeping the Mohammedan power in check; and he felt the necessity of rousing and uniting the nations in a common cause, lest they should, one by one, be overwhelmed by Islamism. Statesmen in those times were unable to form extensive political combinations; and the Popes were often successful where diplomacy failed. Gregory excommunicated Frederic II.

twice; first, for having refused, contrary to his engagement, to go to Palestine; and secondly, for having concluded afterwards a disgraceful peace with the infidels. The irritated emperor, however, obliged the aged Pope several times to escape from his capital as a fugitive. In this way, he fixed his residence by turns at Spoleto, Assisi, and Perugia; but returned to the capital in 1230, after a fearful inundation, which, when it subsided, caused the city to be infested with serpents and disease. He died in 1241, in his hundredth year. He made a collection of Papal decisions, which are commonly called the Decretals of Gregory IX., and form a considerable part of the code of canon law. Though many of the Popes have, like Gregory IX., lived to a very advanced age, it is remarkable that none hitherto has ruled as long as St Peter. Hence it is customary to remind each Pontiff at his elevation that there is little chance of his pontificate lasting twenty-five years. "*Non videbis annos Petri,*" ("Thou wilt not see the years of Peter.") Indeed, of the 259 Popes who have occupied the Roman See, eight only have retained it for a longer period than twenty years, viz., Sylvester, Leo the Great, Adrian I., Alexander III., Urban VIII., Clement IX., Pius VI. and VII. The two latter reigned the longest—the first twenty-four, and the second twenty-three years.

181. Celestine IV., A.D. 1241.

Geoffrey de Castiglione. He reigned only sixteen days. He is reported to have been a man of upright morals, and learned, but old and infirm. After his death the Holy See was vacant about twenty months.

182. Innocent IV., A.D. 1243–1254.

He was elected at Anagni by common consent, and reigned eleven years and a half. Being compelled to escape from Rome, he repaired to Geneva, and sought refuge in vain in England, Aragon, and France. At last, however, he arrived at Lyons, a neutral city then belonging to its archbishop.* His conflict with the Emperor Frederic was long and trying. He caused Henry, Landgrave of Thuringia, and William, Count of Holland, to be elected successively in Frederic's stead; preached a crusade against him, and after his death (1250) declared equally against his son Conrad. At the death of Conrad, however, (1254,) Innocent became the protector of the young Conradin, grandson of Frederic II., against Manfred his uncle. Innocent IV. was concerned in many other disputes in Europe, and was firm and inflexible throughout.

* Fleury, vol. xvii. p. 347.

To throw light on the reign of this Pontiff, it is needful to refer to some preceding events. Frederic II. owed his elevation and his power to Pope Innocent III., who in all circumstances had protected him as a guardian would his ward, and had preserved for him the kingdom of Sicily, of which the Popes were Lords.

When Otho was deposed, the Pontiff proposed his protégé to the suffrages of the electors, and caused him to be recognised as Emperor of Germany. Frederic II. was a prince of great genius, endowed with the most brilliant talents, and took pleasure in rewarding merit wherever he found it. To have eminent qualities in one's self is the best guarantee for appreciating and recompensing them in others. Unhappily, however, for himself and for his people, Frederic united great defects with rare advantages. He was a slave to the most ignominious passions, and his unbounded ambition led him to assail the liberties of Rome and Italy, as his predecessors had done. Ancient Italy was the terror of Germany, and Germany has in turn been for ages the scourge of modern Italy. While Innocent III. lived, Frederic II. remained faithful to his engagements. The ingratitude of his conduct would have been too flagrant if he had arisen against him who had been the protector of his childhood and the author of his elevation. But after the death of Innocent, (1216,) he showed himself the enemy of the Holy See, and troubled himself very little about his oaths and pledges. Thus, for example, he had promised at his coronation to undertake a crusade, and not to unite the kingdom of Sicily to the empire. This last promise he violated in appointing his eldest son Henry, already King of Sicily, to succeed him in the empire. As to the crusade, he always deferred it, and deceived Innocent's successor, Honorius III., with vain pretexts. At length, being urged by the ardent spirit and energetic will of Gregory IX., he put to sea, and returned three days after, alleging an illness as the cause. The Pontiff then excommunicated him. The measure appeared extreme. Crusading was no obligatory part of Christian duty, but Frederic hardened his heart, and was as full of dissimulation as of impiety. He made contracts with Malek-Hamel, Sultan of Egypt, and started on his expedition without being absolved from the sentence of the Sovereign Pontiff, (1228.) When arrived in the East, he entered into negotiations with the Sultan of Cairo, and did nothing for the prosperity of Christian establishments. The tokens of friendship which the emperor and the chief of the infidels exchanged in the course of their mutual relations gave umbrage both to Mussulmans and Catholics. At length Frederic obtained the city of Jerusalem, but on the disgraceful condition of not raising the walls anew, to which was added that of allowing the Turks their freedom of religious worship. Such toleration in the Middle Ages was regarded as a compromise of Christian principles.

The emperor made his public entry ingloriously, in the midst of the murmurs of the faithful, who were scandalised at seeing a mosque standing side by side with the Church of the Holy Sepulchre. It had been his wish to be made King of Jerusalem; but he found no one who would crown an excommunicated prince. He then quitted Palestine, and returned to the West, where the most violent storms, provoked by his numerous faults, were ready to burst on his head, (1230.) During his absence, his lieutenant, Rainald, whom he had left in Sicily, attacked the States of the Pope, and crossed with a numerous army the frontiers of Spoleto. The thunders of the Vatican smote the usurper; but Frederic hastened to make his submission, and to promise all which the Holy See could desire. Alas, these fine words were insincere. Scarcely had he signed the peace, when he let loose on Lombardy a tiger in the form of a man, Eccelino di Romano, surnamed the Ferocious, who reduced all the Lombard cites to servitude, and committed cruelties there which surpass imagination. Inebriated by these successes, the emperor resolved to despoil the Apostolic See of its temporal power. He tore Sardinia from its sovereignty, and robbed the Church of all her liberty in the kingdom of Naples. Gregory IX., driven to extremity by such excess, excommunicated a second time this impious prince, who was not ashamed to form an alliance with the Saracens in order to insure by force the success of his tyrannical designs, (1240.) Frederic appealed from the Pope's sentence to a general council, which Gregory convoked at Rome, and then arrested all the German and French bishops who were on their way to the council, and laid siege to the Holy City. Gregory died unshaken in the midst of all these perils, (1241.) After a dispute of nearly two years' duration, stirred up by Frederic, one of his friends, Cardinal Sinibaldi di Fieschi, was elected. But the new Pope, who took the name of Innocent IV., well understood that private affection must not interfere with public duty. Having without avail, or with trifling success, tried gentle means, he escaped from Italy, where the emperor ordered all his movements to be watched; and fixing his residence at Lyons, under the protection of St Louis, he there convoked in 1245 a general council, the assembling of which in Italy was rendered impossible by the violence of Frederic. This was the thirteenth œcumenical council of the Church. In spite of the emperor's defending himself by means of one who was in his confidence, he was excommunicated in full council, and declared fallen from the imperial dignity, (1245.) On hearing this, he placed his crown on his head, and with a terrible voice cried aloud, "This crown I have it still; and before it is torn from me much blood will be shed." All his threats, however, issued only in some impotent attempts. Broken by reverses, he died in 1250 in a retired part of Italy. His son Conrad survived him only four years, (1254,) and his grandson Conradin, wishing to dispute the crown of Sicily with Charles of Anjou, lost his head on a scaffold. Such was the melancholy end of the dynasty of Hohenstauffen, which had caused so many ills to the Church, (1268.)

Innocent IV. died at Naples on the 7th of December, 1254, and was buried in its cathedral.

183. ALEXANDER IV., A.D. 1254–1261.

The name of his family was Rinaldi; he became Bishop of Ostia. Four years after his elevation, in May, 1258, he was obliged to retire from Rome in consequence of the violence exercised by Brancallen, a senator whom the people, with an English baker at their head,* had released from prison, and whom the Pope had excommunicated. He took part in the long contest which the Holy See had to sustain with the house of Suabia, as represented by Manfred, King of the Two Sicilies. He established inquisitors in France in 1255, at the request of St Louis, and died at Viterbo in 1261, where also he was buried.

184. URBAN IV., A.D. 1261–1265.

Jacques Pantaleon was born in 1185, at Troyes, in Champagne. He was the son of a poor cobbler, and from this obscure rank he arrived at the dignity of patriarch of Jerusalem. He augmented the number of cardinals, and instituted the Feast of Corpus Christi. He offered the crown of Naples and Sicily to St Louis, who refused it. He called Charles d'Anjou, St Louis's brother, to combat Manfred, King of Naples and Sicily—who was deservedly in disgrace with the Holy See—and gave him the crown.

The people of Orvieto having declared against him, he advanced to meet the insugents, took a fortress belonging to the Church, and was carried on a litter to Perugia, where he died on the 2d

* Fleury, vol. xvii. p. 633.

of October, 1264. Among his letters there is one which bespeaks his goodness in a very striking manner. When Archdeacon of Liège, he had been sent by Alexander IV. on a mission into Germany. Some gentlemen of the diocese of Treves laid wait for him, stripped him of all he possessed, and kept him some time prisoner. When he became Pope, they offered to restore what they had stolen, and to make amends by coming in person to ask his forgiveness. The Pope, however, absolved them freely by the hands of the prior of the Frères Prêcheurs at Coblentz, without exacting from them the humiliation they offered.

The works of André Duchesne, *Histoire des Papes*, 1653, &c., and also those of Gregoras, the Greek historian, are of use in ascertaining the events of this period.

185. Clement IV., a.d. 1265–1268.

Guido Fulcodi was born at St Gilles, on the Rhone. He had been a soldier, then a lawyer, then secretary to St Louis. After the death of his wife he embraced the ecclesiastical life.

He was made Archbishop of Narbonne; subsequently Cardinal Archbishop of Sabina; sent as legate to England; and ultimately chosen Pope at Perugia. His elevation did not change his manners and mode of life; he was modest, mild, and disinterested. He signed with St Louis the Pragmatic Sanction, which put an end to the differences between France and Rome. History records his ability as a preacher, and assures us that when Pope he often preached in the cathedral of Viterbo to fortify the people in the faith. During a long period he ate no meat and wore no linen, finding such mortification conducive to his spiritual life. He died at Viterbo in 1268, and was buried in the church of the Preaching Brothers. After his death the Holy See was vacant nearly three years.

186. Gregory X., A.D. 1272-1276.

Thibaut Visconti before his elevation had been Archdeacon of Liège. He was but slightly conversant with letters, but had great experience in secular matters, and was more fond of distributing alms than of laying up treasure. He held at Lyons, in 1274, the fourteenth œcumenical council, at which ambassadors from all the courts in Europe, and some of Asia, assisted, with a view of reuniting the Greek and Latin Churches. Gregory himself presided at the council. Five hundred bishops were present, and a great number of inferior prelates. At the close of the fourth session, the Pope, with gushing tears, intoned the Credo in Latin, which being done, the former Patriarch of Constantinople, Germanus, began it in Greek, and the "filioque" was sung twice over. The healing of the Greek schism was not the only object for which the council of Lyons was convened. It provided for sending succour to the Christians in Palestine, for the more expeditious election of Popes, and for promoting stricter discipline among the clergy. This last article was only put into incipient execution. The angelic doctor, St Thomas Aquinas, was summoned to this council by Gregory X. This Pontiff died at Arezzo, and was buried in its cathedral. Miracles were said to be wrought at his tomb, and a lamp burned constantly before it for many ages.

187. INNOCENT V., A.D. 1276, (January 21 to June 22.)

Pierre de Tarentaise, a Dominican, had already distinguished himself as one of the most celebrated theologians of his order. He succeeded St Thomas Aquinas in teaching theology in the University of Paris. He was made Archbishop of Lyons in 1272, and then Cardinal-Bishop of Ostia. He was interred in the Lateran Church; and Charles, the King of Sicily, assisted at the funeral.

188. ADRIAN V., A.D. 1276.

He was a Genoese by birth, nephew of Innocent V., and raised to the popedom when very aged and infirm. His reign lasted but a month and nine days. He was ill during this time, and when his relations came to compliment him on his election, he said he would rather they had come to see a Cardinal in health than a Pope dying. Indeed, his end arrived before he could be consecrated, and he was still in deacon's orders when he expired at Viterbo.* Dante was at this time ten years old, and, if his account can be trusted, Adrian V., who had during his cardinalate been ruled by avarice, owed his conversion to his new dignity and the responsibilities which it involved. The poet's imaginary interview with this Pope in Purgatory is described in his peculiarly intense and lofty style,† but his political feelings were too strong to admit of his being taken as a good authority in matters of history.

189. JOHN XXI., A.D. 1276–1277.

Peter Julian, or Petrus Hispanus, was born at Lisbon, and in the earlier part of his life distin-

---

* Fleury, vol. xviii. p. 219.   † *Il Purgatorio*, canto xix.

guished himself as a physician and philosopher. He endeavoured to prevent the outbreak of war between Philippe le Hardi and Alphonso of Castile, and he desired, though without success, to induce them to undertake a crusade.

His end was disastrous; he perished at Viterbo, crushed beneath the ruins of the palace which he inhabited, and which fell to the ground in 1277. He has left a work entitled *Sumulæ Logicales*. *The Treasure of the Poor*, ascribed to him, was more probably written by John XXII. It is a medical treatise.

190. Nicholas III., A.D. 1277–1280.

His name was Giovanni Gaetano Orsini. When a child, his father had presented him to St Francis, who predicted that though he might not wear his habit, he would be the protector of his Order, and the ruler of the world.* He caused Imola, Bologna, Faenza, &c., to be restored to the Roman States by the Emperor Rodolph of Hapsburg. He obliged Charles of Anjou to give up the vicariate of the Empire in Tuscany, and the title of Patrician of Rome, an order instituted by Constantine. He was unsuccessful in his endeavours to perpetuate the temporal reunion of the Latin and Greek Churches;

* Fleury, vol. xviii. p. 237.

nor could he fulfil, as he desired, the office of mediator between the King of Castile and Philippe le Hardi. He favoured his own relations, and this gave occasion to Malespini, a Florentine, to write unfavourably of him in this particular.† He died of apoplexy when apparently in the full bloom of health.

191. MARTIN IV., A.D. 1281–1285.

Simon de Brione was a native of France. After his elevation he caused himself to be elected to the chief magistracy of the city, under the title of Senator of Rome. He sustained the rights of Charles of Anjou, King of Sicily, against Peter III. of Aragon, and severely condemned Peter and the other authors of the atrocious Sicilian Vespers, in which eight thousand French perished, (1282) The massacre began on Easter Monday, March 30.

Martin IV. died at Perugia, and was buried in the Church of St Laurence. An author of the time says many miracles were wrought at his tomb in the presence of large multitudes.

192. HONORIUS IV., A.D. 1285–1287.

He was a Roman, and his family name Jacopo Savelli. Being much afflicted with the gout in

† *Ibid*, an. 1278.

his hands and feet, he had great difficulty in celebrating Mass. He espoused the cause of the French in Sicily against the house of Aragon, to which the Sicilians had given themselves after having massacred the French. He regarded the struggle of the latter against the Aragonese as "a holy war." Honorius was a strenuous defender of ecclesiastical immunities. He died in April 1287, in the palace he had built near Santa Sabina.

193. Nicholas IV., a.d. 1288–1292.

Girolamo d'Ascoli, who had been general of the Frati Minori, was elected Pope against his will. He used all his efforts to rekindle crusade zeal, and favoured Charles II. of Anjou's claims on Sicily. He sent missions even to China, and founded the University of Montpellier, 1289. He died at Rome, worn out by old age, on Good Friday, 1292. He was the author of several theological works.

194. St Celestine V., (called the Solitary,) a.d. 1292–1293.

His family name was Pietro di Morone; he was born in Apulia, and had before his election entered the Order of the Benedictines, and founded a new religious order, which was called after his own name, and which followed, with slight variations, the rule of St Benedict. He lived in a cell in the midst of the severest austerities when the tiara was brought to him. After his election he entered Aquila, not, as was the custom on such occasions, on a horse richly caparisoned, but mounted on an ass, while two kings—Charles the Lame and his son—held the bridle on either side. Wholly unacquainted with mundane affairs, he felt his incapacity for the popedom, and abdicated in five months. Boniface VIII., to avoid the danger of a schism, kept him shut up in the Château of Fumone, in Campania,* where he died two years after. "Nothing but a cell did I desire in this world," said the holy recluse, "and a cell they gave me." He was canonised by Clement V. He has left some *opuscula*. His festival is celebrated on the 19th of May. Dante† makes Boniface VIII. say, in speaking of him:

> " Lo Ciel poss' io serrare e diserrare,
> Come tu sai; però son due le chiavi,
> Che 'l mio antecessor non ebbe care."‡

---

* See *Dublin Review*, June, 1856.
† *Inferno*, canto xxvii.
‡ I can the heavens lock—I can unlock—
Thou know'st it well—for those two keys are mine
Which he who ruled before me held not dear.

195. BONIFACE VIII., A.D. 1294–1303.

Benedict Caietan was born at Anagni. He became an advocate and Papal notary at Rome, and canon of Lyons. He obtained a cardinal's hat in 1281.

On his accession Boniface found great disorder in England and in France. The princes, in order to maintain their rivalry, levied taxes, neither usual nor due, on ecclesiastical property. This Boniface resolved to oppose. For this purpose—to repress the encroachments of civil power—he published the bull *Clericis laïcos*, (1296.) Edward I. submitted; but Philippe le Bel resorted to recrimination, and forbade the sending out of France the legacies bequeathed to the Holy Land, and the annual gifts to the See of Rome made by the clergy of his Catholic kingdom. The Pontiff, astonished by this resistance, explained his bull, and proved in a letter that all he had advanced was conformable to the ancient canons, (1297.) Philippe, satisfied with these explanations, revoked his ordinances, and made peace with Rome. He allowed himself, however, to vex in numerous arbitrary ways the Church and the Pope. He received at his court the Colonna, who were the sworn enemies of Boniface VIII., and had been guilty of a rupture with the Holy See. He took possession of

Cambria, of which the temporal and spiritual jurisdiction belonged to the bishop. He appropriated the revenues of the Church of Rheims, and those of the Church of Laon, the bishop of which was cited to Rome. He altered the moneys and exacted enormous sums from convents and churches. He arrogated to himself the investiture of the county of Melgueil, which depended on the Church of Narbonne. Boniface having sent him a legate, Bernard de Saisset, Bishop of Pamiers, to demand an account of these grievances, Philippe had him thrown into prison. The Pope then addressed him a second bull, (*Ausculta fili,*) in which he commanded him to come to Rome with the prelates and the doctors of his kingdom, that his cause might be heard and judged in a council. He also placed France under an interdict. Philippe falsified the Pope's bull, and substituted for it one altogether offensive and violent; and after having thereby excited general discontent with the Holy See, he caused it to be publicly burnt, (1302.) The *Etats-généraux* were convoked for the first time in France; and the three orders— the clergy, the nobles, and the third *état*— repulsed the claims of the Holy See, and wrote highly offensive letters to the Pope. Boniface then held his council at Rome. Forty-five French prelates attended in spite of Philippe's prohibition. The Pope published his third bull, (*Unam sanctam*,) in which he defined the superiority of the spiritual above the temporal power, without, however, condemning any person. In the meanwhile the King of France, bursting every bound of moderation, called together another assembly, in which, by means of Guillaume de Nogaret, his chancellor, he deposed Boniface, and appealed from his decision to a future Pope and council, (1303.) He thus became a schismatic. Boniface, who had borne much patiently, was about to excommunicate the king, when one of the blackest plots was laid against him. Emissaries of Philippe—Pierre Flotte and De Nogaret—scrupled not to go with some troops to Italy, to lay violent hands on the sacred person of the Pope, and retain him captive. Aided by Sciarra Colonna, they shamefully maltreated him at Anagni. They struck him when attired in his pontifical robes, and Colonna would have killed him on the spot if Nogaret had not interposed. Four days after, he was delivered by the people, but died of grief and the ill-treatment he had received in one month, October the 11th, 1303. After his decease, Philippe le Bel made long and fruitless efforts to tarnish his memory.

196. St Benedict XI., a.d. 1303.

He was a schoolmaster, and son of a shepherd, or, as others say, a notary, of Trevigi. He became general of the Frati Predicatori. After his elevation, he withdrew the bulls of Boniface VIII. against Philippe le Bel. It has been said, but untruly, that he was poisoned with figs. He reigned only eight months, and was buried at Perugia in the church of his Order. Contemporary historians, and especially Dino Compagni, speak in high terms of his character and virtues.

197. Clement V., a.d. 1305–1314, (Avignon.)

Bertrand de Goth was born at Villandrand. He was made Archbishop of Bordeaux in 1300, and elected Pope at Perugia by the influence of Philippe le Bel exerted in a divided conclave. He allowed himself to be directed by this prince in many important matters. He transported the papal residence to Avignon, (1309,) "modified the bulls of Boniface VIII. against Philippe le Bel," and instituted proceedings against the knights-templars.

In 1311 Clement presided at the fifteeth œcumenical council, held at Vienne in France. Philippe le Bel was present, as well as Edward

II. of England, and James III., king of Aragon. Three hundred bishops assembled. The main object for which the council was convened was to judge the cause of the knights-templars, who were accused of all sorts of crimes. Their principal delinquency was that of possessing vast riches, which excited the covetousness of Philippe le Bel, by whom a great number of them were seized, plundered, and committed to the flames, October 13, 1307. The Pope, in a secret consistory, suppressed the Order of the Knights-Templars in 1312. Their Grandmaster was Jacques de Molay. He was preparing to recover the losses sustained by the Christians in the East, when, in 1305, he was recalled to France by Clement V., who in, concert with Philippe le Bel, had decided on suppressing the Templars. Being treacherously delivered up to horrible tortures, he made some avowals which he afterwards retracted. He was nevertheless condemned to death, and was burnt alive, on the 18th of March 1314, in Paris. According to a popular tradition, he cited the King and the Pope to appear before the bar of Divine justice within a twelvemonth to answer for their injustice. They both died in 1314.

John Lech, Archbishop of Dublin, obtained from Clement V. in 1312 a brief for the foundation of an Irish University; but the laudable design did not succeed. Clement promoted extensively the study of Oriental languages, with a view to the evangelisation of the East.*

He has been accused wrongfully of cupidity and licentious habits. He has left some constitutions called *Clementines*, which form a part of canon-law, and were published by his successor. He died at La Roquemaure, near Avignon, on the 20th of April.

198. John XXII., a.d. 1316-1334, (Avignon.)

Jacques d'Euse was a native of Cahors in France, and of obscure origin. He was the second Pope who resided at Avignon. He favoured France. He combated the election of Louis of Bavaria as emperor, and offered the imperial crown to John of Luxemburg, King of Bohemia. Louis, in revenge, caused the antipope Nicholas V., a Franciscan, to be elected in his stead at Rome; but the Pope succeeded in taking and imprisoning the antipope at Avignon. He also delivered up to the secular arm the Bishop of Cahors, whom he accused of intending to poison him.

He was well versed in jurisprudence and medicine, and has left several medical treatises, among others the "Treasure of the Poor," Lyons:

---

* Veuillot, *Parfum de Rome*, vol. i. p. 41.

1525. He also published, as already mentioned, the *Clementines* of his predecessor, and gave them the title of *Extravagantes*. He published several constitutions intended to quiet discussions which had arisen in the Franciscan Order relative to their rule. He was inclined to the opinion that the beatific vision of God will not be enjoyed by the just till the judgment-day. When near death he renounced this idea. He had forbidden any one to be molested for holding it; but his successor defined the opposite doctrine as of faith.* He died at the age of ninety years, and was buried in the Cathedral of Avignon.

199. BENEDICT XII., A.D. 1334–1342, (Avignon.)

This Pontiff was a Cistercian monk. He was the son of a baker of Saverdun, and the third Pope who resided at Avignon. He applied himself to the reform of religious houses, rewarded merit, and, as umpire, terminated the disputes of many princes. His writings and decree respecting the beatific vision of God enjoyed by the saints after death deserve particular attention. He was a courageous and worthy Pontiff, and though half a prisoner, asserted in all things the Church's rights. He was buried in the Cathedral of Avignon. Full particulars concerning

---

* *Dublin Review*, January 1865, p. 49.

him may be found in Baluze's "Lives of the Avignon Popes." The writer, however, should be followed with reserve, his book being placed on the Index.

200. CLEMENT VI., A.D. 1342-1352, (Avignon.)

Pierre de Roger was born at Limousin. He was a doctor of Paris, and successively a Benedictine monk, Archbishop of Rouen, cardinal, and Pope. He had a serious dispute with Edward II., King of England, on the subject of investitures. In the war between Edward III. and Philippe VI. of France, Pope Clement VI. had continually remonstrated with the hostile monarchs respecting their sanguinary warfare; and at length he succeeded in persuading them to sign an armistice, which, under his influence, was prolonged for six years, subsequently to the battle of Crecy. He reduced the year of jubilee from every hundredth to every fiftieth year. He was moderately learned, and endowed with a good memory; but historians complain of his private life having been disorderly, especially during the time of his archiepiscopate.* He was the fourth Pope who resided at Avignon, which he bought of Jeanne of Naples, Countess of Provence, for 80,000 florins; and he refused

* Mathieu Villani, tome iii. p. 43; Fleury, tome xx.

to hear the entreaties of the inhabitants of Rome, who, with the famous tribune Rienzi at their head, came to implore him to return to the ancient seat of his predecessors. This Rienzi was the son of a poor person who kept a public-house in Rome. He was born about 1310, and received a careful education. He became apostolic notary, and had formed part of the deputation to Pope Clement VI., already spoken of; after which, in order to put an end to the anarchy under which the city groaned, he proclaimed, on the 20th of May, 1347, a new constitution, drove the Barons from Rome, caused the bandits to be executed, and received the titles of tribune and liberator of Rome, together with dictatorial power.

Rienzi had formed a futile plan of reuniting Italy in a unique republic, of which Rome should be the centre. Perugia and Arezzo submitted to him, and other cities were similarly disposed. The nobles in the country then marched against Rome. They were at first repulsed, but returned to the charge. The people, already disgusted with their liberator, who had made himself odious by his arrogance and tyranny, refused to arm, Rienzi took refuge in the château of St Angelo, and subsequently, in 1348, fled to Prague to the Emperor Charles

IV. This sovereign, instead of protecting him, delivered him up to Clement VI., who was going to have him put to death, when he himself expired in 1352.

Innocent VI., his successor, in order to reestablish his authority in the States of the Church, thought of making use of the eloquence of the ex-tribune. He therefore made Rienzi a Roman senator, and placed him under the direction of the Cardinal Albornoz. He was received at Rome with enthusiasm in 1354, and signalised his second government by wise energy, and beheaded the famous brigand Montreal, who roved through Italy with a troop of 20,000 or 30,000 men; but he alienated many minds from him again, and was massacred in a revolt on the 8th of October, 1354.

Rienzi was, for his epoch, highly lettered, and Petrarch's intimate friend.

There is no inherent alliance between freedom and scepticism. The republics of the middle ages were founded and maintained by some of the most Catholic populations in Europe; and the Catholic Church has, in every age, numbered among her devoted sons some of the most ardent champions of rational liberty and true progress. "With such exceptions," says Bulwer, "as peculiar circumstances necessarily occasioned, the

Papal See was, upon the whole, friendly to the political liberties of Italy." "That movement towards absolutism," says the *Dublin Review*,* "which succeeded the mediæval period seems to us altogether retrogressive, and such as would not have existed had the Church retained due influence. Avignon continued in subjection to the Holy See until the year 1791, when the Legislative Assembly declared it to be annexed to France, together with the Comtat Venaissin. The treaty of Tolentino confirmed this cession; but as the spoliation had in the first instance been sacrilegious, and the treaty had been forced from an unwilling Pontiff, Pius VII, on the 4th of September, 1815, protested against the recognition of this deduction from the Papal territory by the Congress of Vienna.

201. INNOCENT VI., A.D. 1352–1362, (Avignon.)

Stephen d'Albert was born in Limousin. He became professor of civil law at Toulouse, and subsequently Bishop of Clermont. He was "a man of simple habits and exemplary life."† He patronised men of letters, enforced the residence of bishops on their sees, and founded the college of St Martial at Toulouse. He was the fifth Pope who held the Papal seat at Avignon. His body

* April 1865, p. 496. † Sir E. Bulwer Lytton's *Rienzi*.

was interred in the Cathedral of that city, and afterwards removed to the neighbouring Chartreuse, which he had founded.

202. URBAN V., A.D. 1362-1370, (Avignon.)

Guillaume Grimand was member of a noble family of Gloandau, and was the sixth of the Avignon Popes. Though French, he was resolved, in spite of France, to return to Rome, and he resided there from 1367 to 1370.

He succeeded in deciding the Emperor Charles IV. on entering Italy in order to force into submission the usurpers of ecclesiastical fiefs. This prince, however, having come with insufficient forces, Urban found himself obliged to take again the route to Avignon in 1370. He died in that city in the same year, in the odour of sanctity; and, like Clement VI. before him, solemnly re-revoked whatever he might have taught, preached or said, at any time, or in any way, at variance with Catholic faith and morals.* His charity, his justice, his severity with regard to simony and corruption of manners was as great as his desire to free the Papacy from the French tutelage, and to recover for it its dominion in Italy.

When John Wickliffe had been dispossessed of the principalship of Canterbury College in

* Fleury, tome xx. pp. 121, 231.

Oxford—to which he had been elected in 1365—he appealed to Rome; but Urban V. pronounced against him, and his exasperation at this decision appears to have been the commencement of his erratic career.

203. Gregory XI., a.d. 1370-1378.

Pierre Roger, nephew of Clement VI., was born in 1332, near Limoges.

He proscribed the heretical doctrines of John Wickliffe of Oxford, a precursor of Luther, and ordered the Archbishop of Canterbury and the Bishop of London to arrest him. In spite of objections and obstacles on the part of the King of France and Charles V., in 1377 he restored the Papal seat to Rome, after it had been held at Avignon seventy years. During the whole of this time Rome and Italy ceased not to desire their Pastors' return; and on different occasions solemn embassies were sent to them, exhorting their Holinesses to console the Eternal City by their presence for years of widowhood. All French as they were, the Popes of Avignon were moved by these touching addresses. They felt that they could recover their entire independence only by returning to Rome. They strove once and again to break their bonds; but the factions which desolated Italy were always an obstacle to the accomplishment of their designs. The part which St Catherine of Sienna took in bringing it about at last is well described by Dr Coleridge in his "Sketches from the History of Christendom."* Gregory XI., whose health had always been weak, died in Rome before reaching his forty-seventh year.

204. URBAN VI., A.D. 1370–1389.

Barthelemi di Prignano of Naples was Archbishop of Bari. Sixteen cardinals protested against his election, pretending it had been the work of violence, but in fact because he had irritated them by reprimands which, under all the circumstances, seem to have been indiscreet.† They had fully concurred with the six cardinals at Avignon in recognising him as their lawful Pope, when, to their shame, they chose in his place, through French influence, Cardinal Robert of Genoa, Bishop of Cambray. Thus elected, the antipope installed himself at Avignon under the title of Clement VII. This was the commencement of the great schism, which lasted nearly forty years. The larger part of the empire, Bohemia, Hungary, England, and Sicily, adhered to the lawful Pope; while France, Naples, Portugal, Savoy, Scotland, Lorraine, and

---

* *Month*, May and July, 1866. † Fleury, an. 1378.

Spain, declared for the competitor. The rival Pontiffs mutually anathematised each other, and thus became a cause of sorrow, perplexity, and scandal, to all Christendom. Never had the Church experienced so deep an affliction.

Urban VI. created twenty-six cardinals, to replace those who had defected to the antipapal side. He preached a crusade against Clement VII. and his adherents. He called to his aid from Hungary Charles de Curas, and offered him the crown of the Queen of Naples, Jane I., and accompanied him to the conquest of that kingdom. It was not long, however, before he fell out with Charles. He retired to Nocera, where he had to sustain a siege; then to Salerno, and lastly to Genoa, where he caused five cardinals to be arrested and put to death for having conspired against him; nor could he return to Rome until after the decease of Charles de Duras. He was preparing to possess himself of the kingdom of Naples, which he regarded as his own property, when he died in 1389, and was buried in the Church of St Peter's. He fixed every thirty-third year for the return of the jubilee, and instituted the Feast of the Visitation of the Blessed Virgin Mary. The antipope Clement VII., died of grief and trouble at Avignon, without having done anything to terminate the schism, in spite of the efforts made by numbers of the French clergy, and especially those of the University of Paris, (1394.)

205. Boniface IX., a.d. 1389–1404.

He was a Neapolitan noble, named Peter de Romacelli, and was made a Cardinal in 1381. He instituted the *annats*, (year's revenue, or yearly tribute,) paid to the Holy See by those who had benefices, on receiving their *bulla*. He is reproached with avarice and simony;* but in recording such blemishes, I must observe, once for all, that I always quote an authority, and that I vouch for them only so far as that authority is trustworthy.

The antipope, Peter de Luna of Aragon, called Benedict XIII., held his seat at Avignon during this reign. He was a stubborn man, and would not make the least concession for the re-establishment of peace. He reigned—if usurpation can be called reigning—with Pope Gregory XII. when the Council of Pisa assembled to reconcile the contending parties, (1409.) Boniface IX. died on the 3d of October, and was buried without pomp in the Church of St Peter. It was hardly to be expected that the affairs of the Church would right themselves in his day. "The return of the Holy See from its long

* Fleury, tome xx. pp. 447, 458.

sojourn at Avignon was a stroke of profound policy, by which its emancipation from the straitening influences of nationalism was cheaply purchased, even at the cost of the great scandals which followed, and which a calculating politician might have foreseen."*

206. Innocent VII., a.d. 1404–1406.

His family name was Cosimo di Meliorati. He was born at Sulinone, in the Abruzzi, and was elected to the papal chair while the antipope called Benedict XIII. was still in possession of his usurped dignity. Historians speak highly of his attainments, amiable temper, and unsullied life. The competitors made some conciliatory demonstrations, which were not attended with any result. A tumult excited at Rome by Ladislaus and the Colonna obliged Innocent to retire for a time to Viterbo. He subsequently returned, and effected at last a reconciliation with Ladislaus. Innocent died on the 6th of November.

207. Gregory XII., a.d. 1406–1409.

Angelo Carrario belonged to one of the first families of Venice, and became bishop of that

* Rev. Dr Coleridge.

city. He had sworn to lay down the tiara if his rival, "Benedict XIII.," would do the like; but as both delayed to fulfil their oath, the cardinals of each obedience assembed in council at Pisa, and deposed them both, after they had refused to appear, and elected Alexander V., a Franciscan. Gregory XII. some time after adhered to this decision. He retained the title of Dean of the College of Cardinals, and died (1417) in his ninety-first year. The negotiations, which lasted during the three years of his pontificate, were of a very difficult and complicated nature.

203. Alexander V., a.d. 1409–1410.

Philarge was a native of Candia. His pontificate lasted only eighteen months. From a poor beggar he became a gray friar, and Doctor of the Sorbonne. He was elected Pope, when Cardinal Archbishop of Milan, by the Council of Pisa in 1409. He followed in all things the counsels of Belthazar Cossa, afterwards John XXIII. He excommunicated John Huss of Bohemia, who propagated in his country the doctrines of his friend and master, Wickliffe. Huss appealed from his judgment to that of the Council of Constance.

During the early part of this reign, Pope Gregory XII. and the antipope Benedict XIII. persisted in their claims, and found supporters. Castile, Aragon and Scotland remained attached to Benedict. Robert of Bavaria, King Ladislaus, and some cities of Italy, persevered in supporting Gregory XII. The rest of Christendom was neuter, or adhered to Alexander V. Instead of two Popes, there were now three who assumed this august title.

209. John XXIII. a.d. 1410-1415.

Urged by the Emperor Sigismond, he convened the council of Constance (seventeenth œcumenical) in 1414, by which he was deposed, (1415,) and Martin V., (who presided in the 42d, 43d, 44th, and 45th sessions,) was elected Pope in his stead. The antipope Benedict XIII. was likewise deposed. The place of meeting had been chosen by John XXIII. and Sigismond. Three patriarchs, twenty-two cardinals, twenty archbishops, a hundred and twenty-four abbots, a hundred and eighty priests, a multitude of doctors, and upwards of sixteen hundred princes, lords, counts, and chevaliers, assembled there with numerous suites. The Pope opened the council, November 5, 1414.

Forty-five propositions of John Wickliffe, who had been dead several years, and thirty of John Huss, were condemned by the council; and Huss himself was delivered over to the secular power, together with Jerome of Prague. The council did not terminate its sittings till the 22d of April, 1418.

The family name of John XXIII. was Balthazar Cossa, and he was elected at Bologna by sixteen cardinals, while others recognised the antipope Peter de Luna, named Benedict XIII. He had great talents for business, and succeeded in getting back to Rome. Being banished thence by King Ladislaus, he had recourse to the Emperor Sigismond, and at last he consented to defer to the council of Constance for the choice of a single Pope; but no sooner had he arrived in that city than, foreseeing that the election would be unfavourable to him, he betook himself to flight. He was arrested, however, as he fled, deposed, and thrown into prison, where he remained three years. Freed by Martin V., he yielded to him as Pope, and bore, till death, (1419,) the title of Dean of the Sacred College. It was at Florence that he recognised Martin V. with great emotion, and there also, six months after, he died on the 22d of December, 1419. Cosmo di Medici, who had been his intimate friend, celebrated his funeral with extraordinary pomp, and raised a monument to him in the Church of St John.

210. Martin V., A.D. 1417–1431.

His family name was Otho Colonna. He ended the great schism of the West, having been elected for that purpose, as we have seen, by the council of Constance. He died in 1431, at the moment when about to go and open the council of Basle. His virtues were numerous; and the Church, Italy, and Rome, owe him a large debt of gratitude. He was buried in the Church of St John Lateran at Rome. The pretensions of Clement, the antipope, lasted five years, from 1424 to 1429, when he gave in his adhesion to the lawful Pope, and put an end to the schism which had so cruelly torn the Church from September 21st, 1378, to August 24th, 1429. As some compensation for his temporal losses, Martin V. gave the antipope, after his submission, the bishopric of Majorca.

211. Eugene IV., A.D. 1431–1447.

He was a Venetian, and nephew of Gregory XII. He had long disputes with the Council of Basle, which tried to exalt its power above his, and deposed him, choosing the antipope Felix V. This council is received by the Church only as far as the twenty-sixth session.

Eugene pronounced the dissolution of this factious assembly, and called another council at Ferrara, and then at Florence, (1438–1439.) He realised a brief reunion of the Greek and Latin Churches. The seventeenth œcumenical council began its sittings at Ferrara in 1438, under the presidency of Eugene IV. A hundred and forty-one bishops were present, together with the Greek Emperor, the Patriarch of Constantinople, and legates from the patriarchiates of Alexandria, Antioch, and Jerusalem. The council was transferred to Florence in 1439, and the reunion of the Greek and Latin Churches was effected in the "decree of union," which contained four articles :—

1. On the procession of the Holy Ghost from the Father and the Son.

2. On the validity of the consecration of the Body of Christ, either in leavened or unleavened bread.

3. On Purgatory.

4. On the supremacy of the successors of St Peter.

In 1440 Eugene IV. gave to the Armenians, who had hitherto been Eutychians and Monothelites, a compendious form of orthodox instruction concerning the sacraments and other dogmas. he did the like also for the Jacobites, a Monophysite sect of Syria.

Eugene IV. died on the 23d of February, 1447, and was embalmed and exposed in St Peter's, that the people might kiss his feet. By his own desire he was laid near the tomb of Eugene III. "Though not without faults," says Fleury, "he was possessed of great qualities." He rendered important services to the Church, and terminated happily all the conflicts in which he engaged, without interfering in the disputes of other Christian princes. Platina wrote his Life, with that of other Popes down to Sixtus IV. The Abbé Christophe's Histories of the Papacy during the fourteenth and fifteenth centuries are works of great value to the student of this period.

212. Nicholas V., A.D. 1447–1455.

His name was Parentucelli di Sarzama. He had the happiness of seeing the antipope Felix V. abdicate. After the capture of Constantinople by Mahomet II., (1453,) Nicholas V. conceived the project of a crusade of all Christendom against the Turks, and preached to this effect at the congress of Lodi, (1454.) He was actively working towards this end when death cut him off, (1455.) He was learned, fond of letters and lettered men, built several magnificent edifices in Rome, and greatly enlarged the Vatican library. The Vatican palace is situated on a hill of Rome, anciently called Mons Vaticanus, on the west of the Tiber and north of the Janiculum. This hill stood originally without the limits of Rome, and did not form part of the seven hills. The magnificent palace of the Popes now adorns its summit, together with the superb gardens, the celebrated Vatican library, and the Basilica of St Peter. These sumptuous buildings are enriched with the most precious and numerous objects of ancient and modern art which have ever been collected together in one spot. The palace, according to some authors, was constructed by Constantine, but according to others by the Pope Liberius, or by Symmachus, in 495. After having been enlarged and embellished by different Popes, it became the residence of the Sovereign Pontiffs, especially after the return from Avignon in 1377. Nicolas V., Paul III., Sixtus IV., Leo X., Sixtus V., Benedict XIV., Clement XIV., and Pius VI. are those who have done most for the adornment of the Vatican. Among others whose works there excite perpetual admiration, are Bramante, Raphael's master and patron, Michael Angelo, Raphael himself, Perugino, and the architect of the seventeenth century, Bernini, on whom Urban VIII. heaped abundant riches.

213. Calixtus III., a.d. 1455–1458.

Alphonso Borgia was a native of Xativa, near Valencia in Spain. He was uncle of Alexander VI., and was seventy-eight years old at the time of his election. He directed bells to be rung at mid-day, calling the faithful to the recitation of the Pater Noster and Ave.

Jeanne d'Arc had been burnt (1431) by order of an English tribunal, of which Cauchon, Bishop of Beauvais, who had been a creature of Henry V. of England, was the president, and Cardinal Beaufort, brother of Henry IV., one of the members. This iniquitous tribunal had condemned her on the charge of witchcraft. Calixtus III. caused the process (too late, alas!) to be reversed by a commission, and the memory of Jeanne d'Arc to be restored to honour.

Calixtus III. appalled, like his predecessor, by the extraordinary progress which the Turks were making in Europe, after the capture of Constantinople, exerted all his power and influence in making an appeal to the courage of Christians against the Mussulman invasions and aggressions. In spite of his great age, the venerable Pontiff had preserved in his soul all the fire of his youth. He sent preachers through all Christian kingdoms, and, thanks to his own ardent zeal, succeeded in equipping an army of more than 60,000 men, which he sent under the command of John Campestran, his legate, to the help of the noble Hunyad in Hungary, (1456.) Two years after this he died in Rome, on the 6th of August, and was buried in St Peter's in a tomb of marble.

214. Pius II., A.D. 1458-1464.

Æneas Sylvius Piccolomini of Pienza then called Corsignano, was born in 1405. He received the purple in 1456. He fulfilled several political missions, strove hard to organise a crusade against the Ottomans, and formed a league to this end with the intrepid Mathias Corvin, King of Hungary. He pressed the King of France, the Duke of Burgundy, and the Republic of Venice into the cause, and put himself at the head of the movement, but died of a fever when on the point of embarking at Ancona, and in sight of the Venetian galleys waiting to transport him to the foreign shore. In 1461 he had obtained from Louis XI. a nominal revocation of the Pragmatic Sanction of Bourges, (1438,) which confirmed and extended that one which had been signed by St Louis and Clement IV., and was regarded by the French in general as the bulwark of the boasted liberties of the Gallican Church. We shall see further on how undue attachment to these liberties caused just displeasure to the Holy See. Pius II. was at once theologian, orator, diplomatist, canonist, historian, geographer, and poet. He has left behind him, among other works, a "Description of the State of Germany," a "History of the Empire under Frederic II.," some letters, harangues, and a "Romance of Euryalus and Lucretia." He also took part in the Memoirs of his Life, published by his secretary, Gobellini. If his days had not been unexpectedly cut short, he would have presented the extraordinary and unique spectacle of a Pope at the head of an army and navy, going forth in person to combat the colossal force of Mohammedanism—himself the counterpart of Mohammed, unfurling valiantly the standard of the cross, assailing the religion of the false prophet in its stronghold, and struggling with sword and spear to reduce Islamite Constantinople into subjection to Christian Rome. He died in peace on the Eve of the Assumption, aged fifty-nine.

215. Paul II., a.d. 1464–1471.

Pietro Barbo, a Venetian, was elected in 1464. He excommunicated George Podiebrad, King of Bohemia, who had embraced the doctrines of the Hussites, and persecuted the Catholics of his dominions, assigning the crown at the same time to Mathias Corvin, the king's son-in-law, King of Hungary, whom the Catholics had placed at their head, (1468.) He preached a crusade, and held consistories for the defence of Christendom against the Turks in vain. Notwithstanding these generous efforts, a few cavaliers only devoted themselves to the sacred cause; not a single nation put itself in movement; not a king was found to unfurl the Oriflamme, nor to wear on his vest the pilgrim's cross. All nations, eaten up with narrow selfishness, thought of themselves only, and ignored the virtue of that devotion and self-sacrifice which such an expedition demanded. The undecided character of Frederic III. suffered Germany to flutter about in every wind of discord; Louis XI. manœuvred and calculated with no other end in view than that of ruining his vassals. England was swimming in waves of blood in the midst of the anarchical horrors of the wars of the Roses. Italy sadly continued her intestine struggles; and Spain, obliged to bring to an end that portion of Islamism which had so severely afflicted her, surrounded the last Moors in Granada, and forced them to capitulate. Faith had become feeble in the souls of men, and Christian feeling had no longer sufficient energy and force to excite in favour of religion a general rising and movement analogous with that which had drawn on the first crusades.

Paul II. adopted the triple crown, and reduced the jubilee to every twenty-fifth year. He began the restoration of ancient monuments in Rome, raised the Palace of St Mark, and caused games to be celebrated in the capital for the diversion of the people. He died of apoplexy on the 26th of July, when quite alone. With his death Platina brought his History of the Popes to an end, and Onuphrius, an Augustinian monk of Verona, continued the series.

216. Sixtus IV., A.D. 1471-1484.

Brother Francis Albescola della Rovere, a Franciscan general of the Frati Minori, and of a fisherman's family, was created cardinal under Paul II.

In the first place he set on foot useful reforms. He sent an expedition against the Turks under Cardinal Caraffa, who took Attalia in Pamphylia. In the conspiracy of the Pazzi against the Medicis, (1478,) Sixtus IV. saw reason to favour the designs of the conspirators;* and in the war of the Pazzi which followed its partial success, he, together with Naples and Sienna, attacked Florence with the cry, "War to the

* Fleury, tome xxiii. p. 405.

Medicis! peace to Florence!" (1478–1480.) After two years' negotiation he succeeded in re-establishing peace in the Tuscan capital. According to Onuphrius, he was too indulgent as regarded his nephews: he made two of them cardinals; for a third, Peter Riano, Legate and Cardinal-Archbishop of Florence, he procured the principality of Imola and Forli; and for a fourth, John della Rovere, that of Sora and Sinigaglia. By conferring the see of Cuença on his nephew, Cardinal San Giorgio, he gave umbrage to Ferdinand and Isabella of Spain. They threatened him with the convocation of a general council, and succeeded in obtaining a bull in favour of their ecclesiastical nominations.

He instituted by a bull, in 1476, the Feast of the Immaculate Conception of the Blessed Virgin Mary, on which subject he also composed a work; and he authorised the establishment of the inquisition in Castile for the extirpation of heresy, under which term Judaism was included.[*] Sixtus at first censured its intemperate zeal; but afterwards, being better satisfied of its utility, he confirmed its proceedings, and armed it with fresh powers. The standard of the cross in massive silver, which Ferdinand and Isabella planted on the walls of Granada, was a present from this Pontiff.

[*] See Mariana, *Hist. Hisp.* l. 4, c. 27.

Robert Fleming, an Englishman, wrote in his praise a poem, which was published at Rome. He died in that city on the 13th of August, and was laid in St Peter's, in a bronze tomb erected by his nephew, Cardinal Julian.

217. Innocent VIII., a.d. 1484-1492.

John Baptist Cibo was elected through the influence of the Vice Chancellor Borgia, (Alexander VI.) He had been married, and was the father of a family before he took holy orders.

He strove to excite the zeal of the sovereigns of Europe against the Turks, and he caused to be delivered into his hands the young captive Prince Zizim, brother and rival of the Sultan Bajazet II., (1490,) who, after his defeat, had taken refuge with the Knights of St John of Jerusalem, then called the Knights of Rhodes. Innocent received from the sultan a pension for keeping him. He excommunicated Ferdinand, King of Naples, who had exercised cruelties on the Pope's subjects, and declared his kingdom given to Charles VIII. of France. After several combats of little importance, peace was re-established in 1492. Onuphrius speaks highly of Innocent VIII., and applauds his kind and gentle disposition. He died on the 25th of July, in consequence of an apopletic attack received two years before. As nothing availed for the restoration of his health, a Jewish physician was called in, who gave him a draught mingled with the blood of three boys just dead. Innocent's horror at the discovery hastened his end. He was buried in St Peter's.

218. Alexander VI., a.d. 1492–1503.

Roderick Borgia, of Valencia in Spain, was nephew of Calixtus III., by whom he had been created cardinal in 1456, and is numbered by all historians among the few Popes of ill-fame. The conclave that chose him to be head of the Church was much to blame in electing a Pontiff whom they knew to be unworthy, in opposition to the earnest exhortation of Leonelli, who delivered the funeral oration on the death of Innocent VIII.* Before his elevation he had several sons, of whom Cæsar Borgia, afterwards Cardinal and Duke of Valentinois, (1499,) is the best known, and one daughter, the too famous Lucretia Borgia. Alexander VI. played an important part in the political history of his time. He entered into a league with other princes for the purpose of expelling Charles VIII. from Italy. The league, however, failed in its object. The French king entered Rome as a conqueror on the 31st of

* Duchesne, *Hist. des Papes.*

December, 1494, and carried on the government of the city, while the Pope was shut up in the castle of St. Angelo, into which he had thrown himself. The Pope soon came to an understanding with Charles VIII., and subsequently contracted a close alliance with his successor, Louis XII., and, favoured hereby, he succeeded in spoiling his princely neighbours, and restored to the Holy See many of its ancient domains. To satisfy his ambition, and exalt the princes of his own family, he too often outraged the laws of justice. It was with such views that he sought the ruin of the houses of Colonna and Orsini.* When the Spanish general, Gonsalvo de Cordova, came to his relief in Rome during the troubles alluded to above, he bluntly advised his holiness to reform his life and conversation, which brought scandal on all Christendom; and the Spanish ambassador, Garcilasso de la Vega, a few years later, fearlessly followed this bold example. The name of Roderick Borgia is linked by historians with some of the worst crimes, such as simony, treachery, and even poisoning.† He died in 1503; and is affirmed to have poisoned himself by a beverage which had been prepared for one of his victims. The truth of this has been, and is still, contested, but

---

* Mariana, lib. 26.
† Guicciardini, *Hist. Ital.*, lib. 5 Fleury, tome xxiv., p. 444.

Prescott, who is tolerably impartial, says there is very little doubt of it. Dr Von Hefele, in his *Life of Ximenes*, speaks of him as "a very unworthy Pope;" and De Maistre, in his work *Du Pape*, calls him a *mauvais sujet*, and "a sad exception to the long line of virtues which have done honour to the Holy See." His deplorable end is described at length by Duchesne, Mariana, Guicciardini, Daniel,* and Fleury. Ferdinand and Isabella of Spain were confirmed by Alexander VI. in the possession of all lands discovered, or hereafter to be discovered by them in the Western Ocean.† The bulls issued to that effect were in accordance with the belief of the times that Papal confirmation of regal authority was desirable, if not necessary. They authorised the sovereigns, moreover, to receive all the tithes, and collate to all benefices in the colonial dominions, subject only to the approbation of the Holy See. The royal supremacy in the West was thus established on a firm, and, as it afterwards proved, dangerous footing.

219. Pius III., a.d. 1503.

Franco Piccolomini reigned only twenty-six days. He was the son of a sister of Pius II.,

---

* *Hist. de France*, tome v.
† Prescott's *Ferdinand and Isabella*, part i. chapter 18.

who allowed him to take the name of Piccolomini. His election was due to Julian della Rovere, by whom he was succeeded under the name of Julius II. His short reign was deeply regretted, for all good men regarded him as a Pontiff specially raised up to remove scandals and repair the injury that had lately been done to religion.

220. Julius II., A.D. 1503–1513.

Julian della Rovere, nephew of Sixtus IV., was born at Abizal, near Savona. Cæsar Borgia, Duke of Valentinois and son of Alexander VI., having possessed himself of Romana, Julius II. retook the country, compelling Borgia to deliver up all the fortresses. So martial was his spirit, that being asked by Michael Angelo whether he would be represented in the act of blessing, he replied, "Give me a sword." From him was obtained the dispensation for the marriage of Henry VII.'s son, afterwards Henry VIII., with Catherine of Aragon, his brother's widow; the English prelates not being unanimous in their opinion on the subject. He vigorously made war against the Venetians, who had taken from the Holy See many cities in the north of Italy. With Louis XII. of France, Ferdinand of Spain, and the Emperor Maximilian, he formed against the Venetians the league of Cambray, (1508,) and reduced Venice to accept the most disadvantageous conditions. But having occasion to complain of Louis XII, he broke with him, and felt himself obliged to stir up foes against him. In the "Holy League" he joined with the Venetians, the Swiss, Ferdinand, Henry VIII., and Maximilian, in opposition to France. Louis XII. delayed not in marching an army against the Pope, and also assembled a council in Pisa to examine into his conduct. The papal troops were routed at Bologna and Ravenna in 1511 and 1512; and the council of Pisa, which Louis had convoked, declared the Pope to be suspended from his functions. Julius, on his part, called together a general council at Rome, in the Church of St John Lateran, (1512.) He annulled the acts of the insignificant council of Pisa, excommunicated Louis XII., placed his kingdom under an interdict, absolved his subjects from their oath of allegiance, and excited Henry VIII. to invade France. These strong measures did not diminish the popularity of Louis XII., called by his subjects "the good King Louis, the father of his people." Julius II., it is said, was not much regretted after his death, even by those whom he had served, in consequence of his rough address.* He died on the 20th of February, 1513.

* Fleury, tome xxv. 278.

It was he who commenced the present church of St Peter's at Rome; the most spacious, grand, and beautiful religious edifice which the world has ever seen.

"The expulsion of the foreign tyrants," says Lord Macaulay, "and the restoration of that golden age which had preceded the irruption of Charles VIII., were projects which fascinated all the master-spirits of Italy. The magnificent vision delighted the great but ill-regulated mind of Julius; it divided, with manuscripts and sauces, painters and falcons, the attention of the frivolous Leo."* But the bias of Protestant historians in such statements must always be taken into account. The Popes have in every age had enemies ready to magnify their slightest failing, and turn it to their disadvantage. In the absence of any history of their sacred line which can be trusted throughout, the student should in each case lean to the loyal side, and be suspicious of adverse testimony.

221. Leo X., A.D. 1513–1521.

The celebrated Leo X. was born at Florence in the year 1475. He was the son of Laurence de Medicis, and before his elevation to the Papal seat was known by the name of John de Medicis.

* Compare Fleury, tome xxvi. 74.

At the early age of thirteen he was made cardinal, and while still young quitted his native country in consequence of the troubles of his family, fixed his residence at Rome, where he attached himself to Pope Julius II., in whose cause he took arms, fought, and was taken prisoner at Ravenna. In his thirty eighth year he was raised to the Papal dignity, and his pontificate was marked by many extraordinary events, religious and political, as well as by great progress in the fine arts. He made peace with Louis XII. of France, whom his predecessor, Julius II., had excommunicated; yet soon after declared against Francis I., and to cope with him leagued with Sforza, Duke of Milan, and the Swiss. He was compelled to treat with France after the victory of Marignan or Malegnano, (1515,) known in history as the battle of the giants, and the conquest of the Duchy of Milan by the French; but in 1521 he united with Charles V. against him, and aided the emperor in drawing him from the Milanese. Julius II. opened, and Leo X. terminated the Lateran Council, (1512–1517,) famous for the abolition of the Pragmatic Sanction. Leo concluded also with Francis (1516) the concordat which has regulated the Church of France during three centuries, and caused indulgences to be preached throughout Christendom, (1517,) which were dispensed with great profusion at first, with the view of paying the costs of a crusade against the Turks, and afterwards for the completion of the Basilica of St Peter. This distribution gave occasion to quarrels, which brought about the terrible revolutionary movement against the Church, of which Luther, Calvin, Henry VIII., and Elizabeth were the principal leaders. Leo X. excommunicated Luther, and condemned and anathematized thirty-five of his propositions *in globo*, but did not succeed in stifling the new doctrines. It was he who conferred on Henry VIII. the title of Defender of the Faith, (1521.) He fostered sciences and letters, re-established the University of Rome, and richly endowed it, brought to light and published ancient authors, and founded the Laurentian Library. This reign was so illustrious through the progress of arts and letters, that the brilliant epoch in which he lived has been called the age of Leo X. Then flourished the poets Ariosto, Vida, Sannazar, Berni, Ascolti, and Alamanni, Fracastor the physician and poet, Cardinal Bembo, Machiavelli, Guicciardini, Caravaggio, Giulio, Romano, Cardinal Sadolet, Michael Angelo, Raphael, Andrea del Sarto, &c. The Complutensian Polyglot of Cardinal Ximenes was sufficient to render his name immortal in the republic of letters. It exhibited in one view the Scriptures in their various ancient languages, and the compiler was greatly encouraged in his difficult task by Leo X., who threw open to him the precious collection of the Vatican, and supplied him especially with the Greek MSS. But for the labours of such men, Protestants would never have had a Bible at all. Leo X. had just re-established his family at Florence, and invested his nephew, Lorenzo de Medicis, with the Dukedom of Urbino, torn from La Rovere, nephew of Julius II., in 1516, when he died almost suddenly in the midst of his successes, on the 1st of December, 1521, at the age of 44. It was said that he had been poisoned. Leo X's life has been written by Audin and Roscoe. The latter biography is valuable chiefly on literary grounds.

222. ADRIAN VI., A.D. 1522–1523.

Adrian Florent, son of a weaver, was born at Utrecht, (1459,) and taught theology at Louvain; he became vice-chancellor of the university in that city, tutor of Charles V., Bishop of Fortosa, viceroy in Spain conjointly with Ximenes, and Pope through the influence of Charles V. He granted the kings of Spain the right of appointing the bishops in their own kingdom and sent a legate to Sweden to combat Lutheranism. He reformed some abuses which he found in the court of Rome, and restored economy in the administration of its affairs; but unhappily died a year after his election, (1523.) He was not so popular with the Romans as any of his predecessors, owing to his being a foreigner, and frugal in his habits. His virtues, however, were of a high order, and he was the author of several theological works. The epitaph on his tomb in St Peter's is remarkable: "Here lies Adrian VI., whose greatest unhappiness consisted in having to rule." He was inflexibly just in conferring dignities, and said that "he wished to see men given to benefices, not benefices given to men."

223. Clement VII. a.d. 1523–1534.

Julian de Medicis was a cousin of Leo X. He leagued with Francis I., the princes of Italy, and Henry VIII., against Charles V., to break up the treaty of Madrid. This league, which was called the Holy League because the Pope was at the head of it, brought upon Clement nothing but misfortunes. He was besieged in Rome by the army of Charles V., commanded by the Constable de Bourbon, (1527,) who had deserted and betrayed his master, the King of

France. Clement VII. was detained prisoner at Rome seven months, and was only able to escape in the disguise of a merchant. In 1534, after long expostulations, he decided against Henry VIII., who had divorced Catherine of Aragon on the ground of her having been his brother's wife. She had been married to him (some accounts say nominally only) at an early age, and her union with Henry, which had lasted eighteen years, had been solemnised by a dispensation from Julius II. The divorce of this virtuous queen occasioned the separation of England from the Catholic Church. In 1524 Clement VII. sent Martin de Valence and twelve monks as missionaries to Mexico, and approved the order of the Theatines or regular clerks. He died of a slow fever on the 25th of Sept. 1534, aged fifty-six. Several of his letters are extant.

CALVIN.

John Calvin was born at Noyon in Picardy, in 1509, and was son of a cooper named Cauvin. He was educated in the Catholic religion, and was, at first, destined for holy orders, but quitted this career for that of jurisprudence, and went to study at Orleans, and then at Bourges under the famous Milanese lawyer, Alciat. Having allied himself with several of Luther's partisans, he soon embraced the exciting principles of the Reformation, and, in 1532, began to propagate them in Paris. Being threatened with imprisonment, he, at first, took refuge in Angoulême, and then with Margaret of Navarre, who favoured the new sect, at Nérac, and, lastly, at Basle. In this city he published, in 1535, under the title of *Institutio Religionis Christianæ*, an *exposé* of the doctrines of the innovators, which he himself translated into French, and which became the catechism of the Reformés of France. In 1536, he became Professor of Theology at Geneva, the headquarters of the Reformation. Two years after, he was banished from this city for having employed excessive severity. His doctrines were austere. Predestination bordered on fatalism; election engendered phariseeism; reprobation darkened the Divine mercy with a cloud, and his doctrine of final perseverance was presumption itself. Calvin retired to Strasbourg, where he married in 1539, and there propagated his Christianity revised. A few years later he was recalled to Geneva, (1541.) From this time he became all-powerful in that city, insomuch that he was called the Pope of Geneva. He procured the adoption of his articles of faith by the council, together with his ordinances concerning ecclesiastical discipline. He aspired to reform morals as well as belief, and, from ardour falling into intolerance, he caused the unhappy Servetus to be burnt for having assailed the mystery of the Holy Trinity, (1553.) Calvin died at Geneva in 1564. As a revolutionist in religion, he went beyond Luther, destroyed man's free-will, denied the real presence in the Eucharist, and rejected all hierarchy, and all æsthetics in religious worship. Calvin has left a large number of works, all of which are characterised by remarkable learning, and by a severe, and often engaging, style. The principal are the *Institutio*, of which he published several editions, a treatise on the Lord's Supper, and commentaries on the Holy Scriptures, which came out in parts in French and Latin.

224. Paul III., A.D. 1534–1549.

His family name was Alexander Farnese. He was a scion of the house of Boniface VIII., and had received a learned education. A bull of excommunication was published against Henry VIII. by Paul III. after the king's marriage with Anne Boleyn, but its only effect was to render him more implacable. Cromwell was now appointed vicar-general, and it was determined to obtain from the clergy written acknowledgments that they held their authority from the king only. As a first step towards this was the suspension of the powers of all bishops within the kingdom; and when they petitioned to be restored to the exercise of their functions, they each received a commission of authority to act as the king's deputy, and during his pleasure. The only remaining obstacle to Henry's absolute supremacy was the monasteries; he therefore determined to suppress them, but thought it prudent to commence by all the smaller ones. A bill was passed giving to the king all monastic establishments, the annual revenue of which did not exceed two hundred pounds. By this measure three hundred and eighty of them were abolished.

Paul III. formed a league against the Turks with Charles V. and Venice in 1538. He acted as mediator between the Emperor and Francis I., who, thanks to him, concluded the truce of Nice in 1538.

In 1540 he approved the order of the Jesuits, founded by St Ignatius Loyola; and in 1545 opened the eighteenth and last œcumenical council of the Church at Trent during the reigns of Charles V. and Henry II. of France. The sessions of this council were not terminated till 1563. In that year they were brought to a happy conclusion by Pius IV., aided especially by his nephew, St Charles Boromeo. During the twenty-five sittings of the council one hundred and twenty-seven canons were decreed, and their object was three-fold:

1. To form, as it were, a compendium of all the preceding great councils, by setting forth the most explicit and luminous definitions of the several articles of the Christian faith;

2. To repudiate in detail the errors of the German Reformers; and

3. To make abundant provision for the reform of ecclesiastical discipline.

Paul III. took in hand anew the building of St Peter's, intrusting it to Michael Angelo, (1546) He issued in 1536 the "In Cæna Domini," or bull of excommunication of heretics and all contumacious enemies of the Holy See and the clergy, which was read in Rome every Holy Thursday until the time of Clement XIV.; Paul V. gave it its last form in 1610.

Paul III. had been married before his ordination, and he made his son, Peter Louis Farnese, Duke of Parma and Placentia. The duke was unhappily addicted to some degrading vices. The letters of Paul III. to Erasmus, Sadolet, and others, are extant. He died on the 10th of Nov., 1549, at the age of eighty-one.

Luther.

Martin Luther was born in 1483, at Eisleben, in Saxony, and was the son of a poor working miner. He studied at Eisenach, and in 1505 entered an Augustinian monastery at Erfurt; soon after became professor at the University of Wittemberg, and was sent to Rome in 1510 respecting some affairs of his order.

In 1517 Pope Leo X. having published indulgences, with a view of completing St Peter's at Rome, and having charged the Dominicans to dispense them in Germany, the Augustinians were, it is said, jealous of this choice, and Luther, whom they selected as their organ, went so far as to attack the doctrine of indulgences itself. He published on this occasion a programme containing ninety-five propositions, which soon found a number of adherents. Tetzel, a Dominican, who had received a special mission from the Pope to publish the indulgences, caused this programme to be burnt, and Leo X., after having in vain cited the author to appear at Rome, deputed the affair to Cardinal Cajetan, his legate, at the diet of Augsburg. The Cardinal endeavoured, but without effect, to make Luther retract; he then wished to have him arrested, but Luther, warned of this intention in time, succeeded in making his escape. Being protected by the Elector of Saxony, he openly professed more advanced and alarming doctrines. Acknowledging no other authority than that of the Bible — mutilated, however, and interpreted after the dictates of his own reason — he attacked the Pope and the

Roman Church, monastic vows, the celibacy of priests, the ecclesiastical hierarchy, and the possession of temporal goods by the clergy; he rejected the invocation of saints, purgatory, the five commandments of the Church, the doctrine of transubstantiation, the sacrifice of the mass, and communion under one kind; and of the seven sacraments he retained only those of baptism and the supper of the Lord.

In 1510 Leo X. issued a bull of excommunication against him, and at the same time he caused his writings to be burned; but Luther, undaunted, delivered the Pope's bull to the flames at Wittemberg, together with all the decisions which had emanated from the Holy See. In 1521, being cited before the diet of Worms, he went there furnished with a safe conduct of the Emperor Charles V. He there again refused to retract his opinions, and was banished from the empire. He found an asylum in the château of Wartburg, near Eisenach, where the Elector of Saxony, his protector, concealed him during more than nine months. Luther employed this leisure in composing several works to propagate his doctrines, and in the same retreat undertook to translate a version of the Scriptures in German, which was not completed till twelve years afterwards. Having returned to Wittemberg, he there recommenced preaching, made numerous proselytes, drew into his party powerful princes, among others, those of Sweden, Denmark, Franconia, Brandenburg, and the Prince Palatine. He also succeeded in getting liberty of conscience accorded to his disciples in the Diets of Nuremburg (1523-1524) and of Spire, (1526.) After numerous vicissitudes, in which this liberty was by turns restricted or extended, he saw the peace of Nuremburg signed by the Protestant princes and Charles V. This treaty secured to the Lutherans religious toleration until the assembly of the projected council of the Church.

Luther employed the rest of his life in spreading his doctrines by his writings and by his preaching, and also in struggling against the numerous conflicting sects which were engendered rapidly in the bosom of the reformation.

He died in 1546, a little after the convocation of the Council of Trent.

Luther had been married from the year 1525, when he espoused a young nun, Catherine de Bohren, or Bora, by whom he had several children.

This reformer was of a hot, irascible, and indomitable character. He often employed low language, and did not spare his adversaries the grossest abuse. He was master of an impetuous eloquence, by which he exerted an irresistible influence on the multitude.

Luther has left a great number of works, of which many are pamphlets suggested by circumstances of his own time. The principal are his German translation of the Bible, his Catechism, which contains the principles of the Reformation, sermons and Biblical commentaries, the treatise against Erasmus on Free Will, the existence of which he denied, and lastly, his letters.

The doctrines of Luther have been ably exposed and refuted by the learned Bossuet, in his history of the Variations of Protestantism.

225. Julius III., a.d. 1550–1555.

Giovanni Maria Giocchi reopened the Council of Trent, interrupted by the death of Paul III., on whose grandson, Octavius Farnese, Duke of Parma and Placentia, he made war. His death took place on March 23, 1555. His reign, with that of his predecessor, fills a large space in Church histories, owing to the political complications of the time, and the continued struggle with Lutheran errors.

226. Marcellus II., a.d. 1555.

This Pope reigned only twenty-one days, but during that brief period his devout and noble intentions were so plainly manifested, that his death was a subject of deep regret.

227. Paul IV., a.d. 1555–1559.

John Peter Caraffa had accomplished some delicate missions before his accession. He reformed abuses, and evinced much zeal, but the excesses of his nephews Charles, John, and Antony Caraffa, punished too late, irritated the headstrong people who, after his death, profanely hurled his statue into the Tiber.*

He drew up the rule of the Theatines, (regular clerks,) and instituted, it is said, the Congregation of the Index. Paul IV. having leagued himself with the French for the purpose of driving the Spaniards out of Italy, Philip II. made war upon him. His arms were successful, yet so unwilling was he to carry on hostilities against the Pope, that, as Alva remarked, the treaty which followed seemed to have been dictated by the vanquished instead of the victor. All places taken from the territory of the Church were restored; the Spanish troops were immediately withdrawn; the French were allowed a free passage back to their own country, and Alva, who entered Rome on the 27th of September, 1557, had to ask pardon on his knees in order to get absolution for having borne arms against the Church. Paul, however, paid the duke the honour of giving him a seat at his own table; and sent the duchess

---

* Fleury, tome xxxi. p. 390.

the consecrated golden rose, reserved for royal persons and illustrious champions of the Church.*

It may be observed in this place, that the leading doctrines of Christianity have been developed in the Church in a certain historical sequence running parallel to the order of the creed. Thus, the doctrine of the Trinity mainly occupied the two first œcumenical councils; the four next were engaged in expressing accurately the faith of the Incarnation; and the first definition of the Eucharist occurs in the seventh, held in 787. The questions of grace, free will, and justification subsequently presented themselves in full to the mind of the Church, together with that of the sacraments, and issued in the luminous expositions of the Catechism and decrees of the Council of Trent, which continued its sittings under Paul IV. and the two preceding Popes. The errors of our day, being chiefly rationalistic, turn on the last division of the creed, and concern the person and offices of the Holy Ghost, His abiding presence in the Church, the communion of saints, and sacramental forgiveness; and they prepare the way for those predicted mockers, who, in the last day, will pour contempt on the promises of Christ's second coming. Heresiarchs and Popes are the foremost agents in this long warfare, of which the creed is the battle-field.

* *Dublin Review*, June, 1856.

228. Pius IV., A.D. 1559–1565.

Giovanni Angelo Medicis, or Medechino, brother of the Marquis of Marignan, made war with the Turks; confirmed the decrees of the Council of Trent; embellished Rome; re-established the order of the Knights of St John of Jerusalem; and founded the printing-press of the Vatican. He has been reproached with rigour in the sentences he inflicted on the Caraffas, to whom he was personally opposed; but when have the Popes exercised the powers vested in them without raising murmurs in some quarter or other? St Pius V., however, rescinded the act of the Roman senate, which, under Pius IV., declared the memory of the Caraffas abolished. He died on the 8th of December, with the Song of Simeon on his lips, and St Charles Boromeo and St Philip Neri at his bedside.

229. St Pius V., A.D. 1566–1572.

Michael Ghisteri was a Dominican, and prior of the order, in which he restored discipline. He was born at Bosco, in Lombardy, of a noble and distinguished family, in the year 1504.

He was full of zeal against the wiles of heretics, of whom many in his time were delivered up to the tribunal of the Holy Office. The view of heresy taken by the Popes in general, to which I have alluded in the notice of Innocent III., will account for Pontiffs as remarkable for their piety as St Pius V. having countenanced proceedings against innovators which many writers represent as cruel.* It is certain, however, that though "in the long course of 1800 years there are events which need explanation, or which the world might wish otherwise, the general tenor and tendency of the traditions of the Papacy have been mercy and humanity. It has ever been less fierce than the nations, and in advance of the age; it has ever moderated, not only the ferocity of barbarians, but the fanaticism of Catholic populations."† The Papacy being a divine institution, it must of necessity have its severe as well as its merciful aspects.

Pius V. took part in the cost and equipment of the fleet which obtained the victory of Lepanto on the 7th of October 1571. In this battle Don John of Austria commanded the combined forces of Venice, Spain, and the Pope, while Selim headed the Ottoman fleet. The Turks are said to have lost two hundred galleys and thirty thousand men. The letters of St Pius V. were published at Antwerp in 1640. He died on the

---

* See Prescott's *Ferdinand and Isabella*, i. 295.
† Newman's *Lectures on the Present Position of Catholics in England*, p. 203.

1st of May, repeating the paschal hymn, "*Quæsumus auctor omnium*," and he was canonised in 1713.

"Men of a very different class," says Macauly, "now rose to the direction of ecclesiastical affairs; men whose spirit resembled that of Dunstan and of Becket. The Roman Pontiffs exhibited in their own persons all the austerity of the early anchorites of Syria. Paul IV. brought to the Papal throne the same fervent zeal that had carried him into the Theatine convent. Pius V., under his gorgeous vestments, wore day and night the hair-shirt of a simple friar, walked barefoot in the streets at the head of processions, found, even in the midst of his most pressing avocations, time for private prayer; often regretted that the public duties of his station were unfavourable to growth in holiness; and edified his flock by innumerable instances of humility, charity, and forgiveness of injuries; while, at the same time, he upheld the authority of his see, and the unadulterated doctrines of his Church, with all the stubbornness and vehemence [he should have said, firmness and courage] of Hildebrand. Gregory XIII. exerted himself not only to imitate but to surpass Pius in the severe virtues of his sacred profession."*

* Essays. Ranke's *History of the Popes*.

230. Gregory XIII., a.d. 1572-1585.

Buoncampagno was elected by the unanimous voice of the Sacred College, and chiefly through the influence of Cardinal de Granvelli, minister of Charles V. and Philip II.

He sent troops and money to aid Henry III. against the Calvinists.

A seminary had been established at Rome from which Pope Gregory XIII. sent to England in 1580 two Jesuit missionaries, named Persons, and Campian, an Oxford convert. Queen Elizabeth immediately took measures to have them arrested. Campian eluded her vigilance during some time, and boldly published a defence of the Catholic faith; offering to dispute before the court and universities. He was, however, taken, and with twelve others condemned to death on a charge of having conspired to murder the queen and overthrow the State. They were, all but two, cruelly executed.

Gregory XIII. is celebrated for having substituted the calendar which bears his name, and which is in use to this day throughout almost all Europe, for the Julian Calendar, which derived its name from Julius Cæsar, in whose time it came into vogue. In Russia the Gregorian calendar is not accepted, nor did it come into vogue among ourselves until the year

1752.* Gregory died in 1585, aged eighty-three. He was well versed in jurisprudence, in the profession of which science he had distinguished himself in Bologna, his native city. He loved the arts, and adorned Rome with many edifices. The line of conduct he took in regard to the Massacre of St Bartholomew is explained at length in the *Dublin Review* for October, 1865.

231. Sixtus V., A.D. 1585–1590.

Felix Peretti was born in 1521 at Montalte, near Ascoli. He was first a swineherd, whence he was often called "the pastor of Montalte;" and then became successively a Grey Friar in 1537; professor of canon law at Rimini in 1544, and afterwards at Sienna; grand inquisitor at Venice, where he had a disagreement with the senate; adviser of the "congregation" or commission of cardinals appointed by the Pope; procurator-general of his order; theologian of the legate in Spain, (Buoncampagno, afterwards Gregory XIII;) adviser of the holy office; vicar-general of the order of Grey Friars in 1566; bishop of St Agata di Goti; cardinal in 1568; archbishop of Fermo; and, finally, he was raised to the Papal See. Many writers state, but altogether without proof,* that he was elected when

---

* *Month*, May, 1866. English Premiers.
* Ranke's *Popes*, (1493–1700.) Book iv.

supposed to be labouring under serious infirmities. He did much for public peace and morals, and also for the publication of a pure edition of the sacred Scriptures.

He showed true talents for governing; cleared the States of the Church from vagabonds and brigands who infested it; adorned Rome with useful and magnificent monuments; completely reorganised public administration, which was confided to fifteen committees, or "congregations;" took part in almost all that passed in Europe, and, at his death, left in the treasury 5,000,000 gold crowns. He encouraged the "Holy League," formed to defend the Catholic religion in France against the Huguenots, (1576.) He excommunicated Henry III., who had sided with the "moderate" party, and who had caused the Duke de Guise, the head of the league and of the "*Catholiqués Zelés*," to be assassinated close to the royal apartment, on the 23d of December, 1588, and had his brother, the Cardinal de Lorraine, put to death the next day.

Sixtus V. excommunicated Henry IV. also, though he knew how to appreciate the greatness of his character. Henry put an end to the League by abjuring Calvanism and embracing the Catholic faith in July, 1593.

Sixtus V. has left some sermons and other writings.

232. Urban VII., a.d. 1590.

His family name was Castagna. He reigned only thirteen days, but during that short time did much for the welfare of his people. His deathbed was most tranquil and edifying.

233. Gregory XIV., a.d. 1590-1591.

Nicholas Gondrato reigned during ten months. He published a monitory cautioning the French people against Henry IV. and the Calvinists; and he sent aid of all kinds to the League. His habits were exemplary, and both before and after his elevation his private life was without stain.

234. Innocent IX., a.d. 1591.

John Anthony Facchinetti was a native of Bologna. He reigned only two months, and died much regretted by the Romans, whom he intended to relieve of heavy taxes. Indeed, he was full of noble designs, both for the city of Rome and the Church at large.

235. Clement VIII., a.d. 1592-1605.

Hippolytus Aldobrandini was born in 1536 at Fano, in the Roman States. He encouraged piety and knowledge in every part of the Church; condemned duelling; absolved Henry IV. on his conversion; brought back a large number of heretics, and did much for the peace of Vervins, (1598,) between Henry IV. and Philip II. He raised to the rank of cardinal, Baronius, Bellamine, Tolet, d'Ossat, Du Perron, and many other eminent men.

He declined deciding the controversy between the partisans of the Jesuit Father Molina and those of the Dominican, St Thomas, respecting the limits of free will and grace. In his treatise on the agreement between these principles, Molina ascribes a large part to the action of free will, at the risk even of diminishing that of grace; and he supposes in God, in relation to conditional acts, a peculiar kind of knowledge, which he called *scientia media*. His main propositions, which were said to be in contradiction with the teaching of St Thomas Aquinas, divided theologians into two camps, the Molinists and the Thomists, and gave rise to long debates in which Paul V., as well as Clement VIII., wisely refused to interfere.

This Pope published the most accurate edition of the Holy Scriptures.

He seconded Henry IV. in his project for the confederation of the Italian States. The Milanese territory was assigned, in this plan, to the Duke of Savoy, who was to assume the title of King of Lombardy; Sicily was given to the Venetians, and some places of importance to Tuscany; and Naples to the Pope, who was to be the centre and chief of the confederation. A similar scheme was formed in 1848, but failed from various causes, and it was revived more recently under suspicious auspices, in the pamphlet "Napoleon III. et l'Italie," ascribed to the Emperor and the Vicomte de la Guéronnière.

The Cenci family were executed under this Pope.* During his reign also the Roman States were ravaged by Mark Sciarra, a famous bandit chief. He was so hard pressed by Clement VIII. that he quitted the country and went over to the service of Venice, by which power he was sent into Dalmatia with 500 of his own followers to carry on war against the Uscoques. The Venetian Government afterwards, with barbarous treachery, caused Sciarra to be assassinated, because the Pope required that he should be delivered into his hands.

"One cannot," says the Abbé Drioux, "too greatly admire the virtues and talents of the Sovereign Pontiffs whom God placed at the head of His Church during the religious troubles of the sixteenth century. After the death of Leo X. the tiara was given to Adrian VI. This

---

* See *Quarterly Review*, April 1858, p. 377.

austere native of the Netherlands melted into tears over the faults of his predecessors, and set himself to reform in Rome that excess of grandeur and luxury which had scandalised the gravity of the German character. The lamentations of this worthy Pontiff not having sufficed to expiate the ill, Providence punished the eternal city by sending against it, in the reign of Clement VII., Adrian's successor, soldiers excited to fanaticism by the Lutheran Fronderberg. Then, after having thus purified it by suffering, he set over it the celebrated Paul III., who introduced into the sacred college the Contarinis, the Caraffas, the Sadolets, the most holy and the most learned men of their age. Guided by their counsels, he formed the apostolic chamber, the chancery, and the penitentiary. From that time one sees only men of talent and genius seated on the pontifical throne, such as, for example, Pius IV., aided by the learning and the virtues of St Charles Boromeo; St Pius V., victorious at Lepanto through his prayers; Gregory XIII. and Sixtus V., whose abilities have no need of praise. The sixteenth century was closed by Clement VIII., who rejoiced to have at his side Bellarmine and Baronius, the two great lights of Catholicism in their day. These courageous Pontiffs fearlessly took part in all public events, and they alone among all the sovereigns of Europe had the merit of having an avowed object in view, and a policy perfectly consistent with itself. Their principal means of action was through the Council of Trent, the various religious orders, and the genius of men who devoted themselves to the defence of the Catholic faith, which at this period was so vigorously assailed."

236. Leo XI., a.d. 1605.

He was of the Medici family, and reigned only one month. "It is asserted that his new dignity, and the feeling of the arduousness of the office imposed on him, extinguished vital powers already enfeebled by age."*

237. Paul V., a.d. 1605–1621.

This Pope, whose family name was Camillus Borghese, had a disagreement with Venice on the question of ecclesiastical immunity, which was settled by Henry IV. in 1605-7. Suarez was requested by the Pope to write a work on the subject, which was not published till our own time.† He approved the orders of the Oratory, and of the Visitation, and that of St Ursula in 1611. He canonised St Charles Boromeo, and died on the 28th of January, 1621,

---
* Ranke's *Popes*. Book vi.   † *Month*, vol. ii. p. 178.

from the effects of apoplexy, by which he was first struck in a procession to celebrate the victory of the Weissberg.

238. Gregory XV., A.D. 1621-1623.

Alexander Ludovic, a native of Bologna, archbishop of that city, and cardinal, was elected Pope in 1621, at sixty-seven years of age. The Duke de Lesdiguières had said to Gregory XV., before his elevation, "I will be a Catholic when you are Pope." He kept his word, and embraced the faith of his fathers, notwithstanding he had become the leader of the Calvinists.

Gregory raised the See of Paris to be a metropolitan archbishopric.

He founded the Propaganda; canonised Ignatius Loyola; helped the Emperor Ferdinand II. against the Protestants, and died deplored by the poor, who had been the constant objects of his charity. A valuable sketch of the state of Christendom at the time of his decease will be found in Ranke's "History of the Popes," vol. ii.

239. Urban VIII., A.D. 1623-1644.

Maffeo Barberini, before his elevation, had ably filled many important posts. The reunion of the Duchy of Urbino and its dependencies to the

Roman States, (1626–31,) rendered the first part of his reign illustrious; but he was less happy in his dissensions with Venice and Portugal, and in the war of Castro, which seems to have been undertaken for the interests of his family, as well as for those of the State, and was concluded by a disadvantageous peace. "He had," Ranke says, "a favourite notion that the States of the Church must be secured by fortifications, and become formidable by their own arms." He heaped favours and riches on his nephews. For the rest, he fulfilled all that one had a right to expect from a Pope as enlightened as he was virtuous.

He republished the "*In Cœna Domini*" in 1627, and in the "*In eminenti*" a bull scarcely less celebrated, he pronounced the first condemnation of the errors of Jansenius, Bishop of Ypres. He approved the order of the Visitation, and suppressed that of the Jesuitesses who went abroad and preached in churches, as being contrary to sound doctrine. He published, under a new form, the Roman breviary; corrected the hymns of the Church, and cultivated with success Latin and even Italian poetry. His poems were published in Rome in 1640, and in Paris two years afterwards.

240. Innocent X., a.d. 1644–1655.

John Baptist Panfili was a native of Rome, and was elected on the 16th of September. The Duke of Parma being accused of having assassinated the Bishop of Castro, Innocent X. deprived him of his States, and razed Castro to the ground to punish its inhabitants for the part they had taken in the commission of the crime. He exiled the cardinals Francis and Anthony Barberini, notwithstanding they had contributed to his elevation.* In 1653 he condemned the five famous propositions of Jansenius, drawn from his "Augustinus":

"1. Some of the commandments of God, to just men willing and striving, according to their present strength, are impossible; and the grace is wanting to them by which they might become possible.

"2. In the state of fallen nature there is never any resistance to inward grace.

"3. In the state of fallen nature freedom from necessity in man is not requisite for meriting reward, but only freedom from coercion.

"4. The Semipelagians allowed the necessity of preventing inward grace for every action, even for incipient faith; and they were

* Ranke, vol. iii. pp. 40–42.

heretical in that thus, they made grace something which human will may either obey or resist.

"5. It is semipelagian to say that Christ died for all men, or shed His blood for all."

In condemning these propositions of Jansenius, Innocent X. only followed up the work which his predecessor had begun. How wonderful it is to trace such inflexible uniformity of doctrine, ranging over an extensive field of theology, in 259 Pontiffs of character so different, and placed in circumstances so varied and often so exquisitely trying! Those who cannot discern the hand-writing of God in the dogmatical decrees of the Popes, whether affirmative or condemnatory, are blinder than were the Assyrians in the banquet-hall of Baltazar; for how, except on the supposition of an especial providence preserving them from doctrinal error, is it possible to account for a phenomenon so striking and so unparalleled in history as that of which I speak?

Innocent X.'s last years were embittered by family dissensions. He died on the 5th January, and "the corpse," says Ranke, "lay for three days before one of those belonging to him, on whom, according to the usage of the court, this office devolved, took the smallest care for its interment."* Let us hope, for the credit of Innocent's court, that the historian, so accurate in general, may have been misinformed.

241. ALEXANDER VII., A.D. 1655–1667.

Fabio Chigi was born at Sienna in 1599, and elected Pope on the 7th of April. He had always been regarded as a wise and virtuous man. He reformed many abuses, embellished Rome, approved the bull of Innocent X. against Jansenius, and prescribed the famous formulary in 1665, which Louis XIV. obliged his subjects, under heavy penalties, to sign. His successor, Clement IX., terminated this affair by an agreement, which acquired the name of the "Peace of the Church," in 1668. The Duke de Crequi, the French ambassador in Rome, having been insulted by the Corsican guard, the Pope was obliged by Louis XIV. to disband his guard, and to erect a pyramid in Rome with an inscription recording the outrage, and the satisfaction. This was in 1662. Alexander VII. was accustomed to devote his afternoons to literature. Authors resorted to his presence and read their works aloud, and it was one of his favourite recreations to suggest amendments. His brother

* *Popes* vol. iii. p. 50.

Don Mario, and his nephews Flavio and Agostino, were brought by him to the capital and installed in posts of high emolument.*

242. Clement IX., A.D. 1667–1669.

Julius Rospigliosi was born at Pistoia in 1599. He governed the Church wisely, and observed moderation in the advancement of his kinsmen. Ranke says, "It was agreed by acclamation, that it was impossible to find a better or a kinder man." He strove to reunite Christian princes and procure aid for the Venetians against the Turks, who besieged Candia during the long period of twenty-four year, (1645–1669,) and at last took this important place. He died in 1669, aged seventy-one.

243. Clement X., A.D. 1670–1676.

Emilius Altieri was elected at the age of eighty years, after a vacancy of several months, occasioned by some differences among the cardinals. His age prevented him from doing anything by himself. The government was left to Cardinal Anthony Peluzzi.

Like Innocent X. and Alexander VII. he leaned in his policy to the side of the Spaniards.

* Ranke, vol. iii. p. 56.

For this Louis XIV., who could endure no divergence from his own system, avenged himself by incessant encroachments on the spiritual power.

244. INNOCENT XI., A.D. 1676–1689.

Benedict Odescalchi had been a soldier before he entered the priesthood. Several differences arose between him and Louis XIV. One of these regarded the *regale* of the king of France, and another the *droit de franchise* of the French ambassador in Rome, in virtue of which he afforded an asylum to all sorts of offenders and ruffians in privileged districts under his special protection in that city. The *regale* consisted in the crown receiving the revenues of vacant bishoprics, and presenting to the benefices attached to them. The dispute became serious. Adherents of the Holy See were banished from France. Louis made the champions of his authority bishops, and Innocent denied them institution. They took possession of the temporalities, but could not discharge the episcopal functions. Before the end of the struggle, there were in France thirty prelates who could not ordain or confirm. The Pope refused to receive Lavardin, the ambassador of Louis, and having excommunicated him for daring to enter Rome, the king was preparing reprisals when Innocent XI. died. He condemned the errors of Molinos, a Spanish priest, and author of "Quietism," which inculcated an inactive, unsolicitous, and purely contemplative repose of the soul. Innocent XI. had a severe and often inflexible character, but he strove to revive discipline, deprived ignorant and disorderly men of office, and provided for the wants of the poor. In the year 1682, the Gallican clergy, in a general assembly, Bossuet and thirty-five bishops being present, put forth a "Declaration concerning ecclesiastical power," which containing, as it does, the essence of Gallicanism, greatly displeased Pope Innocent XI. The main articles in this document set forth:

"1. That power has been given by God to Blessed Peter and his successors, the vicars of Christ, and to the Church herself, over things spiritual and relating to eternal salvation, but not over civil and temporal matters; the Lord saying, 'My kingdom is not of this world;' and, also, 'Render therefore unto Cæsar the things which are Cæsar's, and unto God the things which are God's.' The Apostle says, likewise, 'Let every soul be subject to the higher powers,' &c. Kings and princes, therefore, in temporal matters are by God's ordinance subject to no ecclesiastical power, nor can they be deposed by the authority of the Keys of the Church, directly or indirectly; nor can their subjects be exempted from their oath of allegiance, or released from fidelity and obedience; and this opinion is necessary for public tranquillity, and not less useful to the Church than to the State, and is to be held fast as altogether consonant with the Word of God, the tradition of the fathers, and the example of the saints.

"2. But full power over spiritual things resides in the Apostolic See, and the successors of St Peter, the vicars of Christ, in such wise as that at the same time the decrees concerning the authority of general councils, which are contained in the fourth and fifth sessions of the holy œcumenical synod of Constance, approved by the Apostolic See, and confirmed by the usage of the Roman Pontiffs and the entire Church, and guarded with perpetual reverence by the Gallican Church, be still in force and stand unshaken. Nor does the Gallican Church command those who in presence of those decrees, as if they were of doubtful authority and little approved, infringe their force or apply the words of the council merely to a time of schism.

"3. Hence the use of the Apostolic power is to be moderated by the canons established by the spirit of God, and consecrated by the respect of the whole world. The rules also, customs, and institutions received from the kingdom and Church of France are in force, and the limits marked by the fathers remain unmoved; and it pertains to the greatness of the Apostolic See that the statutes and usages confirmed by the consent of the Churches and of so great a See should retain their proper stability.

"4. In questions of faith, also, the principal part belongs to the chief Pontiff, and his decrees concern all and each of the Churches; yet his judgment is not irrevocable unless it obtain the consent of the Church."

It is not surprising that these affirmations displeased the Pope. It was hardly the part of a provincial synod to define his power and privileges, and it would be difficult to prove that the Church has not the right of absolving subjects from their oaths of allegiance, when aderence to such oaths would involve shipwreck of a good conscience, treason to the Church, and violation of the laws of God. The fourth article involves a question of great delicacy, and I purposely abstain from attempting to discuss it, as such a discussion would be quite out of place in an elementary book like the present. Suffice it to say, that many theological writers maintain that the Pope is infallible, and his instructions or decrees are binding of themselves whenever he speaks *ex cathedrâ*—*i.e.*, as universal teacher—on matters of faith and morals; while others are of opinion that the express or tacit consent of the episcopate is necessary in order to give them this character.

Innocent XI. recommended James II. of England that moderation and prudence in which he was so distressingly wanting. If, without infringing in any way the liberties of his Protestant subjects, James had contented himself with steadily and unostentatiously promoting the unfeigned principles of civil and religious freedom, and, by the mode of educating his offspring, had rendered such benign government traditional, a Stuart might now be upon the throne of England, and England in great part within the fold of the Catholic Church. Violent and unconstitutional exercise of the royal authority was the rock on which he wrecked himself, his dynasty, and his sacred cause. His ambassador at Rome, Castelmaine, was coldly received by the Sovereign Pontiff. Innocent, after long delay, refused his petition that Father Peter, a Jesuit, should be mitred. Castelmaine hereupon threatened to leave Rome, and the Pope provokingly replied that his Excellency might go if he liked, giving him, at the same time, advice as to the best mode of travelling.*

---

* Macaulay, *Hist. of England*, vol. iii. p. 96.

The invariable principles, however, of the Catholic religion require that heresy should be suppressed whenever it is practicable. Accordingly, in 1685, the Pope addressed a brief to Louis XIV., congratulating him on the Revocation of the Edict of Nantes, and the document, as we learn from Barrillon, the French ambassador in London afforded the King of England great satisfaction.* Notwithstanding this approval of the Revocation, Innocent, in 1688, feeling himself obliged to act on the defensive against Louis, adhered to the Treaty of Augsburg, of which the Prince of Orange was the chief promoter, and by which a formidable coalition was banded against France.†

245. Alexander VIII., A.D. 1689–1691.

Peter Ottoboni was born at Venice in 1610. He published a bull against the four articles of 1682, and withheld his favour from the Gallican prelates who had signed them. In 1690 he addressed several briefs to Madame de Maintenon, authorising the transfer of the revenues of the Abbey of St Denis to the establishment of St Cyr, and expressing the warm interest he felt in that undertaking.

---

* Duc de Noailles. *Hist. de Madame de Maintenon*, vol. ii. p. 450.
† Idem, vol. iv. p. 253.

He sent large pecuniary aid to Leopold I. and the Venetians, to assist them in carrying on a war against the Turks.

246. Innocent XII., a.d. 1691–1700.

Anthony Pignatolli had all the good qualities of Innocent XI., and was elected on account of his inclination to conciliatory measures. He showed himself a rigorous censor of morals, bestowed office on worthy individuals only, and was the father of the poor.

After the necessary concessions made by Louis XIV. and the French clergy, he terminated the differences which had existed between Innocent XI. and France. The articles of 1682 were annulled, and those who had compiled them expressed their grief at having done so.

He also concluded the affair of Quietism, and condemned Fénelon's "Explication des Maximes des Saints," which was tainted with Jansenism.

247. Clement XI., a.d. 1700–1721.

John Francis Albani was born at Pesaro in 1649. He twice refused the tiara. To end the troubles in the Church of France, he condemned the five propositions of Jansenius in the bull "Vineam Domini Sabaoth." He issued the celebrated constitution "Unigenitus," which condemned a hundred and one propositions of the Jansenist Quesnel in 1713, and Benedict XIII. convened a council at Rome to confirm it in 1725. Clement XI. died in 1721, aged seventy-two. He was learned and pious, and ruled prudently in most difficult times. The character of the Popes, and, indeed, of the clergy in general, since the time of the council of Trent, commands increasing admiration and respect.

The War of the succession in Spain caused Clement XI. great embarrassment and trouble. Charles II. had bequeathed the crown to a grandson of Louis XIV., and this testament was disputed by Austria. Though Clement at one time congratulated Philip V. on his accession, he was afterwards obliged to recognise his Austrian rival, Charles VI., as the Catholic king.*

243. Innocent XIII., a.d. 1721-1724.

Michael Angelo Conti, who was elected in May, was the eighth Pope of his family. In 1723 he published the bull "Apostolici Ministerii," concerning discipline. He granted a pension to Prince James Edward, son of James II. of England, and obtained of the Emperor of

* Ranke, vol. iii. p. 180.

Germany the restitution of Comacchio to the States of the Church. During his time, and that of the two succeeding Popes, the Catholic governments of Europe united in a strange hostility to the Roman court, and stripped the Roman See of many of its temporal rights and privileges. This deplorable state of things continued till the time of Benedict XIV. Innocent possessed the advantage of long experience, and was endowed with admirable qualities both for spiritual and temporal government. He died March 7, 1724.

249. Benedict XIII., A.D. 1724–1730.

He was a Roman of the Orsini family. He entered the Dominican order, became Bishop of Manfredonia, Ceseno, and Benevento, and was elected Pope on the 29th May, 1724. Benedict XIII. was eminently pious and charitable, and caused Rome to bless his name. Capello speaks of him as "remarkably resolute, ardent, and active in all ecclesiastical affairs." Always unwilling to resort to extremes, he saw with satisfaction the loyalty with which Cardinal de Noailles, Archbishop of Paris, accepted the bull "Unigenitus," and he issued another called "Pretiosus," in which he explained the former document and its bearings on the doctrines of grace. James Stuart, the heir to the crown of England, had in his time settled in Bologna, and the Pope increased the pension which his predecessor had granted to that prince.

250. Clement XII., a.d. 1730-1740.

His family name was Laurence Corsini. He was a Florentine by birth, and was elected Pope in July, 1730. He invested Don Carlos as King of Naples and Sicily, diminished the taxes in his own States, punished those who had misappropriated public money during the preceding reign, and governed the Church with wisdom He restored the little republic of San Marino to its liberties, which had been infringed. Mocenigo says he was "distinguished by the accomplishments of a gentleman and a magnificent prelate." He died in 1740, aged eighty-eight, and bowed down by many infirmities.

251. Benedict XIV., a d. 1740-1758.

Prosper Lambertini, of Bologna, was born on the 13th of March, 1675.

At an early age he had been remarkable for his aptitude in all branches of science. He became counsellor of the holy office, and canonist of the penitentiary. In 1727 he was made

Bishop of Ancona, cardinal in 1728, and Archbishop of Bologna in 1732. He was the most learned divine of the eighteenth century, had the merit of comprehending the true position of the Church, and by means of wise concessions succeeded in re-establishing peace between the Papal See and some of the disaffected courts of Europe. The Concordat made with Spain in 1753 is an example in point. In this treaty the Roman Curia renounced the patronage of the smaller benefices in that kingdom. Being of an enlightened and conciliating character, Benedict tried to calm religious disputes, and to obviate some inconveniences which had been occasioned by the bull "Unigenitus."

He promoted some reforms among the Jesuits of Portugal, and encouraged and himself cultivated science and letters. His numerous works were published at Bassano in 1788, in fifteen volumes folio. The most important of these were the treatises on the Beatification, on the Holy Sacrifice of the Mass, and on Synods. "It is well known," says Ranke, "how little Benedict XIV. suffered himself to be dazzled or elated by the elevation of his dignity, nor did it destroy his good-humoured jocularity and Bolognese wit. He rose from his work, joined his courtiers, communicated to them some idea which had just entered his head, and returned to his desk. His attention was steadily directed to essentials." He died on the 3d of May, 1758.

252. Clement XIII., A.D. 1758–1769.

Charles Rezzonico was born at Venice in 1693. He was already distinguished for his piety and private virtues when raised to the Popedom in July, 1758. He endeavoured in vain to support the numerous Jesuits expelled from France, Spain, and Naples. He lost the "county of Avignon" through the adverse policy of the King of France, and the Duchy of Benevento through disputes with the young Bourbon Duke of Parma. His successor, however, Clement XIV., smothered away the differences and recovered the possessions. During his pontificate many of the sovereigns of Europe attempted to put such a pressure on him as should constrain him to suppress the Jusuit order. Resistance to ecclesiastical authority was the order of the day, and even Maria Theresa, the Venetian Senate, the Elector of Bavaria, the Dukes of Tuscany and Parma, and the King of Naples caused trouble and annoyance in various ways to the Holy See. In the midst of difficulties which they raised, Clement XIII. died. A splendid mausoleum was erected to his memory in St Peter's by Pius VI. The workmen who were engaged on it eight years, were directed by Canova.

253. Clement XIV., a.d. 1769–1774.

Laurence Ganganelli was born in the Duchy of Urbino, in 1705. He was of the order of the Franciscans. His election was supported by France. His Character was conciliating, and he lived in harmony with the courts of Europe in consequence of his showing a disposition to yield to some of their importunate demands. Urged by several princes, after some years' delay he suppressed by bull the order of the Jesuits, on the 21st of July, 1773. He was said to have been poisoned in 1774, but the story is false. The "Letters" ascribed to him are not authentic. They are one of the most elegant and beautiful inventions which literature can boast, and no one can peruse them without regretting that they should be spurious.

I here subjoin some particulars respecting the Society of Jesus and its suppression, which I have taken principally from two French writers.*

* Bouillet—*Dictionnaire d'Histoire, Corrige et Autorise par le Saint-Siege.* Drioux—*Precis d'Histoire Ecclesiastique.*

The Jesuits.

Of all the Religious orders, the Society of Jesus has been the most illustrious for its learning, its devotion to the Holy See, and zeal in the cause of education and missions. It was founded in 1534 by Ignatius Loyola, of Biscay, in Spain, and was approved in 1540 by Pope Paul III. The propagation of the faith at the time when that faith was vehemently assailed by various foes, was the great object to which all its efforts were consecrated. Its members made a special vow of obedience to the commands of the Sovereign Pontiff. This society, which has acted so important a part in history, is eminently remarkable for its constitution. Its general resided at Rome, and from that spot exercised absolute rule over its members spread throughout Christendom. He had five assistants at hand who formed his council, and a monitor, whose office it was to watch over the words and movements of the general himself. Under his orders in each country were provincials, each of whom had charge of a province. There were in the order three degrees—the professed, who had taken their vows; the coadjutors, temporal and spiritual; and, lastly, the novices and scholars. All members before admission into the society underwent long and varied probation, after which each one was employed in accordance with his particular bent and capacity. The order took rise in Paris, where Ignatius Loyola had come to study theology. Together with him, among its first apostles, were Laynez, Salmeron, Bobadilla, Francis Xavier, and Rodriguez, all Spaniards, and Peter Favre of Savoy. It was instituted under the title of Clerks of the Company of Jesus, and was first established at Rome, in which city the Pope gave to the society the church which took the name of Il Gesù. The society spread rapidly in Italy, Spain, and Portugal. Although Paris had been its cradle, it was not admitted into France till after long debates; it had to sustain strong opposition on the part, above all, of the parliament and the university, and it was not till 1562 that it obtained at last permission to teach in the kingdom of France. The Jesuits have rendered incontestable and great services to humanity; they have obtained signal success in the education of youth, and also in preaching. By their courageous missions, which no dangers or difficulties could arrest, they have carried the faith of Jesus Christ into the most distant lands, and among the most barbarous people, from whom they have received innumerable crosses and crowns of martyrdom. The have numbered in their ranks some of the most eminent men that have ever lived, eminent not in one field of science only, but in the most varied attainments; such were the fathers Bourdaloue, Bouhours, André, Bolland, and a multitude beside. Though they have been accused of being implicated in various plots and conspiracies, of mixing too much in politics, and of teaching a system of loose morality, nothing has ever been proved against them so as to substantiate these charges. The hostility they have met with has been mainly due to the unworldly character of their order, the inflexibility of their principles, their courageous zeal, and the purity of their lives. They have been banished at different times from many of the States into which they had been admitted, and this from various causes according to the caprice of rulers, or the pressure of political troubles. They were driven from England in 1581 and 1601, from France in 1594 and 1762, from Portugal in 1593 and 1759, from Russia in 1717 and 1817, from China in 1753, and from Spain and Sicily in 1767. The society, as mentioned above, was suppressed in 1773 by Clement XIV. A useless endeavour had been made to induce the Jesuit fathers to consent to an alteration of their statutes. Laurence Ricci, their general, is said to have replied to this proposition in the following firm and pithy terms: "*Sint ut sunt, aut non sint,*" ("Let them be as they are, or not at all.") Notwithstanding the formal suppression of the order by Ganganelli, they continued to exist under different names in certain countries, and particularly in Russia, where the Empress Catherine II. granted them an asylum in 1779. They were solemnly re-established by Pius VII. in 1814, and very soon were recalled by many of the States which had banished them, and found they had exiled their most faithful servants and best friends. They re-entered France at the restoration of the Bourbon dynasty, under the name of Fathers of the Faith, and during some years they had flourishing colleges, which were closed in the latter part of the reign of Charles X., (1828.) Many of these have been reopened since 1848.

The Coalition Against the Jesuits.

Even sovereigns in the eighteenth century took part with the fashionable philosophy of their time, and formed a coalition against the suspected order. The Marquis de Pombal, who governed Portugal in the name of Joseph I., gave the signal. He began by spreading throughout Europe a multitude of libels in which the Jesuits were calumniated in the blackest manner. They were accused of being accomplices in a frightful conspiracy against the king his master, and

Pombal demanded the suppression of the order from the Sovereign Pontiff. Not being able to obtain it, he caused them to be interdicted in Portugal; he surrounded their houses by soldiers who arrested them and conducted them to dismal prisons and dungeons, whence they were soon dragged in order to be packed together in vessels which deposited them, deprived of everything they possessed, on some wild coasts of the Roman States. Spain closely followed the example thus set by Portugal, and France was not slow in doing likewise. Without hearing them, without admitting their complaints, their constitutions were declared impious and sacrilegious, their colleges were closed, their novices dispersed, their goods seized, and their vows annulled. It seemed but little to the enemies of religion to have driven away the Jesuits from their peaceful homes; they were bent on obtaining from the Pope the suppression of the entire order. The Roman Church possessed in different kingdoms lands which kings had given from time to time to the Holy See. At the same moment these were confiscated, and the ambassadors of the sovereigns in question at the court of Rome declared that they would not be restored so long as the Jesuits existed as a religious order. Besides all this, they uttered in the Pope's ears still more terrible menaces, and feared not to declare that the annihilation of the society was the only means of re-establishing union between the Holy See and the foreign courts.

Clement XIV. was intimidated, but he prolonged the affair to the utmost, and anxiously sought means of saving the persecuted religious from the impending blow. But at length, being more hardly pressed than ever, he consented to publish the fatal brief which suppressed the Society of Jesus. . The philosophy of the times applauded and extolled the Pontiff who had the weakness to consent to this measure. Ganganelli discovered his mistake; and his death is thought by many to have been occasioned by the sorrow which it caused him.

The suppression of the Jesuits became a signal for discord and insurrection against the Holy See. On all sides pamphlets were published and libels propagated against the Papacy; rash and headstrong writers misunderstood its rights, despised its authority, and attacked directly the hierarchy of the Church. It was in Germany above all that these dangerous novelties attracted the largest number of partisans. Joseph II., son and successor of Maria Theresa, protected and emboldened these innovators, with a view of forming a national church and of separating his subjects altogether from the Church of Rome. The policy of the free-thinking emperor was so far completely identical with that of Protestant princes before him. He forbade recourse to the Sovereign Pontiff for dispensations of marriage, and by his own authority suppressed a multitude of convents and appropriated their revenues, forbade the bishops during a certain period from conferring holy orders, abolished processions, rescinded certain festivals, and regulated the ceremonies of religious worship and the number of masses. Pius VI. went himself to Vienna to check the emperor in his scandalous and rash undertakings. Joseph II., however, delayed not to excite new troubles for the Pope in Lombardy, in reference to the nomination of the Archbishop of Milan; and he had the audacity to go to Rome, under pretext of returning the Pontiff's visit, but in reality in order to form a league against him. Some private interviews which he had with Azara, Minister of State in Spain, caused him to renounce this last project. Nevertheless, he still continued to disquiet the States which were subject to his sway, and to counteract the Papal intentions.

254. Pius VI., a.d. 1775–1799.

John Angelo Braschi was born at Ceseno in 1717. He distinguished himself by useful reforms and great undertakings, such as the draining of the Pontine Marshes, and the construction of the Appian Way. But he was soon interrupted in these peaceful projects by the misfortunes of his time. He had to combat the hostile dispositions not only of Joseph II., the Emperor of Austria, but also of Leopold, Grand Duke of Tuscany, and, above all, of revolutionary France.

Joseph II dealt blow after blow at the system of ecclesiastical discipline which prevailed in the empire, and enforced irregularities which neither the entreaties of Pius VI. nor his journey into Germany were able to cancel or arrest. " What shall we say," asks De Maistre, " of the Pope being first despoiled on *terra firma*, then taken to Venice by the apostolic cabinet under the plausible pretext of the most august hospitality, and there required to deliver up his states, and at last treated with sulks and slights because he took the liberty of refusing to accede to this Catholic proposition ?" On the 12th of July, in the year 1790, a "civil constitution of the Gallican clergy" was published by the National Assembly, and all bishops and other ministers of religion were ordered to accept it on oath. It provided a bishop for each department, election of bishops and *curés* by the people, a salary provided for them by the State, and an annual dotation of only 77,000,000 francs as a substitute for the former revenues and benefices of the clergy. The king, much against his will, accepted this decree on the 26th of December. Some ecclesiastics adhered to it, and were called *assermentés;* the greater part nobly refused, and were called *nonassermentés.*

In a brief of the 11th of March, 1791, and in a monitory letter of the 13th of April in the same year, Pius VI. condemned this presumptious constitution as heretical and sacrilegious, and stigmatized the civil oath as the source of all kinds of poisonous errors, and the especial cause of the distress of the Gallican Church. In this all the bishops of France concurred, with four exceptions.

After the accidental murder of a French envoy, Basseville, on the 13th of January, 1793, the States of the Pope were invaded, and he was forced by General Bonaparte to sign the treaty of Tolintino, February 19, 1797, which deprived him of thirty-one millions of francs, several provinces, and the most precious objects of art. By this treaty Bologna, Ferrara, and Romagna were yielded to the Cisalpine Republic.

This Pope was distinguished in every way, in family, knowledge, piety, prudence, and liberality to all who were in want. God chose him to preside over His Church in the most difficult times, and he proved himself worthy of the arduous task.

255. Pius VII., A.D. 1800–1823.

Barnabas Chiaramonti was born at Cesena in 1740. He was a Benedictine. He became Bishop of Tivoli in 1780, cardinal and bishop of Imola in 1785. He was elected after an interregnum and long conclave in Venice in 1800.

He reorganised his States, signed a concordat with Bonaparte in 1801, and went to Paris to crown him in 1804. Soon, however, he had cause to complain of the emperor, and excommunicated him in January, 1809, when Rome had been invaded. On the 10th of June in that year Napoleon published a proclamation in the Pope's capital, declaring that, for several reasons, or rather pretexts, the Papal territory was annexed to that of the French Empire, and the Pope's yearly revenue fixed at two million francs. Soon after this outrageous act, Pius VII. was carried off by force to Savona and then to Fontainebleau, where he endured a hard captivity. "Never," says Count de Maistre, "has any sovereign laid hands on any Pope whatsoever, either with or without reason, (which I do not now examine,) and been able afterwards to boast of a long and happy reign. Henry V. suffered all that a man and a prince can suffer. His unnatural son died of the plague at forty-four years of age, after a very stormy reign. Frederic II. was poisoned by his son after having been deposed. Philippe le Bel died of a fall from his horse at the age of forty-seven. My pen refuses to cite more modern instances."*

In 1813 Pius had made some concessions which he soon retracted. His chains were not broken till the beginning of 1814, when England and Russia, in opposition to the desires of Austria, concurred in re-establishing his temporal throne. He returned to Rome, where he generously gave an asylum to the family of his greatest persecutor.

"Here is a book of facts," says Dr Newman, speaking of Cardinal Pacca's Memoirs of Pope Pius VII's captivity, "here is a narrative, simple and natural. It does not give you the history of a hero, or of a saint; but of a good religious man, who would rather have died any moment than offend God; who had an overpowering sense of his responsibility, yet a diffidence in his own judgment which made him sometimes err in his line of conduct. Here, too, is vividly brought out before you, what we mean by Papal infallibility, or rather what we do not mean by it. You see how the Pope was open to any mistake, as others may be, in his own person, true as it is, that whenever he spoke *ex cathedrâ* on subjects of revealed truth, he spoke as its divinely ordained expounder."†

* Letters, &c., du Comte J. de Maistre, tome i. p. 241.
† See also *Dublin Review*, January, 1865, p. 51.

The Abbé Drioux gives the following summary of the wrongs inflicted upon Pius VI. and Pius VII.:

The convention being exhausted by the excess of its own violence, France was given over to a new government which took the name of the Directory. The armies of this assembly having invaded Italy, hastened to proscribe religion in that country, and to spread abroad the destructive principles which had caused so many disasters in France. They received orders to penetrate into the States of the Church, and there to proclaim the republic and the abolition of the pontifical government. In the first instance, the Pope was assured that he would be respected and recognised always as Bishop of Rome, but these promises were soon forgotten. General Duphot having been killed in a sedition at Rome, it was attacked by the French, and on the night of the 19th or 20th of February, 1798, Pius VI. was torn from his palace and carried off from that city. A great number of cardinals and bishops shared the same fate, and a military government, which weighed the people down with exactions, took the place of the pacific authority of the Sovereign Pontiff. The head of the Church, captive and despoiled of everything, was dragged about from one place to another as an exile at the will of his enemies. The venerable old man had at least the consolation of seeing the people throng around him on his way, and solicit with tears the blessing which they felt it their happiness to receive. Having been conducted to Grenoble, and afterwards removed to Valence, he was there attacked at the end of six weeks with an illness, the consequences of which brought him to the grave. His strength was completely exhausted, and he died on the 29th of August, 1799, at the age of eighty-two, after having filled the Holy See more than four-and-twenty years. Pius VI. was no more, and the cardinals, dispersed or in captivity, could not reunite to give to the Church a pastor and to Rome a worthy and suitable sovereign. But an over-ruling power provided for this extremity. Suddenly the French were driven from Rome and Italy. The Emperor of Germany convoked the cardinals in order to appoint a successor to Pius VI. They assembled at Venice, formed a conclave, and elected the Cardinal Barnabas Chiaramonti, who took the name of Pius VII. The new Pope signalised the commencement of his reign by wise and honourable measures; he hastened to establish order in the Roman Church, and very soon entered into negotiations with the new French Government respecting ecclesiastical matters. Bonaparte was at the head of the Republic, which he administered under the title of First Consul. His penetrating genius saw that it was time to restore to France her religion and worship, and that the people were weary of the reign of impiety. He laboured, therefore, to overcome the resistance of the *Corps Legislatif* which maintained with all its might the constitutional church of 1790, and showed itself profoundly imbued with Voltairian doctrines. In this project he succeeded, and the concordat which he had made with the new Pope (1801) was adopted as the law of the land. At the same time, two bulls of the Pope were published; the first developed and ratified the conventions made with the French Government; the second suppressed all the Sees of France, and formed in their stead sixty new ones. Before publishing this bull Pius VII. had addressed a brief to the old bishops soliciting their resignation. Some had refused, but these for the most part afterwards submitted. As soon as the concordat was publicly known, the exercises of worship was re-established throughout France. On Easter-day the cardinal-legate celebrated mass at Notre Dame, in the presence of the consuls and all the *Corps de l'Etat*. The *Te Deum* was chanted as a thanksgiving for these happy changes, and for the re-establishment of the Catholic faith and worship. Peace and confidence began to revive. The pastors of the widowed churches returned from foreign lands where they had groaned in exile, and reappeared in the midst of their flocks. Congregations of the *filles hospitalières* and of

Christian doctrine were formed, and permission was given even to some brotherhoods to reunite for the service of the Church. The priests spread through the towns and villages, instructed the people, and revived the faith in their hearts. The Sovereign Pontiff, consoled by this grand spectacle, had his eyes at the same time fixed on the churches of Piedmont, Italy, and Germany. He hastened to provide them with pastors, to re-establish discipline, and to cause religion to flourish in the provinces from whence the disasters of recent wars had banished both.

Napoleon meanwhile, who had thus restored to the Catholic religion her temples and her altars, marched on from victory to victory, and France, dazzled by his glory, threw herself at his feet and invested him with absolute power. He had taken the title of Emperor, and had been recognised as such by all the nations of Europe. In order to render his authority more imposing in the eyes of the people, he resolved to be crowned by the Sovereign Pontiff. Pius VII. crossed the mountains and came to Paris. He received on his road every testimony of veneration, and was astonished to find so much faith among a people whom the enemies of religion had tried so hard to pervert. He remained four months in France, and during this time occupied himself with the affairs and interests of the Church. When returned to Rome he expressed his satisfaction to the cardinals, and recounted all that Providence had enabled him to effect. Unhappily Napoleon, after having rendered such great service to religion, allowed himself to be dazzled by his own glory, and scrupled not to have recourse to violence in order to oblige the Pope to approve his projects. From his imperial camp in Vienna he decreed the reunion of the States of the Church with the French empire, and on the 6th of July, 1809, the very day on which he achieved one of his most brilliant victories at Wagram, General Radet received orders to carry off the Pope from Rome. The venerable old man was successively transferred to Valence, Avignon, Nice, and finally to Savona, which was the place appointed for his exile. The elated conqueror approved a commission of bishops who were to report upon the difficult situation of affairs. The authority of the Sovereign Pontiff was indispensably necessary to sanction the proceedings of this assembly, but no one dared to suggest to Napoleon any expedient by which he could escape from the course marked out by his own head-strong will. He convoked a council at Paris, but this synod declared that nothing could stand in the place of the Papal bulls, (1811.)

14

Napoleon caused Pius VII. to be transported to Fontainebleau, in hopes that he might thus be able to master his will more easily. In truth, he obtained some concessions from the unhappy Pontiff, but these were no sooner made than regretted by the Pope as an act of weakness, and his faith supplied him anew with fortitude and resolution superior to the infirmities of his age. But after the fearful reverses which befell the French arms during the campaign of 1812, the emperor hastened to put an end to all these differences which he had with the Sovereign Pontiff, in order that he might have no other care than that of defending France against a foreseen invasion. After five years' exile Pius VII. returned to Rome amid the acclamations of his people, and completed his reign in peace.

A few words respecting the changes seen at Rome during the Papal history must not be thought a digression; for, in a Manual like the present, recapitulations of this sort are often indispensable.

The Vicissitudes of Rome.

When Italy had become Greek again, Rome, which, since the year 404, had no longer been even the capital of Italy, became the chief city of a separate Duchy, called the Duchy of Rome, and this, being one of the provinces of the Pentapolis, was subject to the exarchs, or viceroys of the Greek Emperors; but the delegate of the exarch had in reality less authority there than the Pope. Under Leo III. the Iconoclast, Rome, and all the duchy rebelled against the exarchate, and formed, in fact, an independent republic, governed by the Popes, in 728; being in turn menaced by the Emperors of Constantinople and the Lombards, she solicited the aid of the Frank sovereigns. After the fall of the exarchate in 752, and of the kingdom of the Lombards in 774. Rome and its duchy, which Pepin had in some sort given to the Pope, were, by the illustrious son of this Prince, Charlemagne, who had confirmed his father's donation, placed under the powerful protection of France. But under the feeble successors of this great monarch this protection would have been invoked in vain; and the authority of the Pope in Rome was more than once despised or annihilated by powerful parties.

In the tenth century the family Marosia held the dominion and disposed scandalously of the Papacy, until the Emperor Otho I. re-established order by suppressing the reigning factions in the year 962. Nevertheless, Rome did not cease to be agitated under Otho II. and III., and still more in the reign of Henry II. The evil had reached its highest pitch, when the Emperor Henry III. remedied it in a violent manner, by making Rome bend to the law of the Emperors, and by imposing on the See Pontiffs of his own choice. From that time stricter morality reigned in the apostolic line, but the Pope soon had to defend the liberty of the Church and of Italy against the Emperors. Rome, with Milan, was the soul of resistance. Unhappily the Popes, while they combated the emperors, often saw their own authority shaken in Rome; sometimes imperial troops, and sometimes powerful families or demagogues, expelled them or reduced them to flight. Henry IV., after three sieges in 1081, drove out St Gregory VII., the illustrious Hildebrand.

During the quarrels of Innocent II. and Anacletus II., (1140,) Arnold de Bressia established a republic and senate at Rome, and the city did not submit to its lawful sovereign until 1149.

Gregory IX. fled before Frederick II., when marching upon Rome in 1241; in 1281 the nobles, who had become masters of Rome, refused to receive into the city the Pope Martin IV.; in 1347, favoured by the absence of the Popes, who since 1309 had resided at Avignon, the famous Rienzi, the last of the Tribunes, established a republic in Rome; but this state of things had but a momentary duration. The

Popes, however, did not immediately become masters of Rome again, and when Albornoz (from the year 1364) was preparing the return of the sovereign Pontiffs, (which took place in 1377,) the great families, and especially the Colonnas and the Orsini, exercised greater authority than did the lawful sovereigns, and continued to exercise it in various degrees down to the beginning of the sixteenth century.

The end of the great schism commenced the re-establishment of the Papal power in Rome. Alexander VI. and Julius II. and the two Popes of the Medicis family, Leo X. and Clement VII., consolidated it in the period between 1492 and 1534. In the interval Rome was nearly taken by assault by Charles VIII., when on his way to the conquest of Naples in 1495; and in 1527 it was actually taken by the Constable de Bourbon. When the domination of the Spaniards in Italy had at length restored order there, Rome passed through another phase. Already the Popes Julius II. and Leo X. had embellished it, and their successors, especially Sixtus V., trod in their steps. Rome became more than ever the resort of pilgrims, of travellers, of artists, and of learned men. The French revolution alone troubled this tranquility. Berthier, with the soldiers of the Republic, wrested Rome from the Pope, and by proclamation in 1798, declared it to be subject to the dominion of France. By the peace of Lunéville, in 1801, Rome was restored to Pius VII., but in 1808 Napoleon united it together with a great part of the States of the Church, to the French Empire; he declared Rome to be the second city of the imperial territory, and made it the capital of the department of the Tiber, in which he appointed a French *Prefet*.

Such were some of the most remarkable vicissitudes in the history of Rome until the forced abdication of Napoleon in 1814.

256. Leo XII., a.d. 1823–1829.

His family name was Annibale della Genga. He was born at Genga, near Spoleto, in 1760, and was vicar general of Pius VII.

He embellished Rome, encouraged letters, enlarged the library of the Vatican, and died universally venerated in February, 1829. It was he who reorganised the university of the Sapienza at Rome, which consisted of five colleges or faculties, theology, law, medicine, philosophy, and philology, increased the number of professors, and raised their salaries. He also reformed the administration and the *procedura civile*, and fixed the fees of the litigants. Chateaubriand was the French ambassador in Rome during eighteen months of this Pontificate, and, in his letters to Madame Récamier, written during that time, gives interesting accounts of the events of his embassy, the death of Leo, the Conclave, and election of Pius VIII.

257. Pius VIII., A.D. 1829–1830.

Saverion Castiglione was born at Cingoli, in the States of the Church, in 1761. He was Bishop of Frascati at the time of his election in March, 1829, and reigned only one year and eight months. Many interesting particulars respecting him and his predecessors may be found in Cardinal Wiseman's "Recollections of the Four Last Popes," and in their Lives by M. Artand de Montor, the author of a work on fifteen of the Popes Gregory.

258. Gregory XVI., A.D. 1831–1846.

Mauro Capellari was born in 1765.

While still very young, he entered the Contemplative Order of Camaldoli, and resided in the monastery, of St Michael, of Murano, near Venice, of which he became Abbot; he was subsequently made Procurator, and Vicar-General of the Congregation. He was appointed by Leo XII. Apostolic Visitor of the Universities in the

States of the Church; was made cardinal in 1825, and lastly, Prefect of the Congregation of the Propaganda. He preserved on the Pontifical throne the most simple habits of life. Opposed to all innovations, he saw violent insurrections burst forth in the beginning of his reign, and was unable to suppress them without invoking the assistance of Austria, which led to the occupation of Ancona by the French troops in 1832. He showed himself favourable to the order of the Jesuits; did everything in his power for the encouragement of foreign missions; created many new bishoprics, particularly in America; ruled the matter of mixed marriages, and, in two celebrated encyclical letters of August 15th, 1832, and June 25th, 1835, reproved the paradoxical doctrines of the Abbé de Lamennais, who, after having challenged for the Holy See an extension of authority it had never claimed, stood up in arms against it, and fell from the faith.

Having received a visit from the Emperor Nicholas in 1845, he pleaded before him energetically the cause of the persecuted Catholics of Poland and Russia, nor did his remonstrances fail to produce some happy results.

Gregory XVI. was esteemed for his knowledge of canonical and ecclesiastical matters. He has left among other writings, "The Triumph of the

Holy See," (1799,) and "Discourses on the Foundation of Religion," read before the Academy of the Catholic Religion, founded by Pius VII. in 1801. He created the Order of Gregory the Great, and remodelled that of the Golden Spur, to which he gave the name of St Silvester.

259. Pius IX., A.D. 1846.

Giovanni Maria Mastai Ferreti was born at Sinigaglia on the 13th of May, 1792. In early youth he entered the Pope's Noble Guard, but, in consequence of an epileptic fit, resolved to renounce the profession of arms and devote himself to the Church. His pastoral duties were discharged with assiduity. He was sent by Pius VII. on a mission to the government of Chili, shortly after the recognition of the independence of that Republic. He performed with success the duties of this delicate mission, and, immediately after his return to Rome, was appointed by Leo XII. to a high post of administration in the capital. Not long after the accession of Gregory XVI. he went as Apostolic Nuncio to Naples, where the cholera was raging, in 1836. His efforts to relieve the sufferings of the poorer inhabitants are still remembered there with gratitude. In 1840 he was created cardinal, having previously been made Arch-

14*

bishop of Spoleto, and translated to the See of Imola in the Romagna. He devoted himself to the duties of his diocese with such zeal and self-denial as could not fail to procure him the affections of the people. On the 16th of June, 1846, Cardinal Ferreti was elected to the Papacy under the name of Pius the Ninth. His election was hailed by the Romans with great satisfaction. On the evening of the same day he wrote to his three brothers in the following modest terms:—"It has pleased God, who exalts and who brings low, to raise my insignificance to the highest dignity on earth. I feel all the immensity of the charge, and all the feebleness of my ability."

The reforms introduced into the Roman administration by the new Pope raised him to a high pitch of popularity, but he knew how to estimate the value of popular applause. One of his first acts was to issue a decree of amnesty, by which all past political offences were blotted out. His clemency was miserably abused. The most extravagant ideas of change were formed by persons utterly ignorant of the nature of the Pontifical Government, which is essentially patriarchal and absolute, and never can, like those of other countries, be shared with the people. Restless and revolutionary spirits, assembling from all parts of Italy, inflamed the minds of the Romans, and sowed among them the seeds of rebellion. The object of these ambitious men was not so much to co-operate with the Holy Father in his benevolent efforts for the welfare and happiness of his subjects as to dictate to him what measures he should adopt, and even to overrule his objections by parliamentary authority. The French Revolution of February, 1848, gave a new impetus to the demands of the Romans. The Pontiff was compelled to enter on a policy of reaction, and from that moment his popularity began to decline. He had convened a council, chosen by the provinces, to render his reforms more effective and permanent, to assist him in his administration, and give its opinion and advice on all matters connected with the general interests of the country. This assembly, however, made propositions such as he had never contemplated, and could not sanction. The constitution, which he had granted under the pressure of circumstances, soon brought him into collision with the Democratic party. It had been framed in the hope of satisfying the requirements of the Liberals, and, at the same time, of preserving intact the spiritual authority and incommunicable prerogatives of the Head of the Church, which Pius IX. had not the smallest idea of compromising for a moment.

The agitators were not so scrupulous. Eager for war with the Austrians, they importuned their ruler to take arms against that State, but while the Pope consented to General Durando's leading a Roman corps to concert with Charles Albert, he declared positively that he could not, as Pontiff, proclaim war against a Christian power.

Durando exceeded his instructions, and published an address to his soldiers so exaggerated in its terms that the Pope was obliged to disown it,—a circumstance which produced intense agitation at Rome. The populace now became, according to the advice they had received from Mazzini, "more exacting" every day; and as the only chance of protecting what remained of his own authority against the dictation of the clubs and the lawless violence excited by demagogues, the Pope called to his counsels Count Pelegrino Rossi. This statesman being but a moderate Liberal, sincerely attached to the person of his sovereign, and zealous for true liberty in contradistinction to popular despotism, was exceedingly disliked. His efforts to restore order were responded to by yells of rage from the revolutionary press, and by ferocious denunciations of the clubs. He assumed the direction of affairs on the 16th of August, and on the 15th of November he was brutally assassinated on the steps of the Cancellaria, where the Parliament held its sittings. No attempt was made to arrest the murderers. The Gendarmes and National Guard, who were on the spot, did not interfere, and the Assembly continued to read its minutes as if nothing had occurred!

On the following day a furious assault was made on the palace of the Quirinal by the military and the people. One prelate was shot, and all the inmates, his Holiness excepted, were threatened with death unless the demands of the deputation were granted within an hour. A list of ministers was proposed, at the head of which figured Mamiani, Sterbini, Galetti. This the Pope accepted under protest, declaring, that "he would not grant anything to violence."

"His authority," to use the words of the French ambassador at Rome, "was now absolutely null. It existed only in name, and none of his acts could any longer be free and voluntary." There was but one course left to the outraged sovereign, namely, flight; and this he effected in the dress of an ordinary priest, under the escort of Count Spaur, minister of the King of Bavaria. He took refuge in Gaeta, and enjoyed the hospitality of the King of Naples during the seventeen months that he remained in his dominions. Immediately after his arrival at Gaeta, the Pope sent an ordonnance to Rome protesting energetically against the Junta of the State appointed to supersede his sovereignty, and declaring all its acts lawless and null. This protest the Junta treated with contempt, and when published in Rome it was torn down and trampled upon. Mazzini, the high priest of insurrection, now rose into eminence. He was led to a seat of honor beside the president in the new Constituent Assembly, and Rome became a centre of attraction to the refuse of Italian society.

Though invited by his rebellious subjects to return to his capital, the Pope wisely refused to trust himself in their power, and on the 18th of February, 1849, he appealed to the great Catholic powers, and demanded their armed assistance.

The profanities and atrocities committed under the rule of the Triumvirs—Mazzini, Armanelli, and Saffi—excited the indignation of Europe, and on the 25th of April, 1849, the French squadron, having on board General Oudinot's expeditionary army, anchored before Civita Vecchia. The bravest and most desperate resistance was made by the besieged, but the French arms proved irresistible; and on the 2d of July Oudinot entered Rome with his army, Garibaldi having quitted it on the previous night with some 5000 men. The grateful task of laying the keys of the liberated city at the feet of the Pontiff devolved upon Colonel Niel. On the 4th of April, 1850, Pius IX. departed from Portici, and on the 14th he re-entered Rome amid the tumultuous acclamations of the people, who had not long before shouted as vehemently "Long live Mazzini!"

After the horrible ingratitude and outrage with which the Pope had been treated by his subjects, and especially by those to whom he had, on his accession, conceded an amnesty, no one can feel surprised that he should, after his restoration, have been less ready than before to inaugurate political changes. His attention, however, has been ceaselessly devoted to remedying the disastrous effects of the revolution, and improving the charitable, educational, and ecclesiastical institutions in his States. On this subject very copious and valuable information may be found in Mr. Maguire's "Rome: its Ruler and its Institutions."

Among the more remarkable of his Holiness's official acts may be mentioned his condemnation of the principle of mixed education in the Queen's Colleges of Ireland, his bull for the re-establishment of the Catholic hierarchy in England in 1850, and his promulgation of the doctrine of the Immaculate Conception of the Blessed Virgin Mary as an article of faith on the 8th December, 1854. To these may be added the Encyclical Letter of December the 8th, 1864, in which his Holiness exposed the popular errors of the times, and an appendix in which eighty erroneous and wide-spread propositions were distinctly condemned. It is one of the most important and valuable documents which has issued from the Holy See for many years. Nor ought I to omit mentioning a Brief issued in the same year in reference to the Munich Congress. It severely censured the practice of representing faith and science as essentially distinct, and to be pursued irrespectively of each other's conclusions; and it reprehended as dangerous and irreverent the habit of perpetually insisting on the wide difference between the dogmatic and the infallible decisions of the Church, and those which emanate from the Congregation of the Index, or are the result of common consent among Catholic divines. While fully admitting the difference in the abstract, the Brief maintains that the method objected to is calculated to foster a sad indifference to authority, and the indulgence of wild and erroneous opinions.

Since the outbreak of the war with Austria in 1859, the Pope has encountered great difficulties in retaining the temporal possessions of the Church, notwithstanding the veneration in which he is held in consequence of his personal benignity. The Romagna has revolted from his sceptre, and the excommunications he has launched on sacrilegious spoliators has not prevented his States from being invaded by the Piedmontese legions and annexed to the crown of Sardinia. The patrimony of St Peter only is now left to him. In the preservation of this portion of his dominions, he is protected by the French army of occupation,* while the suffrages of all the faithful Catholics are offered for his ultimate success in this arduous struggle for the security and independence of the Holy See.

The States of the Church.

It will not be out of place before closing this Manual, to resume briefly the history of those ecclesiastical States which have in our day become the object of so much anxiety and dispute. The donation made by Constantine to the Holy See does not appear to have had any great importance, and up to the eighth century the bishops of Rome seem to have possessed merely a spiritual authority. Their temporal power dates from the pontificate of Gregory III. who rendered himself independent in Rome when it had been abandoned by the Emperors of the

East. Pepin le Bref having conquered the Lombards, made a donation to Pope Stephen II. of the exarchate of Ravenna and Pentapolis in 755. Charlemagne added the province of Perugia and the Duchy of Spoleto in 774. The Emperor Henry III. in 1053 ceded to the martial Leo IX. the Duchy of Benevento. By a celebrated gift made in the year 1077, the Countess Matilda, sovereign of Tuscany, added to the States of the Church the cities of Bolsena, Civita Castellana, Bagnara, Montefiascone, Viterbo, &c., which formed the district entitled "The Patrimony of St Peter." Nevertheless, the Popes did not enjoy these possessions undisputed. At different epochs the Emperors of Germany claimed the right of exercising a sovereignty over Rome and the ecclesiastical States; some of them even drove the Popes from Rome or nominated them at their pleasure, and reduced them to a sort of vassalage, as we find, for example, in the history of Otho I. and of Henry III., the first of whom intruded Leo VIII. into the Holy See; and the last, after causing the abdication of Gregory VI., procured the election of the three succeeding Pontiffs. Innocent III. obliterated the last traces of dependence in making the Perfect of Rome pay homage to him, though this functionary had hitherto been appointed by the German emperor, (1198.) In 1274, Gregory X. obtained from the

King of France the countdom of Venaissin. The city of Avignon was added in 1348, Clement VI. having bought it of the Countess of Provence, Jeanne de Sicile.

During the residence of the Popes at Avignon, from 1309 to 1377, Rome was for a moment raised into a republic under Rienzi in 1347, and the temporal authority of the Pope was some time rendered null in Italy. The legate Albornoz re-established it in the name of Innocent VI., in 1353–1365, but at first only nominally. Almost all the cities had become small principalities, belonging each to one family. Thus the Alidosi reigned at Imola, the Malatesta at Rimini the Montefeltri at Urbino, and Bologna continued a republic. These different countries were one after another reunited to the Holy See after various revolutions: Citta di Castello, in 1502; Imola, Faenza, Forli, and Rimini, in 1509; Bologna, in 1513; Perugia, in 1520; Camerino, in 1538; Ferrara and Comacchio, in 1598; and the Duchy of Urbino, in 1626. The ecclesiastical States lost Avignon and its county in 1791, and the peace of Tolentino, while it ratified the cession of these countries to France yielded also to the Cisalpine republic Bologna, Ferrara, and Romagna, (1797.)

In 1798 the remainder of the States of the Church was shaped into a Roman republic, but in 1799 the Papal Government was renewed. The peace of Lunéville in 1801 re-established the stipulations of Tolentino. Bonaparte in 1808, by two decrees, united to the kingdom of Italy, (which was nothing more than the old Cisalpine republic enlarged,) the provinces situated on the Adriatic, and annexed all the rest to the French empire.

The peace of Paris in 1814 restored to the Holy See all its possessions except Avignon and *Le Comtat.*

It would have been well for Napoleon if he had always adhered to the words of wisdom which he pronounced when he was First Consul: "The institution which maintains the utility of the faith, viz., the Pope, the guardian of Catholic unity, is an admirable institution. This chief is reproached with being a foreign sovereign; a foreign sovereign, in fact, this chief is, and we must thank Heaven for it. The Pope is not in Paris: that is well. He is neither at Madrid nor in Vienna, and this is why we support his spiritual authority. At Vienna and at Madrid, they have a right to say the same. Does any one suppose that if he were in Paris, the Viennese and the Spaniards would consent to receive his decisions? One is only too happy that he lives away from our homes, and that, in living far from us he does not reside with our rivals, that he dwells in that old Rome, far from the hands of the emperors of Germany, far from those of the kings of France or the kings of Spain, holding the balance between Catholic sovereigns, leaning always a little towards the stronger, and soon regaining his ascendancy if the stronger becomes an oppressor. Ages have wrought this, and they have wrought it well. For the government of souls it is the best, the most beneficent institution that can be imagined. I do not maintain these things through bigotry, but with reason."

We enjoy in one respect a great advantage over those who lived in the early ages of Christianity. If they were nearer to the sources of divine tradition, and almost within hearing of the great founders of the faith, we can point to the accomplishment of those promises which they took on trust, and see in the history of St Peter's successors the strongest confirmation of the doctrines originally delivered. The gates of hell have opened wide, and errors in every shape, refined and gross, violent and seductive, have assailed the Church without finding in her one vulnerable point. Never was her faith so accurately defined as it is now; never were the lives of her bishops and clergy more exemplary, never was more peace within her borders, nor the voice of her supreme pastor obeyed more readily over a wider extent of territory than at the present time. Empires perish, and the boundaries of kingdoms are effaced, the aspect of society changes, savages become civilised, knowledge spreads, arts decay, continents are being submerged beneath advancing tides, and new lands are rising out of the sea; but amid all this ceaseless mutation, political and social, mental and material, there is one thing on earth, and one only, which is immutable—the chair of the apostles—the See of St Peter. Through ages of persecution and of prosperity, with or without secular adjuncts, it maintains one unchanging standard of faith and morals, and varies only in the application of fixed principles according to the circumstances that arise. The strength of God is made perfect in an old man on the Vatican, who confesses his sins and bewails his imperfections over the tomb of the apostles; and when he speaks from the chair of St Peter, his voice is authoritative as that which proclaimed the law from Sinai, or which delivered the Sermon on the Mount.

ALPHABETICAL INDEX.

	PAGE
Adeodatus	95
Adrian I	106
" II	117
" III	122
" IV	167
" V	199
" VI	243
Agapetus I	79
" II	132
Agatho, S.	96
Alexander I	26
" II	149
" III	168
" IV	194
" V	221
" VI	235
" VII	271
" VIII	278
Anastatius I	51
" II	71
" III	129
" IV	166
Anicetus, S.	28
Anterus	32
Benedict I	84
" II	97
" III	114
" IV	126
" V	134
" VI	135
" VII	136
" VIII	141
" IX	142
" X., Antipope	148
" XI	207
" XII	210
" XIII	281
" XIV	282
Boniface I	56
" II	78
" III	89
" IV	90
" V	91

	PAGE
Boniface VI	123
" VII., Antipope	136
" VIII	204
" IX	219
Caius, S.	39
Calixtus I	31
" II	161
" III	228
Celestine I	58
" II	164
" III	178
" IV	189
" V	202
Christopher	127
Clement I	25
" II	145
" III	175
" IV	196
" V	207
" VI	211
" VII	244
" VIII	262
" IX	272
" X	272
" XI	279
" XII	282
" XIII	284
" XIV	285
Cletus, S.	25
Conon	98
Constantine	100
Cornelius, S.	34
Damasus I	47
" II	145
Deusdedit, S.	90
Dionysius, S.	37
Domnus I	95
" II	135
Eleutherius, S.	29
Eugenius I	94
" II	111
" III	165
" IV	224

ALPHABETICAL INDEX.

	PAGE
Eusebius, S.	41
Eutychian, S.	30
Evaristus, S.	26
Fabian, S.	32
Felix I.	38
" II.	47
" III.	68
" IV.	77
Formosus	123
Gelasius I.	70
" II.	160
Gregory, St, I.	86
" II.	100
" III.	101
" IV.	112
" V.	138
" VI.	144
" VII.	150
" VIII.	175
" IX.	187
" X.	197
" XI.	216
" XII.	220
" XIII.	259
" XIV.	262
" XV.	267
" XVI.	307
Higinus, S.	27
Hilary, S.	67
Honorius I.	91
" II.	162
" III.	184
" IV.	201
Hormisdas	75
Innocent I.	54
" II.	163
" III.	178
" IV.	189
" V.	198
" VI.	214
" VII.	220
" VIII.	234
" IX.	262
" X.	269
" XI.	273
" XII.	279
" XIII.	280
John I.	75
" II.	79
" III.	84
" IV.	93
" V.	98
" VI.	99
" VII.	99
" VIII.	118
" IX.	126
" X.	129
" XI.	131
" XII.	133

	PAGE
John XIII.	135
" XIV.	136
" XV.	137
" XVI.	137
" XVII.	140
" XVIII.	141
" XIX.	142
" XX., Antipope	144
" XXI.	199
" XXII.	209
" XXIII.	222
Julius I.	46
" II.	238
" III.	253
Landon	129
Leo the Great	62
" II.	96
" III.	107
" IV.	112
" V.	127
" VI.	130
" VII.	131
" VIII.	134
" IX.	146
" X.	240
" XI.	266
" XII.	306
Liberius	41
Linus, St.	24
Lucius I.	35
" II.	164
" III.	173
Marcellinus, S.	39
Marcellus I.	41
" II.	253
Mark, St.	46
Martin I.	94
" II. or Marinus	121
" III.	132
" IV.	201
" V.	224
Milchiades, St.	41
Nicholas I.	114
" II.	148
" III.	200
" IV.	202
" V.	226
Peter, St.	15
Pascal I.	110
" II.	150
Paul I.	105
" II.	230
" III.	247
" IV.	254
" V.	266
Pelagus I.	83
" II.	85
Pius I.	28
" II.	229

	PAGE		PAGE
Pius III	237	Stephen III	104
" IV	256	" IV	105
" V	256	" V	110
" VI	292	" VI	122
" VII	295	" VII	124
" VIII	307	" VIII	131
" IX	309	" IX	132
Pontian, St	32	" X	148
Romanus	125	Symmachus	72
Sabinian	89	Telesphorus, St	27
Sergius I	98	Theodorus I	93
" II	112	" II	126
" III	127	Urban I	31
" IV	141	" II	156
Severinus	92	" III	174
Silverius, St	80	" IV	195
Silvester I	42	" V	215
" II	139	" VI	217
Simplicius	69	" VII	262
Siricius, St	51	" VIII	267
Sisinnius	100	Valentine	111
Sixtus I	27	Victor I	29
" II	36	" II	147
" III	50	" III	155
" IV	232	Vigilius	81
" V	260	Vitalian	94
Soter, St	28	Zacharias, St	102
Stephen I	35	Zephyrinus, St	30
" II	104	Zozimus, St	55

CHRONOLOGICAL LIST OF THE POPES.

WITH THE

DATE OF THE ELECTION OF EACH.

No.		A.D.	PAGE
1	St Peter	33	15
2	St Linus	68	24
3	St Cletus	78	25
4	St Clement	91	25
5	St Evaristus	100	26
6	St Alexander	109	26
7	St Sixtus I	119	27
8	St Telesphorus	127	27
9	St Higinus	139	27
10	St Pius I	142	28
11	St Anicetus	157	28
12	St Soter	168	28
13	St Eleutherius	177	29
14	St Victor I	193	29
15	St Zephyrinus	202	30
16	St Calixtus I	219	31
17	St Urban I	223	31
18	St Pontian	230	32
19	St Anterus	235	32
20	St Fabian	236	32
21	St Cornelius	251	34
22	St Lucius I	252	35
23	St Stephen I	253	35
24	St Sixtus II	257	36
25	St Dionysius	259	37
26	St Felix I	269	38
27	St Eutychian	275	39
28	St Caius	283	39
29	St Marcellinus	296	39
30	St Marcellus	308	41
31	St Eusebius	310	41
32	St Milchiades	311	41
33	St Silvester	314	42
34	St Mark	336	46
35	St Julius I	337	46
36	Liberius	352	46
37	Felix II	355	47

CHRONOLOGICAL LIST OF POPES.

No.		A.D.	PAGE
38	St Damasus	366	47
39	St Siricius	384	51
40	St Anastasius I	398	51
41	St Innocent I	402	54
42	St Zozimus	417	55
43	St Boniface I	418	56
44	St Celestine	422	58
45	Sixtus III	432	59
46	St Leo the Great	440	62
47	St Hilary	461	67
48	St Simplicius	468	67
49	St Felix III	483	68
50	St Gelasius	492	70
51	St Anastasius II	496	71
52	Symmachus	498	72
53	Hormisdas	514	75
54	John I	523	75
55	Felix IV	526	77
56	Boniface II	530	78
57	John II	533	79
58	Agapetus	535	79
59	St Silverius	536	80
60	Vigilius	537	81
61	Pelagus I	555	83
62	John III	560	84
63	Benedict I	574	84
64	Pelagus II	578	85
65	St Gregory the Great	590	86
66	Sabinian	604	89
67	Boniface III	607	89
68	Boniface IV	608	90
69	St Deusdedit	614	90
70	Boniface V	617 or 618	91
71	Honorius I	625	91
72	Severinus	640	92
73	John IV	640	93
74	Theodore I	642	93
75	St Martin I	649	94
76	St Eugenius I	654	94
77	Vitalian	657	94
78	Adeodatus	672	95
79	Domnus	676	95
80	St Agatho	678	96
81	St Leo II	682	96
82	Benedict II	684	97
83	John V	685	98
84	Conon	686	98
85	Sergius I	687	98
86	John VI	701	99
87	John VII	705	99
88	Sisinnius	708	100
89	Constantine	708	100
90	St Gregory II	715	100
91	Gregory III	731	101
92	Zacharias	741	102
93	Stephen II	752	104
94	Stephen III	752	104
95	Paul I	757	105
96	Stephen IV	768	105

328 CHRONOLOGICAL LIST OF POPES.

No.		A.D.	PAGE
97	Adrian I	772	106
98	Leo III	795	107
99	Stephen V	816	110
100	Pascal I	817	110
101	Eugene II	824	111
102	Valentine	827	111
103	Gregory IV	827	112
104	Sergius II	844	112
105	St Leo IV	847	112
106	Benedict III	855	114
107	Nicholas I	858	114
108	Adrian II	867	117
109	John VIII	872	118
110	Marinus or Martin II	882	121
111	Adrian III	884	122
112	Stephen VI	885	122
113	Formosus	891	123
114	Boniface VI	896	123
115	Stephen VII	896	124
116	Romanus	897	125
117	Theodore II	898	126
118	John IX	898	126
119	Benedict IV	900	126
120	Leo V	903	127
121	Christopher	903	127
122	Sergius III	904	127
123	Anastatius III	911	129
124	Landon	913	129
125	John X	913	129
126	Leo VI	928	130
127	Stephen VIII	929	131
128	John XI	931	131
129	Leo VII	936	131
130	Stephen IX	939	132
131	Martin III	942	132
132	Agapetus II	946	132
133	John XII	956	133
134	Leo VIII	963	134
135	Benedict V	964	134
136	John XIII	965	135
137	Benedict VI	972	135
138	Domnus II	974	135
139	Benedict VII	975	136
140	John XIV	983	136
141	John XV	985	137
142	John XVI	986	137
143	Gregory V	996	138
144	Silvester II	999	139
145	John XVII	1003	140
146	John XVIII	1003	141
147	Sergius IV	1009	141
148	Benedict VIII	1012	141
149	John XIX	1024	142
150	Benedict IX	1033	142
151	Gregory VI	1044	144
152	Clement II	1046	145
153	Damasus II	1048	145
154	St Leo IX	1049	146
155	Victor II	1055	147

No.		A.D.	PAGE
156	Stephen X	1057	148
157	Nicholas II	1058	148
158	Alexander II	1061	149
159	St Gregory VII	1073	150
160	Victor III	1086	155
161	Urban II	1088	156
162	Pascal II	1099	159
163	Gelasius II	1118	160
164	Calixtus II	1119	161
165	Honorius II	1124	162
166	Innocent II	1130	163
167	Celestine II	1143	164
168	Lucius II	1144	164
169	Eugene III	1145	165
170	Anastatius IV	1153	166
171	Adrian IV	1154	167
172	Alexander III	1159	168
173	Lucius III	1181	173
174	Urban III	1185	174
175	Gregory VIII	1187	175
176	Clement III	1187	175
177	Celestine III	1191	178
178	Innocent III	1198	178
179	Honorius III	1216	184
180	Gregory IX	1227	187
181	Celestine IV	1241	189
182	Innocent IV	1243	189
183	Alexander IV	1256	194
184	Urban IV	1261	195
185	Clement IV	1265	196
186	Gregory X	1271	197
187	Innocent V	1276	198
188	Adrian V	1276	199
189	John XXI	1276	199
190	Nicholas III	1277	200
191	Martin IV	1281	201
192	Honorius IV	1285	201
193	Nicholas IV	1288	202
194	St Celestine V	1292	202
195	Boniface VIII	1294	204
196	St Benedict XI	1303	207
197	Clement V	1305	207
198	John XXII	1316	208
199	Benedict XII	1334	210
200	Clement VI	1342	211
201	Innocent VI	1352	214
202	Urban V	1362	215
203	Gregory XI	1370	216
204	Urban VI	1378	217
205	Boniface IX	1389	219
206	Innocent VII	1404	220
207	Gregory XII	1406	220
208	Alexander V	1409	221
209	John XXIII	1410	222
210	Martin V	1417	224
211	Eugene IV	1431	224
212	Nicholas V	1447	225
213	Calixtus III	1455	228
214	Pius II	1458	229

15*

CHRONOLOGICAL LIST OF POPES.

No.		A.D.	PAGE
215	Paul II	1468	230
216	Sixtus IV	1471	232
217	Innocent VIII	1484	234
218	Alexander VI	1492	235
219	Pius III	1503	237
220	Julius II	1503	238
221	Leo X	1513	240
222	Adrian VI	1522	243
223	Clement VII	1523	244
224	Paul III	1534	247
225	Julius III	1550	253
226	Marcellus II	1555	253
227	Paul IV	1555	254
228	Pius IV	1559	256
229	St Pius V	1566	256
230	Gregory XIII	1572	259
231	Sixtus V	1585	260
232	Urban VII	1590	262
233	Gregory XIV	1590	262
234	Innocent IX	1591	262
235	Clement VIII	1592	262
236	Leo XI	1605	266
237	Paul V	1605	266
238	Gregory XV	1621	267
239	Urban VIII	1623	267
240	Innocent X	1644	269
241	Alexander VII	1655	271
242	Clement IX	1667	272
243	Clement X	1670	272
244	Innocent XI	1676	273
245	Alexander VIII	1689	278
246	Innocent XII	1691	279
247	Clement XI	1700	279
248	Innocent XIII	1721	280
249	Benedict XIII	1726	281
250	Clement XII	1730	282
251	Benedict XIV	1740	282
252	Clement XIII	1758	284
253	Clement XIV	1769	285
254	Pius VI	1775	292
255	Pius VII	1800	295
256	Leo XII	1823	306
257	Pius VIII	1829	307
258	Gregory XVI	1831	307
259	Pius IX	1846	309

INDEX OF GENERAL MATTER.

Albigenses, account of, 168, 185.
Ammianus Marcellinus on the Roman Pontiffs, 49.
Annats, 219.
Arabian figures, introduction of, into Europe, 140.
Arius, account of, 44.
Arnaud of Brescia, 163, 165, 167.
Attila, king of the Huns, 63.
Augustine, St, sent by Pope Gregory the Great, to England, 87.
Avignon Popes, 207–215.
Avignon annexed to France, 214, 284.
Baldwin I., II., III., IV., V., 177.
Baptism, validity of heretical, 35.
Barbarossa, Frederic, 169.
Berengarius, his errors, 149.
Boniface, St, sent by St Gregory II. to Germany, 100.
Britain, conversion of Great 29, 87.
Bulgaria, conversion of, 115.
Calvin, 245.
Campian, the Jesuit, 259.
Canon of Scripture, when fixed, 70.
Catacombs of Rome, 34, 37.
Catherine of Aragon, 245.
Cardinal-priests, 174.
Centuries, the eighteen ecclesiastical, 54.
Charlemagne, 105, 106, 108.
Chrysostom, St John, in exile, 54.
Chronological discrepancies, 14, 68.
Church, zeal of the, in defending the outworks of the faith, 107.
Confederation of Italian States, 264.
Constantine, Emperor, his alleged gift, 42.
Constitutions of Clarendon, 171.
Council of Basle, 224.
" of Chalcedon, 64.
" of Clermont, 157.
" of Constance, 221.
" 1st, 2d and 3d, of Constantinople, 48, 82, 96.
" of Ephesus, 58.
" of Florence, 225.

Council of Frankfort, mistake of, 106.
" 1st, 2d, 3d, and 4th Lateran 162, 164, 169, 180.
" 1st and 2d of Lyons, 193, 197.
" of Nice, 42.
" 2d, of Nice, 106.
" of Sirmium, first formula of, subscribed by Liberius, 47.
" of Trent, 248.
" of Vienne, 207.
Councils, the Eighteen Œcumenical, 53.
Crusades, 157, 175, 185.
Dante, quotations from, 43, 80, 181, 199, 203.
Decretals of Gregory IX., 187.
" of Isidore, 40.
Discipline, local varieties in Church, 30.
Dispensations, 137.
Divorce, 117.
Donatists, 41.
" Droit de Franchise," 273.
Dynasty of Hohenstauffen, 194.
Easter, time of keeping, 30.
Ecclesiastical histories, 25, 81, 86, 125, 144, 160, 232.
Ecthesis, the, 93.
Emperors of Germany, their influence on the Church, 102.
England's only Pope, Adrian IV., 167.
Etats généraux, 205.
Eutyches, account of, 61.
Ferdinand and Isabella, grants in the West made to them by Alexander VI., 237.
Fleury, his character as a historian, 81.
Gallican Church, declaration put forth by the, 229, 275.
Gallican clergy, civil constitution of the, 294.
Genseric, king of the Vandals, 60, 64.

NEW AND POPULAR TALES, &c.

New and Improved Editions of most of the following Books, have recently been issued, printed on Fine Paper, and in neat, and attractive Bindings, which renders them very

Suitable for Presents, Premiums, and for Parochial and Sunday School Libraries, &c.

CHEAP EDITIONS OF
HENDRIK CONSCIENCE'S SHORT TALES,

In 8 vols. demi 8vo. —cloth, 75 cts.; cloth, gilt sides and edges, $1.
The complete set, in boxes, 8 vols. cloth, $6.00. cloth, gilt sides and edges, $8.

The Publishers have the pleasure of announcing a NEW, CHEAP AND UNIFORM EDITION of the SHORT TALES of M. HENDRIK CONSCIENCE, the distinguished Flemish Novelist. PONTMARTIN, the acute French Critic and Reviewer, has likened the Stories of Conscience, to "pearls se' in Flemish gold," and in point of delicacy of treatment and high moral value, they richly justify the comparison.

There is a pure morality throughout the works of this author, happily blending Entertainment with Instruction, and unmarred by Controversy, which makes them peculiarly fitted for the perusal of the young.

1. *The Poor Gentleman.* By H. Conscience.
2. *The Conscript and Blind Rosa.* Two Tales in one volume. By Hendrik Conscience.
3. *Happiness of Being Rich.* By H. Conscience.
4. *The Miser.* By Hendrik Conscience.
5. *Ricketicketack and Wooden Clara.* Two Tales in one volume. By H. Conscience.
6. *Count Hugo of Craenhove.* By H. Conscience.
7. *The Curse of the Village.* By H. Conscience.
8. *The Village Innkeeper.* By H. Conscience.

MORAL & INSTRUCTIVE TALES, &c.
UNIFORM SERIES—SQUARE 16o.

Tales of the Angels; or, Ethel's Book.
By F. W. FABER. 3d edition.

square 16mo............cloth.........	60
do. do. do. cloth, gilt edges	80

The Queens & Princesses of France.

square 16mo............cloth.........	60
do. do. do. cloth, gilt edges	80

Father Laval; or the Jesuit Missionary
A Tale of the North American Indians.

square 16mo............cloth.........	60
do. do. do. cloth, gilt edges	80

Lorenzo; or, the Empire of Religion.

New edition, square 16mo........cloth.........	60
do. do. do. cloth, gilt edges	80

MURPHY & Co. *Publishers and Catholic Booksellers, Baltimore.*

MORAL AND INSTRUCTIVE TALES, &c.

The Oriental Pearl, a Catholic Tale,
By Mrs. ANNA H. DORSEY.
New edition, square 16mo........cloth..........	60
do. do. do. cloth, gilt edges	80

Fenelon on the Education of a
Daughter. New ed., square 16mo...cloth..........
	60
do. do. do. cloth, gilt edges	80

The Catholic Bride—
Translated from the Italian by Dr. PISE.
New edition, square 16mo........cloth..........	60
do. do. do. cloth, gilt edges	80

The Flower Garden—
A Collection of Short Tales and Historical Sketches. From the French of EMILE SOUVESTRE. By S. J. DONALDSON, Jr. Cloth...................... 75
cloth, gilt edges............................ 1 00

This collection is written in that happy style that cannot fail to please alike young and old. The author—the Washington Irving of France, and already favorably known to the American public by his Attic Philosopher, and other Popular Tales—has in this collection been peculiarly happy in combining useful instruction with delicate and refined humor. All these stories breathe that spirit of pure sentiment and innocent playfulness which pervades the other productions of his graceful pen.

A NEW SERIES of JUVENILES, Square 24o.
Suitable for Parochial and Sunday School Libraries, Premiums, &c.

Price in flexible cloth, 20; cloth, 25; cloth, gilt edges, 40 cts. per vol.

1. *The Mother of Washington, and other Tales.*
2. *The Little Orator, and other Tales.*
3. *A Visit to Ancient Rome.*

CATHOLIC TALES, NOVELS, &c.

Pauline Seward—
A Tale of Real Life. By J. D. BRYANT, M. D.
Fifth Revised Edition, two vols. in one, 12mo. cloth	1 50
do. do. do. cloth, gilt edges	2 00

Father Oswald—a genuine Catholic Story.
cloth..	75
do. do. cloth, gilt edges and sides	1 00

LADY FULLERTON'S TALES.

UNIFORM EDITION, in 3 vols. 12o. cl. $ 50; cl. gt. edges, &c. $2.00. per vol.

Lady Bird.   Ellen Middleton.   Grantley Manor.

No less accomplished as an Authoress than pious and unostentatious in private life, Lady Fullerton gives her works a character of instructiveness and practical wisdom which we look for in vain in many of our professedly religious Tales. The young of her sex will find in her pages entertainment of the highest order, interest, beauty of style, elegance of description, without a line to pamper the silly or romantic ideas that too often unfit them for real life. The signal success of her works, not only in England, but in America, and their translation on the Continent, are the best evidence of their decided merit.

MURPHY & Co. *Publishers and Catholic Booksellers, Baltimore.*

TALES, BIOGRAPHIES, &c.

The Catholic Youth's Magazine,

Complete in Four Volumes, small 4to., with upwards of 150 Fine Illustrations.

A few Complete Sets, may be had *neatly bound in Cloth*, with a Beautiful Ornamental Title Page.

Price, per vol......1 25   Cloth, gilt edges, &c., per vol.   1 50

☞ The contents are made up of Innocent, Plain and Instructive *Moral Tales, Interesting Biographies, Sketches of History and Travels, Natural History, Amusing Anecdotes, Poetry, Moral Lessons on various subjects, Fables, Riddles, &c. &c.* Each volume contains 384 Pages. Embellished with Fine Engravings.

☞ It can be recommended with confidence, as one of the most attractive, edifying and instructive Juveniles that can be placed in the hands of Catholic Youth.

☞ It should find a place in every Catholic Household.

☞ It is admirably adapted for a *Premium* or *Gift Book*.

Panegyric of the Blessed Aloysius—
small 8vo. Printed in red and black...flexible cloth   30

Life of Christ—by St. Bonaventure.
To which are added the Devotion to the Three Hours, Agony of our Lord on the Cross, and the Life of the Glorious St. Joseph. A new ed., 18o. cl.   75
    do.   do.   do. cloth, gt. sides & edges   1 00

Life of Mrs. Seton—
Foundress of the Sisters of Charity in the U. S., and an Historical Sketch of the Sisterhood, from its Foundation to the time of her Death. By Rev. C. I. WHITE, D. D. 6th Revised Edition, with a Fine Portrait of Mrs. Seton......12mo. cloth, gilt back   2 00
    do.   do.   cloth, extra gilt sides and edges   2 50

Life of Saint Patrick—
Apostle of Ireland—to which are added the Lives of St. BRIDGET, Virgin and Abbes, and ST. COLUMBA, Abbot and Apostle of the Northern Picts. Embellished with a fine Portrait of St. Patrick. 12mo. cloth   75

Life of St. Alphonsus M. de Liguori,
Compiled from the published Memoirs of the Saint. By ONE OF THE REDEMPTORIST FATHERS. Embellished with fine steel Portrait of the illustrious saint. 12mo. cl   1 50
    do.   do.   cloth, gilt sides and edges...   2 00
Another Edition............fine paper, 8vo., library style   2 50

Short and Familiar Answers to the
Objections most commonly urged against Religion. From the French of the Abbe de Segur, formerly Chaplain of the Military Prison of Paris. 18mo. cloth   60

The Means of Acquiring Perfection.
By LIGUORI. 32o....................................   25

Bishop Ullathorne on the Immacu-
late Conception of the Mother of God. 18mo. cloth   60
    do.   do.   cloth, gilt sides and edges..   80

MURPHY & Co. *Publishers and Catholic Booksellers, Baltimore.*

www.ingramcontent.com/pod-product-compliance
Lightning Source LLC
Chambersburg PA
CBHW032049220426
43664CB00008B/919